PRAISE FOR
REINVENTION ROADMAP

"Kick-start your job search or job change with an entirely
new set of skills in *Reinvention Roadmap!*"

MARSHALL GOLDSMITH
New York Times **bestselling author of** *Triggers*

"Liz Ryan's smart, down-to-earth advice is a pleasure to read.
Whether you're just starting your first career or trying to figure out
your next one, this is an essential guide. Don't miss it!"

ANNE FISHER
"Ask Annie" career advice columnist for Fortune.com

"Liz Ryan leads you on a reinvention journey that can not only redefine your
career path, but also your life. A wonderful book that gives you the power and the
tools to navigate career and life challenges in the new millennium."

JONATHAN ZAKIN
technology visionary

"If you need a job, you need Liz Ryan. Short of having the actual job offer
in hand, having Liz Ryan in your corner is the next best thing. Her approach to
job hunting is unique. Her job hunting tips are not only original and powerful,
but they are highly effective. Instead of groveling for a job, she will help you stand
out. She will help you realize your true worth. She will empower you to seize a job
interview and turn it to your advantage. No book can absolutely guarantee that
you will land a job, but Liz Ryan gets darn close. I have interviewed countless
HR experts and I could say Liz Ryan is one of the best but I won't say that.
She is not just one of the best. She is THE best."

TOMMY SCHNURMACHER
host of the Tommy Schnurmacher Show and radio host for CJAD

BREAK THE RULES TO GET THE
JOB YOU WANT AND **CAREER** YOU DESERVE

LIZ RYAN

BenBella Books, Inc.
Dallas, TX

FOR LIZ SHULL

BenBella Books, Inc.
10440 N. Central Expressway Suite 800
Dallas, TX 75231
www.benbellabooks.com
Send feedback to feedback@benbellabooks.com

Printed in the United States of America
10 9 8 7 6 5 4 3

Library of Congress Cataloging-in-Publication Data
Names: Ryan, Liz (Elizabeth), 1959- author.
Title: Rreinvention roadmap : break the rules to get the job you want and career you deserve / Liz Ryan.
Description: Dallas, TX : BenBella Books, Inc., [2016] | Includes bibliographical references and index.
Identifiers: LCCN 2016037697 (print) | LCCN 2016051588 (ebook) | ISBN 9781942952688 (trade paper : alk. paper) |
    ISBN 9781942952695 (electronic)
Subjects: LCSH: Vocational guidance. | Job hunting. | Career development.
Classification: LCC HF5381 .R798 2016 (print) | LCC HF5381 (ebook) | DDC
650.14--dc23
LC record available at https://lccn.loc.gov/2016037697

All text and artwork by Liz Ryan
Copyediting by James Fraleigh
Text design and composition by Kit Sweeney
Proofreading by Kimberly Broderick and Michael Fedison
Cover design by Sarah Dombrowsky
Cover artwork by Liz Ryan

Distributed by Perseus Distribution
www.perseusdistribution.com
To place orders through Perseus Distribution:
Tel: (800) 343-4499
Fax: (800) 351-5073
E-mail: orderentry@perseusbooks.com

Special discounts for bulk sales (minimum of 25 copies) are available.
Please contact Aida Herrera at aida@benbellabooks.com.

Foreign Rights are represented by: Global Lion Intellectual Property Management, Inc.
Attn: Peter Miller, President, P.O. Box 669238, Pompano Beach, Fl 33066 USA
Email: Peter@GlobalLionMgt.com

CONTENTS

FOREWORD

Several years ago, I had the honor of sharing a platform with His Holiness the Dalai Lama. As the leader of one of the world's great faith traditions, he speaks profoundly about the nature of human life and fulfillment. Like all gifted teachers, his observations can seem deceptively simple. He once said, "To be born at all is a miracle. So what are you doing with your life?" It's a simple question that has deep implications for all of us.

Each one of us is a unique moment in history. No one has ever lived our life and no one ever will. Of course our lives are affected by chance and circumstances, but they're also shaped by our own attitudes and expectations and by whether or not we discover and develop our unique talents and passions. I know many people who live lives that excite and fulfill them. Many others settle for much less. They don't enjoy their lives or especially the work they do; they just aim to get through the week and make it to the weekend. Often they say they have no choice, but they almost always do.

Most of us have pressing obligations and difficult circumstances to deal with. Even so, there's often more room for flexibility and creativity in our lives and work than our well-worn habits of thinking typically suggest. If we are to change, we do need to think differently and take practical steps to identify what we want from our work and how to get it. And that's what this book is about.

Reinvention Roadmap is a customized guide to help you review, rethink, and reorient yourself to the new world of work and the many roads to fulfillment within it. It is based on three core ideas. The first is that we all create our own lives, and we can recreate them if we have the will and the confidence to do so. The second is that the world around us is changing at an exponential rate, and in the process is generating many new opportunities for how we can live and work. The third is that there are many simple, practical steps we can take to match our personal talents and passions to these opportunities.

Liz Ryan is uniquely placed to offer this roadmap. The advice and techniques she gives us here are distilled from a lifetime of guiding people in all areas of work to more fulfilling ways of earning their living. Written with her trademark passion, wit, and humanity, *Reinvention Roadmap* offers her straightforward, human, and road-tested wisdom to help you answer that simple yet often hardest of questions, "So what *are* you doing with your life?"

Ken Robinson
Los Angeles, March 2016

INTRODUCTION

For many years, the working world was relatively simple to understand and to navigate. When you needed a job, you applied for jobs and got one, and then you kept the job for a long time. Some of us walked into a job and stayed at the same company for 20 years or more.

Those days are gone! The job market has changed, and job security is no longer a given. In times past, company loyalty was such that if you wanted to, you could focus on being a good employee and working your way up the internal hierarchy; you could manage your *job*. But in today's world, where job security is a thing of the past, that is no longer enough. You must manage your *career*. In this new working world, you must learn to break the old rules and learn some new ones, too.

This book, *Reinvention Roadmap*, will teach you how to take control of your career and run it like a business—your business. You'll learn how to brand yourself for the jobs you want and how to get a job without begging for it.

IS THIS BOOK FOR YOU?

- Are you looking for a job for the first time or for the first time after many years?
- Are you sick of filling out online job applications that disappear into the void?
- Do you want to or need to change careers but aren't sure how to do it?
- Do you want to feel more power and control over your career path?
- Are you unemployed or underemployed (working in a job below your capability)?
- Are you not being considered for jobs at which you know you could perform well?
- Have you recently been laid off or made redundant from a job?
- Do you want to create a plan and goals for your career but need guidance on how to do it?

If you've answered yes to one or more of these, *Reinvention Roadmap* is for you.

WHAT IS REINVENTION?

Reinvention is a process. Reinvention is the process that begins when your life changes, either because you want it to change—for instance, when you decide to leave one career path and try a new one—or when life forces changes on you whether you're ready for them or not.

Change can be scary, but it doesn't have to be paralyzing. It can be more fun than it is scary, and an opportunity for personal and professional growth. In this book you'll learn how to deal with the anxiety that can creep in when you're not sure what your future has in store for you, and how to step through reinvention and get all the amazing learning and growth that the process offers. I'll teach you the steps to get stronger and more resilient so you're able to deal with the curveballs life throws at you.

Most of all, through this book, you will have an opportunity to reflect on your path so far. You'll look back at your life and see how far you've already come; you will see how many obstacles you've already surmounted. If you're like most people, you don't have a lot of people around you telling you how talented and capable you are, but trust me, you are. You are mighty and amazing! You can navigate your career; you just need a roadmap. That is where *Reinvention Roadmap* comes in.

WHAT IS THE REINVENTION ROADMAP?

The Reinvention Roadmap is the path you'll follow, both in this book and in your life. Your path will be different from everyone else's. Whatever your career history and your background, the Reinvention Roadmap equips you with the tools you'll need to become CEO of your own career. You'll learn a completely new way to manage your career and your job search.

The following are just a few of the many things you will learn in this Reinvention Roadmap project:

- Cool and fun, new-millennium job-search techniques that will let you take back the power the broken recruiting system has stolen from you

- How to reach hiring managers directly with a new kind of resume that brings your power across on the page

- How to stop pitching applications into soul-crushing automated recruiting sites and reach your hiring managers directly at their desks with a twenty-first-century kind of cover letter

Reinvention Roadmap is a job-search and career-planning book with a self-discovery twist. As you go through the book's chapters and exercises, you will look back at your life so far and look ahead at your path going forward. You will realize that you have much more power than you thought you had—and you will learn how to bring that power across on your job search to get the job you deserve. Plus, you will learn how to manage your career the way every CEO manages his or her business. You won't let your employer manage your career for you anymore—you'll manage it yourself! You'll realize that the only people who deserve your talents are the people who "get" you: those who resonate at your frequency and see the value in your experience and gifts.

WHY DID I WRITE THIS BOOK?

I wrote *Reinvention Roadmap* because in my travels, writing, speaking, singing, and drawing about the changing workplace, I heard from thousands of people who were frustrated with their careers. They told me, "The job-search process is broken. I know I'm qualified, but I can't get a job interview!"

I've been writing about the changing workplace, careers, and how to get a job for 20 years. I've been speaking about these same topics in live appearances and on TV and the radio. I wrote this book to make these concepts accessible to working people and job-seekers all over the world.

I'm passionate about helping people remember their gifts and talents, because the working world is a tough place to navigate. It's easy to lose your mojo (life force) and your self-esteem as a job-seeker. It's easy to feel alone and worthless, but I want you to know that you are anything but worthless. You are mighty and powerful. It can be hard to remember that when you get discouraged on the job-search trail, but it's true!

I wrote this book (and drew the illustrations in it) to wake you up and inspire you, to make you smile and laugh, and maybe even cry when you remember that you have much more going for you than your recent job-search experiences might suggest. We all get down and lose our mojo. We all forget our gifts. This book will remind you about things you've forgotten about yourself—important and worthy things!

My mission in this book is to shift the way you look at yourself, and to remind you of the power that you have to run your own life and career.

That was my prime motivation for writing this book. But I have more in store for you here than helping you to know yourself and your talents better—though that is very important! I also lay out practical tips about the actual job search and how you can best navigate this new working world. I show you how to break the rules.

My background is Human Resources leadership. I ran the Human Resources function for a Fortune 500 company, one of the largest companies in the world. I hired thousands of people, and now I consult with employers who hire thousands more people. Here's one thing I noticed about recruiting: The traditional recruiting process—the way companies find and choose people to work for them—is broken. In fact, it needs major fixing, and that's one reason my colleagues and I at Human Workplace are so busy. Still, if you need a job, you can't wait for employers to fix their broken recruiting systems. You need to know how to leap over the broken recruiting system. You need a "side door" to reach your next boss directly instead of pitching resumes and job applications into faceless mechanical recruiting websites. You'll learn how to do that in this book. I'll also show you more rules to break.

10 RULES YOU'LL LEARN HOW TO BREAK:

1. "The only acceptable resume language is stiff, formal, and governmental. Resumes are supposed to say things like 'Results-oriented professional with a bottom-line orientation.'" ★BREAK! THIS RULE.

2. "The way to apply for jobs is to find job ads that interest you and respond to them in exactly the way spelled out in the ad." ★BREAK! THIS RULE.

3. "Your value and worth are set by your employer, not by you." ★BREAK! THIS RULE.

4 "Once you choose a career path, you have to stay in that career path throughout your career." ★BREAK! THIS RULE!

5 "When you're applying for a job, you have to do whatever the company's representatives tell you to do (and fast!)." ★BREAK! THIS RULE!

6 "Your best brand is a listing of your past employers and your skills." ★BREAK! THIS RULE!

7 "Never contact a department manager directly." ★BREAK! THIS RULE!

8 "When you apply for a job, use your cover letter to explain how your background matches the job description in the job ad." (You won't write cover letters at all.) ★BREAK! THIS RULE!

9 "The way to succeed in your career is to work hard at your job and, when you need a new job, to take the first job offer you get." ★BREAK! THIS RULE!

10 "Your education, your professional training, and your past job titles dictate what kinds of jobs you can get or can perform." ★BREAK! THIS RULE!

Are you ready to break these rules and take charge of your career? Good, because while you're breaking these rules, you'll grow new muscles, too. You'll stop looking at yourself as a bundle of skills and qualifications and instead see yourself as the vibrant, talented, creative, and awesome person you are—a person any company would be lucky to have on its team.

HOW IS REINVENTION ROADMAP ORGANIZED?

Reinvention Roadmap is organized into 25 chapters. Each chapter includes lessons and exercises for you to complete. The chapters are organized into four parts: Getting Altitude, Finding Your Path, Taking Steps, and Growing Muscles & Mojo.

In **Getting Altitude**, you'll look back at your path in life so far and look ahead at the future stretching out before you.

In **Finding Your Path**, you'll dig into the question, "What is the best career for me and how do I pursue it?"

In **Taking Steps**, you'll start dreaming up the life and career you deserve. This dreaming stage is fun, but you also have to take steps to make your vision real. You'll learn the steps to getting the job you want and the career you deserve.

In **Growing Muscles & Mojo**, you're going to keep growing and learning throughout your life. Once you step into your reinvention, you'll never stop reinventing yourself.

Throughout the book you will need a journal—I call it a Mojo Journal—to record your thoughts and reactions to the text as you go along. Get yourself any journal you like with plenty of space for writing down all your reflections and "Aha!" moments on your *Reinvention Roadmap* journey. I'll discuss your journal in more details in Chapter One.

THE REINVENTION ROADMAP GLOSSARY

In the back of the book is a comprehensive glossary with the special terms used in this book, along with their definitions. Some of the terms may be familiar to you, while other terms will likely be new. Some of the terms also may have different meanings in *Reinvention Roadmap* than the definitions you're familiar with. If you come across a term in the book you don't know, check the glossary in the back of the book to see if it's defined there. You're stepping into a whole new world, and like any new place you visit for the first time, there's a new language to learn!

ARE YOU READY?

This is a book, as you can see—it is full of words and images on pages. However, *Reinvention Roadmap* is more than a book. It is a path for you to follow as you learn a new way to manage your career. It's a course in book form and a methodology for you to first explore, and then master. You won't be a backseat passenger as you follow the Reinvention Roadmap path. You'll be driving! You'll be actively learning as you read the lessons in this book and then complete the exercises in your journal.

By the time you've completed *Reinvention Roadmap*, you will know how to do the following:

- Take control of your career and run it like a business;

- Use the powerful concept of Business Pain to your advantage;

- Break old-fashioned job-search rules and step into a new perspective on your career, your skills, and your value to employers and clients;

- Choose your own career path and brand yourself for the jobs you want;

- Directly reach hiring managers (aka your future boss!); this means you'll stop applying for jobs through awful online recruiting websites;

- Start a consulting business, either a part-time business alongside your full-time job or your job search, or a full-time consulting business; and

- Get altitude on your career: to see each job and professional assignment as a step on your path, a path that belongs entirely to you!

MY OWN REINVENTION ROADMAP STORY

I traveled the Reinvention Roadmap path myself, starting about 40 years ago. I was a punk rocker with half a degree in vocal performance. I had no idea what to do with my life or career. Little by little I figured it out, and realized something very important that I want you to understand, too. Here's what I learned: "Only the people who get you, deserve you."

You don't have to get every job you apply for. You don't need everyone in the world to like your brand of jazz. No matter how hard you try, everyone won't appreciate you or see your talents.

That's okay. Some people will see your talents, and your job is to find those people and then let the folks who don't get you go and live happy lives without you. You don't need them. You have something powerful to bring to the world, and in this book you'll figure out what that powerful gift is.

Enjoy the journey!

CHAPTER ONE

THE REINVENTION ROADMAP AND YOUR MOJO JOURNAL

Most of us haven't been running our own careers. That's not good, because no one else will run your career if you don't. We have been taught to get a job and then let our employer run our career for us. That's dangerous! You can take charge of your own career and make short- and long-term career decisions for yourself.

Taking charge of your career means running your career like a business. The Reinvention Roadmap is a path that will take you from the state of "I'm not running my career, and no one else is running my career, either!" to the state of running your career like a business.

Here are some things you will learn throughout this book as you begin to take charge of your own career:

- You'll decide what you want to do next in your career and what you want over the long term. You'll think about your whole life, not just your job. After all, what good would it do you to have a great job if that job didn't support your goals for your life?

- You'll decide what kind of work you want to do—work that you enjoy, that you're good at, and that will pay you what you're worth.

- You'll brand yourself for the kind of work you want—whether you've performed that work in the past or not. (You are much more qualified than you think, after all!)

- You'll make a list of target employers and clients to pursue.

- You'll explore becoming a part-time or full-time consultant. When you begin to grow your consulting muscles, you'll watch your mojo and your marketability increase dramatically!

- You'll reach out to employers in a new way—not by completing time-wasting and mojo-sucking automated application forms, but by reaching your own department manager directly at his or her desk with a powerful message you've composed just for him or her.

- You'll learn about the value of your services, and you'll learn to talk about money in your job search and your consulting conversations as comfortably and easily as you talk about the weather today.

- You'll get used to spotting Business Pain in the environment around you, so that you can talk to people about the pain (problems) they're experiencing in their businesses and your ability to solve their pain—rather than branding yourself this way: "I'm a Bookkeeper with eight years of experience." (No one cares about that!)

- Whether you consult for money or not, you'll adopt a consulting mindset regarding your work. You'll see each new job or assignment as a problem to solve—not as a set of tasks to repeat over and over (how would you learn anything new that way?).

- You'll grow your muscles and mojo to keep learning and keep feeling more confident every day!

What are your reactions to this list of goals? Do they seem daunting, or simple? You may find them a little of both as you keep moving down the Reinvention Roadmap.

WHAT IS MOJO?

Mojo is your life force and your energy level. When your Mojo Fuel Tank is full, you feel like you can climb mountains! When your fuel tank is nearly empty, it's hard to do anything—even to get out of bed.

THE REINVENTION ROADMAP STEPS

Let's break down the steps in taking control of your career.

Step One: Get Altitude

Getting altitude means thinking about your life and your career with perspective.

It is hard to get out of our day-to-day to-do list and our immediate concerns to think longer term, but that is what your reinvention and "mojo-fication" as a working person requires! To get altitude, you have to step back and look at your whole life. You have to ask the questions, "What do I want to accomplish while I'm alive? How can I take a step toward my life goals by getting a job that supports those goals?"

Getting altitude means giving yourself permission to dream as expansively as you like.

No one will judge you if you don't hit all your goals, or if you don't get to your dream scenario right away. Your path is not a straight line and it doesn't run on a timetable, at least not one that you can control. You will be more successful (by any measure) and feel stronger when you let go of external yardsticks and judgments about what you *should* be doing with your career or your life.

Your job is to walk your path according to *your* mission, soaking up the learning along the way. You're going to decide what to do with your life and your career. It's wonderful to have people around you who support you, but this is your reinvention. It's your journey! You are going to take control of your career and run it like a business, making all the important decisions yourself.

Step Two: Choose a Place to Put Your Canoe in the Water

Choice is an important concept in your reinvention, career change, or job search. You get to choose your next step and the one after that, but the flip side is that you must choose.

When we wake up in our own reinvention, it often hits us that the months, years, or decades of sleepwalking through our careers was a choice, at some level.

We didn't realize that doing nothing about our careers was also a choice, but it was. That's okay! We get a new chance to choose now, and we're going to grab it and take control. You can design the life and career you want, and your flame will grow tremendously when you do. It's magnificent that you've jumped into this Reinvention Roadmap project. It means you value yourself enough to stop and think about your career and your life with perspective, or altitude.

Do you feel that you get to decide where to travel on your path, or do you feel that you do not have that much control over your life?

Most of your learning as a job-seeker will come through your interactions with the real world and with hiring managers, Human Resources people, recruiters, and other folks you'll deal with in your job search. The place you choose to put your job-search and reinvention canoe in the water may not be your ultimate, "dream job"–type career, although it could be. It will be a step on your path. Your goal is to get into the water and start navigating. Your perspective will be very different once you're in the water than it is from the shore.

In this book you'll learn how to put your canoe firmly in the water and take off in whichever direction you choose. It's a mojo-boosting experience to job-hunt when you know how you can help employers solve their problems.

Step Three: Brand Yourself for the Jobs You Want

A lot of people feel uncomfortable about the idea of "branding" themselves. You might think, "I'm not a brand of toothpaste! I don't need a brand."

Here is a way to think about your personal brand. It is the way that people think about you and what they know of you. There's nothing evil or tacky about a personal brand.

You can say, "I don't want a personal brand!" but that is like going out for a walk on a sunny day and saying, "I don't want to cast a shadow!" You will cast a shadow whether you want to or not. You have a brand whether you like the idea of branding or not.

You can use a different word to describe the way people encounter you if you don't like the term "branding." You get to choose the words you use to describe yourself to people who don't already know you. Those words are very important.

The way you describe yourself to people you're meeting for the first time—including your possible next boss and/or possible new clients, if you work for yourself—is very important. You'll brand yourself as a living, breathing, and talented human being, not a bundle of disconnected skills and credentials.

You'll brand yourself like an individual, because you are individual! There is no one like you. Why should you sound like a robot or a zombie when you're obviously funny, interesting, smart, wise, and creative?

You'll brand yourself in a way that's relevant to the people you can help! You'll think about the people who will be meeting you for the first time by reading your Human-Voiced Resume or your LinkedIn profile. You'll ask yourself, "What will those people—those hiring managers and possible new clients—be interested in? What's the best way for me to describe myself to them, given that they don't know me yet and they are busy people?"

Step Four: Create Your
Target Employer and/or Target Client List

You want to begin to zero in on and research particular organizations—the ones you might want to work with and for. You won't let your job search and reinvention be ruled by the Help Wanted and published job advertising! You can get a job and/or get consulting work whether you pay attention to published job ads or not.

Step Five: Think about How You Could Work for Yourself

Think about the question, "What could I do for money that doesn't involve working for a salary or wages?" In this step, you'll explore your entrepreneurial side. That doesn't mean you will launch a business, although it would be fantastic if you did. Rather, it means that you'll think of your business and its future (which is your future!) the way an entrepreneur does—the way every business owner thinks about his or her business.

If you were going to start a business working for yourself, what sort of business would it be?

Step Six: Learn the Whole Person Job Search

As you follow the Reinvention Roadmap, you'll learn the basic elements of a nontraditional and very powerful job-search method called the Whole Person Job Search. You'll bring your whole personality and your talents—not just the list of qualifications that an employer's job ads ask for!—to your job search.

You'll use Pain Letters (not cover letters!) and your Human-Voiced Resume to get a new job, instead of completing soul-crushing online job applications and waiting for months to hear back from employers. Not every hiring manager has to get you. You only need one job at a time, or just a few consulting clients. Only the people who get you, deserve you!

Step Seven: Know the Value of Your Services

One thing every business owner knows is the value of his or her services. You are a business owner, and you will learn the value of your services, too! What do you think your talents are worth to your employer and/or to your consulting clients, right now?

Step Eight: Learn to Spot Business Pain

You'll practice spotting Business Pain in your environment. What is Business Pain? It's any problem that a businessperson or any organizational decision-maker is struggling with. Every organization has pain. Your power in the hiring equation, whether you work for yourself or for someone else, is in your ability to spot Business Pain around you (or individual pain, if you provide services to individuals) and to solve it!

Most of us tend to think about ourselves as job titles. We say, "I'm an Administrative Assistant" or "I'm a Warehouse Manager," but in reality we are problem-solvers and experts who solve big, expensive problems for our employers every day.

Step Nine: Base Short-Term Actions on Your Long-Term Plans

Now that you are taking charge of your career and running it like a business, you'll look out over the long term and you'll base your short-term actions on your long-term plans and your vision. You won't be a victim of circumstance, if you ever were one. You're in charge! You're the star of your movie!

Step Ten: Grow Your Muscles & Mojo

As you walk the Reinvention Roadmap path you will gain confidence in your own abilities and realize that you are much, much more talented and capable than you think. Your muscles and mojo will grow, and as they grow you will help other people grow their flames, too!

YOUR MOJO JOURNAL

While you're working on this Reinvention Roadmap program, it's a great idea to keep a journal. A journal is any notebook that feels comfortable to write in. It could be a kid's school composition book or a journal with a cover that pleases you. It doesn't matter what kind of journal you choose. It only matters that you write in it every day or as often as you can!

Your Mojo Journal will be your place to capture your thoughts and ideas as you complete this Reinvention Roadmap program. Capture every "Aha!" that occurs to you. Put it in your journal. Write about what was happening when you got the "Aha!"

You'll see Mojo Journal prompts throughout this book. Every time you are asked to write in your Mojo Journal, you'll see this image.

When you write in your Mojo Journal, just write. Don't worry about writing perfectly. Your Mojo Journal is not for publication (at least not yet). It's for you! When you get used to putting your ideas down on paper, new ideas will flow more easily through your body and out through your fingers and your pen onto the page.

You'll think about things differently and recall things differently when you start to write regularly in your Mojo Journal. Don't worry if you don't like what you write at first. It doesn't matter. You are stepping into new territory—don't judge yourself harshly!

What Does Personal Growth Have to Do with My Career?

We are talking about personal growth as we talk about careers. What is personal growth?

It's nothing scary. Personal growth is nothing more complicated than looking at your place in the world and seeing how you can shift anything that isn't working for you and live a healthier life. Growth and change are two sides of the same coin.

We can tell when we need to make a change—when something (or someone) in our lives isn't meeting our needs anymore. That's all personal growth means. We don't need to shy away from it! We all grow and change every day, the same way every living thing does. When we take charge of our own personal growth, we pay conscious attention to it. We don't fall asleep and let life events wash over us. We take charge of our own lives.

Once you see that you have a path and that it's your job to figure out what that path is and follow it, you'll feel stronger. You'll feel more confident. Your career will get easier then, and so will any other areas of your life that are stressing you out. You will grow muscles thinking about the topics you'll explore in this book, and working on the exercises and completing the assignments at the end of each chapter.

It's an awesome feeling to notice yourself learning. It's a feeling we used to have many times a week or even many times a day when we were little kids. A lot of us haven't had that feeling lately! We haven't felt challenged. That's how our muscles got flabby. That's okay! Now we're growing our muscles again, and stretching them and feeling stronger all the time.

What have you learned lately? To get you started, here are some things others on the Reinvention Roadmap journey have learned:

- I learned how to cook meals on a tight budget. I lost my full-time job last year and I've been working part-time as a school health room aide. It's great to see my kids during the day, but the money is very limited and our finances are tight. I must say I'm excited about learning to make healthy and tasty dinners for my kids for a few bucks. I'm saving a ton of money and I'm very excited about what I've learned.

- I learned how to calm myself down when I'm stressed out. That has been such a huge problem for me, especially lately, since I've been job-hunting. I started practicing deep breathing and stretching, and it really helps. I'm proud of myself for that.

- I realized that I've taught myself how to use LinkedIn—and I wasn't even trying! I realized it when I showed my sister-in-law how to use LinkedIn last week. How did I get so good at LinkedIn? Just trying stuff, I guess!

What ideas did you get from these three stories? Write your ideas in your Mojo Journal.

20 Mojo Journal Writing Prompts

What should you write about in your Mojo Journal? Here are 20 ideas to get you going. You can write about each one of these ideas at a time, or you can pick a few topics you enjoy thinking and writing about and stick with those—or you can write about anything you want!

1. Write about what made you begin this Reinvention Roadmap program.

2. Write about your ideal job.

3. Write about the things you know you're good at, and about times when you knew you saved the day or did something important and valuable at work.

4. Write about your memories of your childhood. Write about what you thought you'd like to be when you grew up.

5. Write about the people who most inspire you. What is it about those people that makes them inspirational to you?

6 Write about your career so far. How did you choose the career path you're currently on? What other career paths have you been interested to explore?

7 Write about the most important life lessons you've learned.

8 Write about your favorite movie and why you like it so much. What element of your personality does your favorite movie speak to?

9 Write about your favorite memories from work—memories from any job you've held, whether it was just recently or years ago. What makes those memories so powerful for you?

10 Write about the people who taught you how to do your first job or first several jobs. What lessons did those early coaches and mentors teach you?

11 Write about your ideal living situation. What sort of home would you choose for yourself if you could choose any living situation? Why does your ideal living situation suit you so well?

12 Write about the novel or nonfiction book you will write when you have time.

13 Write about the worst or most embarrassing job interview you ever had. Can you see the humor in your awful memories now that some time has passed?

14 Write about a problem that you especially love to solve at work. Why is this kind of problem your favorite problem to solve?

15 Write about what friends and relatives tell you you're especially good at. Can you use some of your hidden talents in your next job or the next step on your path?

16 Write about your beliefs. What issues or causes do you care about? How do these issues and causes connect to your mission here on earth?

17 Write a story about a young person who follows a path very much like the path you have followed so far. What advice would you give that person on his or her path?

18 Write about something that you heard or saw during the day that made you stop and think.

19 Write about your dreams—the dreams you remember when you wake up in the morning and your dreams for your life as well.

20 Write about your life as you'd like to experience it five years or 10 years in the future. How will your life change during that time?

Choose a Mojo Journal you like and start writing in it! That's a big step.

Don't censor yourself as you write or worry about your penmanship, spelling, or grammar. No one will be grading you—just write! If you aren't sure what to write, use the 20 Mojo Journal Prompts to get started.

PART 1

GETTING·ALTITUDE

Part One of your Reinvention Roadmap journey will guide you to get altitude on your life and career. What does it mean to get altitude? It means thinking about your life and career from a new perspective and asking important questions about where you've been so far in your life and where you're headed.

Are you ready to get altitude? Let's begin!

IT'S YOUR LIFE, AND IT'S YOUR CAREER

Years ago, it was a very big event to get your first "real" job. It's still a big deal to get your first "real" job today, but 25 or 30 years ago your first "real" job was a much bigger deal than it is now!

Here's why: Back then, you might well have stayed at your first "real" job for decades. Many if not most working people got a good job at a young age and stayed in the same company until they retired. That's why it was such a big deal to get the job initially.

At age 21 or 22 you might already know, "This is what I'm going to do for the rest of my career." Once you got that first career-type job, you might have expected to stay with that first employer for many years—and maybe you did just that.

Maybe you are still working at the first job you took as a young person—or maybe one day, that job went away in a puff of smoke!

Have you had a career shock or had a job go away suddenly? That's not an uncommon occurrence these days! The workplace has changed dramatically over the past two decades, but our ideas about work and about how to find a job have not kept pace with those changes.

Most of us still look for a new job the way we did years ago. We still pretend that when we get a new job, we might stay at the job for years on end. That isn't very likely, but most of us still have an old-fashioned mindset when it comes to our careers. We don't plan our careers very far ahead. We think, "I just need a job right now—any job!"

Once we have a job, we forget about our careers again.

What's your career story? Your career story holds tremendous wisdom for you. Your career story is a lot more than just job titles and company names and dates. Your career story is a big part of your life story!

Have you ever told your career story to anyone before? If not, now is a great time to do it! Tell your story to someone, or write about it in your Mojo Journal. You'll see how helpful it is to write down your ideas, hopes, feelings, memories, and plans!

LOSING A JOB

When you're a young person and you lose a job, even if you get fired, you may not really worry about it. You might figure, "I'll get another job—it's no big deal!" When you get older and you have obligations—like kids or animals to feed, a big rent check due on the first of the month, or house or car payments—losing your job becomes a much bigger problem.

When your job disappears, it can rock your whole world. Sometimes it's not only your income that goes away when you lose your job. Sometimes your sense of identity disappears at the same time!

That has happened to a lot of people.

ELENA'S STORY

Elena got laid off when she was 53, after 22 years working in the same job.

She said, "Losing my job was horrible. It was like a death in the family. My co-workers were my best friends. My job was a huge part of my life. I cared more about that job than I should have . . . I watered the plants in our office. I knew my co-workers' kids' names and their stories. Our kids grew up together, in a way. I was sick when my job went away."

What are your thoughts about Elena's story? Have you experienced something like what Elena did, or has someone close to you had an experience like hers? Write about them in your Mojo Journal.

Feelings of Loss

It's a big deal to lose a job suddenly.

It's traumatic, and I don't use that word lightly. It's a major, and often devastating, life event. Sometimes when you lose your job, it's not just your job that goes away but your entire career path.

It might be the career you've set your sights on or one that you've invested decades in that evaporates into thin air.

The real world is always changing. Industries grow and shrink. Organizations evolve (or fail to evolve, at their peril). New job descriptions emerge and old jobs go extinct. Positions get eliminated, shipped overseas, or replaced by technology. The business world shifts, and people get caught between the moving gears!

It's a huge blow when the future you were planning on goes up in a puff of smoke.

Your sense of stability in the world can be seriously rocked when your career path vanishes. More fundamentally, your understanding of what a hardworking person can expect from his or her economic environment can be shattered. You might feel angry and resentful on top of feeling sad about the loss of your job and/or career path.

Here are some of the emotions people feel when their world is rocked by a sudden, unexpected job loss:

- Sad

- Discouraged

- Hopeless

- Tired

- Confused

- Overwhelmed

Does any of this sound familiar? If so, write about your feelings in your Mojo Journal.

Jobs That Aren't a Good Fit

Your whole world is rocked when you lose a long-term job. It's equally disappointing when you work at a series of jobs only to find that none of them is right for you.

this job is not a FIT

Have you tried one or more jobs that were obviously not the right fit for you? Write about that in your Mojo Journal.

CAREER CONCERNS

It can be frustrating navigating the working world today. A lot of people are stressed out about their careers—and who can blame them? Your career pays your bills, and your landlord, or the bank that holds your mortgage, doesn't care whether you're working or not.

The grocery store doesn't care. You still have to buy groceries, even when you're out of work or working in a low-paying job.

Here are some of the most common career concerns I hear about from working people and job-seekers:

- I'm worried that my career path, which used to be so solid and clear, is going away or splintering. I'm not sure how I'll stay employed from now until the end of my career.

- I'm concerned that I might be stuck in the career path I have now, because that's the only career field I have credibility in. Who will hire me in any other field, where I have no experience?

- I'm worried that employers might not consider me because of my age.

- I'm concerned that I might not be able to earn what I'm worth.

- I'm not even thinking about my career—I just need a job, now!

Nearly everybody has worries and concerns about his or her career. When I talk with people on the radio or at live speaking events or in our coaching practice, I hear these concerns over and over. That's why I wrote this book!

What concerns do you have about your career?
Write about them in your Mojo Journal.

FALLING ASLEEP ON YOUR CAREER

We used to think that the biggest question we had to answer (or worry about) at any point in our career was, "Do I have a job right now?" We thought that if the answer to that question was, "Yes, I have a job," then we could go to sleep on our careers. We wouldn't have to think about our careers. Why think about your career when you have a job, right?

We used to believe that we only had to think about our careers when our jobs went away.

Have you felt in the past that if you had a job, you didn't need to think about your career? Most of us have fallen victim to that myth at one point or another. We didn't think we had to worry about our careers, as long as we were employed at the moment.

What does it mean to fall asleep on your career? When you fall asleep on your career, you stop thinking about it. When you fall asleep on your career, you pretend that your job is stable and secure. In reality you have no way to know whether your job is really secure, but when we go to sleep, we forget about that.

When you fall asleep on your career, you forget what you're good at, what you want from your life and career, and the incredible range and variety of things you could be doing professionally (far beyond whatever kind of work you're doing now).

I wrote this book for people who are still asleep (but who want to wake up and run their careers differently!) and for people who have woken up and are looking around them now and asking, "Now that I'm awake, what should I do about my career or my job search?"

The good news is that waking up to see the reality of your career in the new-millennium workplace is the first and most important step in getting to the career and life you want.

How would you describe your sleeping-or-waking state right now, where your career is concerned? Have you been asleep on your career? Have you just woken up suddenly? Write about this in your Mojo Journal.

If you see that you've been asleep on your career and have just woken up, welcome to the waking world! We are all learning together how to manage our careers.

KEITH'S STORY

I was completely asleep where my career was concerned. On the one hand I felt lucky to have a good job. I'm 52. I worked in my company for almost 30 years.

My wife would ask me, "How are things at your work?" and I'd say, "Things are fine at work—it's the same old, same old."

I wasn't really paying attention. I was fast asleep. A lot of things were changing. Two of our competitors went out of business. In our company we said, "Good, that's more business for us!" The whole industry was changing, and our company wasn't responding to the changes fast enough.

I can't blame our leaders for that. I was asleep, myself. I never thought about the question, "What do I want from my career?" I never tried to answer the question, "What would I do if this job went away?" I figured my boss and his boss knew more about our business than I did. I tuned out.

I don't know why I fell asleep and stopped paying attention to my career. Somehow I convinced myself that nothing could happen to my job. I guess it's because I couldn't deal with the huge problem I would have if I got laid off. It was a bad move on my part to tune out that way, because my job did go away. My whole company went away. My company was sold to a bigger company and all of us were out of work.

I had never made a plan about what to do if my job disappeared. I had been earning a pretty big salary. I had no idea about how to replace that salary and get a new job. I woke up fast when they told us, "Today is your last day on the job."

I'm still recovering from the mistake I made, when I fell asleep on my career. Now I'm working through the steps in the Reinvention Roadmap.

I go back and forth between feeling confident and bold, and feeling discouraged and wishing I could get my old job back. I feel like I'm on an emotional see-saw.

I can tell you this—I'll never fall asleep on my career again!

What are your thoughts about Keith's story? Tell them to a friend or write about them— or draw or paint about them.

Keith is like thousands of other people. Nobody ever told Keith he had to manage his career. Nobody ever told any of us that! Keith is in reinvention. He feels like he's on an "emotional see-saw."

What did Keith mean when he said that he feels like he's on a see-saw? He meant that his emotions go up and down. One day Keith feels excited about the next chapter in his career, and the next day he feels discouraged.

Keith also sees some positives in his sudden career jolt. Now he gets to try something new. He's going to learn a lot as he looks for his next job and takes a new step on his path.

Have you ever thought about changing careers or trying work that is more interesting, higher-paying, and/or more fun than the work you've done so far? Write your thoughts in your Mojo Journal.

THE TALENT MARKETPLACE

We can see that the working world is changing fast. The talent marketplace has changed. What is the talent marketplace? It's an imaginary space, but it has a big impact on working people.

The talent marketplace is the set of physical and electronic spaces where employers meet job applicants and vice versa. When you send out a resume or fill out a job application, you are stepping into the talent marketplace. When you go to work, either on the bus, in your car, on the train, or on a bicycle, you are stepping into the talent marketplace again. When you work virtually for people who might be thousands of miles away from wherever you are, you're in the talent marketplace, too.

The talent marketplace is any place where people perform services for other people—whether they work as employees, consultants, contractors, or in some other way. As long as work is being performed and people are being compensated for their work, we're talking about the talent marketplace.

The talent marketplace has changed dramatically over the past several years. Nearly everything we know about getting, having, and keeping a job has changed. Every single aspect of employment has changed dramatically.

What changes have you noticed in the working world lately? Here are some of the biggest changes that have taken place in the working world over the past 20 years, or even more recently.

- Working people stay at their jobs for shorter time periods than they used to.

- The traditional "career ladders" that working people often followed at work have disappeared. It is harder to get promoted to a higher-level job.

- Companies are changing their employees' job descriptions, titles, and job responsibilities more often than they used to do.

- Long-term employment with the same company doesn't have as much value as it used to. Years ago, having worked for one company for a long time was a kind of protection against getting laid off—but it's not anymore.

- Companies are less loyal to their employees than they were before, and employees are also less loyal to their employers. Relationships between working people and their employers have become more "just business" and less "one big, happy family."

- Even after working for one company for years, you can still be laid off at any time, or outsourced to a contracting firm with no benefits and a lower rate of pay.

- More employers are hiring contract labor instead of employees.

- Many of the new jobs that are being created are low-wage service jobs, rather than higher-wage manufacturing jobs or white-collar office jobs.

- Companies have changed their hiring processes. Most medium-sized and large employers use automated recruiting processes that are slow and unfriendly to job-seekers.

PART ONE

- Human Resources department budgets and head count have been slashed over the past several years. That means that Human Resources people have more job-seekers to deal with and less time to spend with each person. Communications with job-seekers have become more formal and less friendly.

- Job-seekers are fed up. Many working people are fed up, too.

Do any of these changes sound familiar, from your own experience? How can we respond to these changes to take our careers to a higher level, feel more secure and more marketable, and become more confident about seeking out and finding work we want to do?

A NEW WAY TO VIEW YOUR CAREER

I wrote this book and designed the Reinvention Roadmap career program because I heard from working people all over the world that they were frustrated and unhappy with their careers.

That makes sense. Most of us are still trying to use a 50-year-old model for career management, and it doesn't work anymore! The old model is broken.

This book, *Reinvention Roadmap*, will introduce you to a new way to think about your career. It will teach you a new way to find a job, and also nudge you (over and over again—so get ready!) to start thinking about your career as a business.

What is that new way to think about your career? It's that you are a business owner. Whether you've ever thought about yourself that way, or not, you are the CEO of your career and, even more importantly, the decision-maker in your life.

In your Reinvention Roadmap journey, you're going to take charge of your career, rather than letting employers (or anybody else) run your career for you. It's your life, and it's your career.

Tell someone you like and trust that you're thinking about your career. Talk over your career ideas with them. Ask them about their career thoughts and plans, too.

REINVENTION AND THE HUMAN WORKPLACE

I have a job description that didn't exist when my career started. My job is to study the workplace and try to understand why people behave the way they do at work. That's the kind of work I've done for over 30 years. I was a Human Resources person for a long time, and then I started to write and speak to audiences about the workplace. Maybe that sounds like a boring job, but it's not boring to me. I love it! I don't want to do anything else. I write columns about the workplace, and I speak, sing, and perform for groups around the world, always about careers and leadership in this new millennium. I draw pictures about working people and the crazy things we do at work. Together with my workmates at Human Workplace and a few million other people who have joined the global Human Workplace movement, I am on a mission to reinvent work for people.

REINVENTING WORK

Reinventing work for people means remembering that people go to work, not machines. It means remembering how people operate.

People are amazing, and they can outperform any machine on earth, but they can only do that if they are excited about what they're doing. People are incredible, but they can only achieve great things if their work is valued by the people they work with and work for.

I have been talking with people about their work for ages, and for years I have listened to people who said, "There must be new rules to running a career today, because the old rules don't work. If there are new rules for this new-millennium workplace, I'd love to know what they are. Working people and job-seekers need a new playbook!"

The old ways don't work anymore, and it is foolish to teach the old, out-of-date career rules to each new generation of job-seekers and working people.

Why teach people methods that haven't worked for years?

Common wisdom teaches job-seekers and students to build their careers around "secure jobs," but there is no security in any job today! We carry our security around with us.

I have seen otherwise-reputable colleges and universities advertising their degree programs to prospective students and their parents using the advertising message, "We grant the degrees that employers want!"

That's despicable! These colleges are saying, "Your kid will be employer-worthy once the kid gets our college's stamp on his or her backside!" They're saying, "Without our fancy degree, your kid doesn't have anything valuable to offer!"

I hope we have higher aspirations for our kids than to send them to college to become acceptable to some big corporation. Maybe they could go to college and find out who they are and what they care about. Maybe they could learn who they are without going to college.

Employers Treat Job-Seekers Poorly

In our society, at colleges and workforce development centers and elsewhere, people are taught to find a job. In institutions, everywhere you look, our society teaches job-seekers to be doormats and to put up with horrible treatment from employers. They are taught to beg for a job. They are taught that they are just one out of many, many qualified people who apply for every job opening.

That's not true! I was on the employer side of the hiring equation for decades. I was a Human Resources executive. No company ever has enough qualified applicants. That was true even during the recent recession, but few employers want to admit it.

There are never enough qualified job applicants for the jobs that employers

STOP BEGGING FOR A JOB

advertise, and there is always a level of hiring (or contracting for services) in nearly any going concern, company, or institution.

When the economy is strong, employers need more help, and when the economy is weaker, organizations' problems get bigger and they need sharp people to solve those problems.

It is hard to find great people, and hard to keep them on board. Most people who advise job-seekers don't tell them that, but they should!

When companies have a hard time filling their job openings, you'd think they would work especially hard to invite job-seekers warmly into their recruiting processes and to keep them interested in their job opportunities.

Unfortunately, way too many employers have done just the opposite. They've made it so difficult and so unfriendly to apply for jobs in their companies that many talented people who could help those companies won't put up with their broken recruiting processes. A recruiting process is the set of steps that a company or another organization follows when they need to hire a new person or more than one new person to add to their teams.

Job-seekers know that most recruiting processes are horrible—unfriendly, slow, and even insulting. Employers ask intrusive personal questions and often treat job-seekers like dirt, starting the moment you begin completing the employer's online job application form. Then, after investing a lot of time and energy completing the form, you may hear nothing back from the employer—for weeks, or perhaps ever! You can send out resumes and fill out job applications until you're exhausted, and still hear nothing back.

That's not just a poor recruiting practice. It's poor business leadership. If a company's recruiting process is broken, then the company's leaders aren't doing their jobs.

Working people know that recruiting is not the only part of the corporate and institutional worlds that doesn't work well.

Many organizations struggle to lead their employees in a human way. It isn't hard to lead an organization with a human voice and to attract and keep great people on your team, but it requires a level of honesty and attention to human topics that many organizations struggle to attain.

It's no wonder that working people are spooked. Many people have had the rug pulled out from under their feet at least once during their careers. You can work in the same place for years and then one day be told, "Your job has been eliminated."

A New Roadmap for Job-Seekers

Who can run a career with that much uncertainty? We need a new roadmap for work in the twenty-first century. CEOs of international corporations can see that working people and job-seekers are burnt out on the old working world of crushing rules and policies and a fear-based leadership. For one thing, managing through fear is incredibly expensive. The ice is beginning to break and that is a great thing.

In 2012, we launched the Human Workplace movement to reinvent work for people, and a million people follow the movement now. More and more employers are seeing the passion–performance connection and taking steps to put a human voice in their leadership practices and their recruiting.

The shift from mechanical work to the Human Workplace is happening slowly. What are job-seekers supposed to do in the meantime? People need to know how to find work and, more importantly, how to navigate a career in the new-millennium talent marketplace.

People who read my columns and came to our workshops told me, "The working world has changed, obviously. Where is the roadmap for the new world of work? How do I brand myself for the jobs I want, and take control of my career rather than letting my employers decide what I get to do next?"

I listened to them and wrote this book and the Reinvention Roadmap program to answer that need.

WHERE DID THE REINVENTION ROADMAP COME FROM?

When I was a corporate HR person for many years, I saw a lot of interesting things and met amazing people, and my biggest "Aha!" as an HR person was this:

The more energy we spend growing the good energy (we call it Team Mojo) in an organization, the better every business result will be. Our customers will be happier, better informed, and more loyal to us when our culture makes it easy to hire great people who want to provide great service to our customers. We'll make more money in our companies when our workplaces are more human. Work will be more fun.

As a leadership team, it's easy to create your own Human Workplace, no matter what kind of business you're in. It isn't hard to make any workplace a Human Workplace. To step onto the Human Workplace path, we only have to stop pretending that we can accomplish anything good at work by making people afraid. We have to stop pretending that it's responsible and businesslike to write policies that treat employees like children. We have to have enough confidence in ourselves to hire people we can trust, and then to trust them.

We have to be brave enough to lead through trust instead of fear.

Employers who want to become Human Workplaces have big changes to make in their approaches to leadership.

Individual working people and job-seekers who want the benefits of the Human Workplace path have changes to make, too! They have to shift their views about their own careers, and begin to manage their careers the way business owners manage their businesses.

As I wrote and spoke to groups over the years about the Human Workplace vision over the past few years, I saw a lot of excitement among readers and audiences, but I also saw a lot of fear and finger-pointing. Working people said, "My employer has to change, before I will change!"

Job-seekers said, "Big companies make it so hard for job-seekers!"

Everyone I talked with wanted the benefits of the Human Workplace, but they didn't necessarily want to look in the mirror and make personal changes to get those benefits.

Here's the secret to your reinvention and to having the career and life you want: Everything will start to shift when you take the brave step of looking in the mirror! You are the star of the movie! It's your life, and it's your career.

The techniques and approaches you'll learn in this Reinvention Roadmap program will only work for you when you do the personal reflection that will allow you to see how your path has unfolded the way it has.

You have to look at your power in every relationship you have—including your relationship with your job and with your career. When you get that "Aha!"—when you see that you have arranged your life the way it is now for a variety of reasons, but that nobody is responsible for your life or career except you—you'll gain tremendous power.

You'll see that you have gotten yourself here, wherever you stand right now on your path, and that you've learned an amazing number and variety of things along the way to getting here. Nothing you've experienced has been wasted. You have nothing to feel regret about or to feel embarrassed about. Whatever you have done in your life has led you to this spot—so you can learn from it!

You'll see that you get to choose where your path leads from here. Nobody controls you unless you let them. You'll take responsibility for your path when you realize that taking responsibility is the only way to get the things you want.

WHAT IS REINVENTION?

Reinvention is a career or life shift during which you leave one state or chapter in your life and step into a new one.

Sometimes people reinvent themselves because they get tired of their old life or career. Sometimes reinvention is forced on them because their job goes away or some other life event requires them to start over in a new situation.

What does reinvention mean to you?

Here's what reinvention means to me.

Reinvention means change. Personal reinvention is the process that any living thing goes through when the world around it has changed such that the creature has to adapt, or as the living thing (even you!) reaches a new stage in life. You are in reinvention when you can tell that you have to make changes—especially if you're not sure exactly what those changes are. If the changes were obvious, you wouldn't stop and wonder. You wouldn't explore. You wouldn't be in reinvention! But you are.

Maybe you need a new job.

Maybe you need to change your location.

Maybe you're tired of the work you've been doing and you're ready for a change.

Maybe you want to get maximum perspective on your situation and decide what you want from your life and career.

Have any of these changes shown up in your life recently?

- You lost your job.

- You realized that you needed to get a new job or find a new career path.

- You left a long-term personal relationship.

- You moved to a new place.

- You finished a degree or training program and are ready for a new start.

- You took charge of your health, your finances, your relationships, or another important area of your life. You are making changes!

As they become aware that their world is shifting and they're in reinvention, some people say, "I had been feeling antsy or dissatisfied for a few years, but then _____ happened and I knew I had to make changes." How would you fill in the blank in that sentence?

People in reinvention often say these things:

- I feel as though I've been sleeping and now I'm just waking up.

- As I look back at my path, I can see certain mistakes that I made earlier in life. I didn't realize they were mistakes when I was making them, of course. Now I see how I goofed up back then—but I learned something from the mistake, so that's good.

- I am starting to think about what I want from my life, not just what other people expect from me.

- I can tell that I've been asleep where my life and career were concerned. I tuned out. Now I'm tuning back in!

- I don't mind going to work. I want to go to work. I want a job that makes me look forward to going to work. I feel like I deserve that!

- I want to know more about my own talents. I know I can get a job when I need one, but I'm tired of holding a job that's just like the other jobs I've had.

- I want to go further in my life. I want to expand my vision for myself.

What are your thoughts about these common reactions to personal reinvention?

WHO CONTROLS YOUR PATH— YOU, OR SOMEONE ELSE?

We always have a choice, even when we don't think that we do. We always have the choice to say, "My life is under my control" or "I'm being blocked and trapped by forces that are bigger than I am!"

Almost everyone has had a lousy job, a demanding boss, a difficult family situation, an empty bank account, or another big problem that got in our way. It's very easy and tempting when big problems arise to say, "What do you expect me to do about it? I can't control everything!"

When we decide, "This problem is bigger than I am, so there's nothing I can do about it," something terrible happens. We become victims. We aren't in control anymore—not because somebody took control from us, but because we gave it away.

Almost everyone has done the same thing at some point. Here is a story about Paddy, who thought there was nothing he could do about his career situation.

PADDY'S STORY

Paddy was a Supervisor in a distribution company. It was a great job. Then Paddy got laid off. He thought, "I need a job fast—like tomorrow!" and he took a retail job. The job was okay, but it didn't pay enough for Paddy to live on. He couldn't pay his bills.

Paddy moved in with his parents, which was a hardship for him and for them. Paddy's dad told him, "Why don't you get a better career?" and Paddy said, "Dad, you think it's easy?" There was a lot of tension in the house.

Paddy decided, "I can't change my situation, so I'm going to make the best of things." He worked at his job on his scheduled workdays, then went home and played video games. He tuned out. Paddy told his friends, "The deck is stacked against me, because I don't have a college degree."

When Paddy said that, he believed it. He believed that the deck was stacked against him. Paddy had never been told, "Our company won't hire you because you don't have a college degree." Paddy had never applied for a job that required a college degree. When he lost his job at the distribution company, Paddy had immediately applied for three retail jobs, and he had taken the first job he got.

Still, Paddy's idea that the deck was stacked against him remained in his mind, and to him, that idea justified his decision to tune out on his career, keep his retail job, play video games, and forget that he had ever had plans or aspirations.

One day Paddy's mom told him, "Paddy, I want to be a good mom. We aren't doing you any favors by letting you live with us and pretend that you are not an adult, because you are an adult. It's time for you to get back into the game. It's time for you to take some steps and take responsibility for your situation."

Paddy was shocked, but he had no choice. He mentioned to his manager at work, "My mom said I have to get a better job."

"What does 'a better job' mean to you?" asked Paddy's manager.

"I don't really know," said Paddy. "I haven't thought about it much."

"You should think about it," said Paddy's manager. "We have team leader jobs available here, but I had never thought of you as a team leader because, frankly, you seem kind of tuned out."

Paddy was shocked to hear his manager say that Paddy seemed to be tuned out at work. Back in his old supervisor job before he got laid off, Paddy was on top of everything. He took a lot of pride in his work.

Paddy did a lot of thinking over the next few days. He told his mom and dad, "I got knocked on my knees when I lost my job, and then when I lost my apartment. I didn't see how I could influence what was happening. Now I'm getting back on my feet."

Paddy told his manager, "I'm going to apply for the team leader job you have available. I also want to know what you would like to see from me in the job I have right now that would give you the confidence to promote me to a team leader job."

"Wow!" said Paddy's manager. "This is a whole new Paddy."

"You're right," said Paddy. "This is a whole new me! I guess I lost more mojo than I realized when I got laid off. Now I'm getting my mojo back!"

 How does Paddy's situation relate to your own? Write about that in your Mojo Journal.

It's empowering to think, *I'm in perpetual reinvention now. I'm not going to fall asleep on my life and career again. My eyes are going to stay open!* At the same time, there are messages everywhere that tell us, "Forget the reinvention. Just get a job—any job!" You may feel that trying to change your career or life situation is hopeless or impossible, the same way Paddy did when he got laid off and lost his apartment. People around you can sometimes make your getting-altitude process harder, although they don't mean to. They might tell you, "Forget all the navel-gazing and just get a job!"

Even people who love us may tell us to take the first job we can get and be happy to have a job at all. Sometimes the people who are closest to us give us the worst career advice, because they just want us to be employed! If they've fallen asleep on their own careers, they may want you to go back to sleep, too.

Even people very close to us can tell us, "Why do you need to reinvent yourself? If it ain't broke, don't fix it!"

Sometimes the people who are closest to us get fearful. They think, "If you design the life you want and step toward it, what if that new life doesn't include me?"

They might think, "If you look in the mirror and learn important things about yourself, you'll change. I'm not sure I want you to change. If you start making changes, I'll feel pressure to shift my life, too. I don't want to do that!"

Sometimes the people who are closest to us resist our reinvention. They might tell us to stop reaching for the stars. They might say, "Why aren't you happy with what you've got?"

 What are your thoughts about people around you supporting your reinvention? Write them in your Mojo Journal.

This Reinvention Roadmap program is designed to guide you through the steps to taking control of your career (and your life, as a bonus!). As you may have noticed, this program includes exercises and assignments for you to complete on your own. The more thought and energy you put into this program, the greater your benefits will be!

 What idea from this book has made the biggest impression on you so far? Write it in your Mojo Journal.

YOUR ASSIGNMENT

Your body is important in your reinvention. Sometimes we forget about our bodies and let our minds run the show! Get outside and ride your bike, take a long walk, or work in your garden. Do something physical and get out of your busy mind.

YOUR LEARNING AND YOUR PATH

We learn throughout life. If we stay awake and pay attention, we'll never stop learning.

Sadly, some people don't want to stay awake and keep learning. They stopped learning when they left school, and their mind closed to new ideas.

Only the people who keep learning, keep growing! They get smarter and more confident because they stay awake and pay attention to what's going on around them. They stay nimble and tuned in to the real world around them.

If you're alive, you're going to have experiences every day, but you won't learn from them unless you let the learning in.

Sometimes we try to keep the learning out!

Maybe your friend asks you, "Want to go see a foreign film with me tomorrow night?" and you say, "No, I don't want to read subtitles. It's too much trouble."

What does it mean when you experience a strong, negative reaction like that? It may mean, "I don't want to try anything new. I don't want to stretch myself. Learning new things is a pain."

When your friend asks you, "Want to go see a film with me?" or "Want to go try a new Ethiopian restaurant I found?" or "Want to go to a networking event with me and meet some people?" try saying, "Yes!"

When you say "yes" to something new, your opportunities for learning grow fast!

The more you think about the learning that you've already accumulated in your life, the more you'll keep learning!

We learn a huge amount as we go through our lives, but most of us seldom stop and think about what we're learning. We're too busy attending to our "to do" list.

  To begin thinking about your learning, grab your Mojo Journal and write your answers to these questions about your learning and your path in life so far:

1 What are the talents you most enjoy using, at work or anywhere? Here are a few ideas:

- Your problem-solving talent
- Your gift for working with other people
- Your customer service know-how
- Your writing or editing abilities
- Your computer talent
- Your way with mechanical and operational things
- Your financial aptitude
- Your mathematical smarts
- Your creative genius
- Your skill at leading and managing people

2 What talents would you love to use in your work but haven't had the chance to use, so far?

Grab the Learning

3 What are you good at doing that most people aren't good at?

As you think about what you're good at, you are getting altitude on your career, and a big part of the getting-altitude process is to know yourself.

Whether you stay in your traditional career path or choose a new one, you want to choose a career path that celebrates your talents, right? That's why we're talking about talents right now.

You know what you're good at. Think about your talents and abilities as you get altitude on your career situation. Why not focus on job opportunities that will make the most of your gifts?

You get to decide on your career path.

WHAT DO YOU LOVE TO DO?

PART ONE

If you've worked at one or more jobs already in your career, you may know that there are things you're capable of doing but have no interest in. You may know "I never want to create another spreadsheet if I can help it!" or "I never, ever want to have a job that keeps me on the phone all day."

What are some things you never want to do, or have tried and never want to do again?

What are some of the things you love to do? If you were independently wealthy and didn't need a regular paycheck, what would you do all day? What would you like to learn about or try?

What are some of the things you've taught yourself to do, so far in your life? Maybe you taught yourself how to work on cars or how to use spreadsheets.

What are some of the things you've learned from other people? Maybe your grandmother taught you to knit or your seventh-grade science teacher got you to fall in love with science.

What are some things you've learned recently? Maybe this morning you learned not to take a chance hitting the snooze button on your alarm clock or your phone. Maybe yesterday you learned a new way to get downtown and avoid the rush-hour traffic. As you look back at the past year or the past few years, what are some things you learned that you didn't know before?

Why is it important to think about your learning? The more you know about your path so far in life—the more you look back and think about where you've come from and what you've learned along the way to get here—the more altitude or perspective on your path you will have.

Also, when you think about your learning so far in life, you'll remember that you are on a path. Just because you are an adult—even someone who has lived a long time, like me—it doesn't mean you are done learning. You are a pie that is still baking.

You will never be done baking! If you sometimes feel, as most people do, that you've made mistakes or messed up in your path so far, you can let those feelings go.

BE AWARE OF YOUR LEARNING

Everything you've done in your life so far was perfect because those things that you did brought you here. Now you are awake and noticing your path and the learning you've collected along the way.

Your awareness of the learning you've gained so far in life is the key!

My four boys love video games. Only our younger boys play them now. The older boys don't play video games anymore, but they still talk about and pay attention to the latest games that come on the market. In many video games, you finish one level and you get to jump up to the next level. At each level there are cooler and fancier treasures to find or to win.

At the same time, each higher level in a video game brings greater challenges. If every level were easy, no one would want to keep playing the game. Things that are too easy for us get boring fast!

It's the same way in life. The more time you spend here on our planet, the more treasures you can find or earn. You can't mess up, as long as you're learning!

What are three of the most important things you've learned in your life so far? Write them down in the form of statements.

Here are examples:

I've learned that my family is more important than anything else.

I've learned that you can't judge a book by its cover.

I've learned that most people are really nice when you get to know them.

WHY DIDN'T WE LEARN THIS IN SCHOOL?

Sometimes when people begin thinking about their careers and their path, they wonder, "Why haven't I learned these ideas before? It is odd that I grew up from childhood to adulthood and no one ever told me, 'You get to choose what your grown-up life will be like.' I didn't have those lessons, or anyone guiding me!"

PART ONE

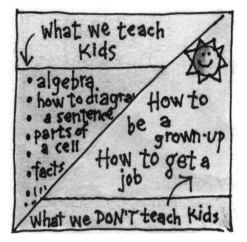

Most working people of all ages don't know how to manage their careers. They haven't been taught to do that. If these ideas are new to you, don't panic! It's not just you who hasn't learned how to run a career like a business. It's everybody!

In our society, we don't teach people to manage their careers—not in primary school, middle school, high school, or college. In our society—and I'm lumping every person, organization, and institution in this category who wants to be included in it—we do a horrible job of preparing young people for the working world.

In school, the subjects we choose to teach and the way we teach them tell kids, "Don't worry about what your life will be like when you're a grown-up. Just do well in school and get good grades! That's all you need to think about!"

This is an irresponsible way to prepare kids for the constantly shifting working world.

Sadly, our educational systems keep kids from exploring the critical question, "What do I want my life to be like when I'm an adult, and what steps can I take to have the life I want?"

Instead, we teach kids mathematics and science and social studies from a very old model. We teach them facts instead of teaching them how to think on their own. We teach the traditional school subjects in nearly the same way our grandparents learned them. Kids learn a lot of cool stuff in school, but they don't learn the essential skills they need to survive as adults.

How crazy is that? We don't teach kids how to choose a career, or how to get a job. We don't teach them how to know what they're good at and how to investigate new passions they discover. We tell them that the best thing they can do in school is to get good grades. That's a horrible thing to teach a kid!

The message we send to kids is, "Get good marks and please your teachers." We should be teaching kids, "Please yourself!"

We don't teach kids to explore the world and discover for themselves what they want to do in their adult lives.

We train kids to seek praise from their elders. We should teach kids how amazing it feels to learn something by doing it, and how to solve real-world problems. We don't teach kids to grow their muscles or to value their own feelings over the opinions of others, especially authority figures.

What are your memories of school? What do you wish you would have learned in school that you had to learn on your own once you were out of school? Write your thoughts in your Mojo Journal.

CAREER PATHS

We do a poor job of educating kids about possible career paths, but we do an even worse job of helping people navigate their careers once they're out of school.

We don't even talk about careers or career planning as a critical life skill for adults, even though everybody goes to work. For most people their career is their biggest financial concern.

Tons of hospitals offer free or low-cost workshops to teach people how to manage their health. It's great that they do that. Banks and credit unions put on workshops to teach people how to manage their finances. That's a great idea, too.

Where can people go to learn how to manage their careers?

Your career will almost surely end up having greater financial impact on your life and the lives of the people you care most about than your house or your retirement savings will. Still, we talk endlessly about mortgage loan rates and good and bad investments. Magazines and websites share great advice about your finances. What about the much more significant financial impact of career ownership? Why aren't we talking about that?

It's good that you bought this book and are following this program. Your career is an important topic!

Hats off to you!

You are to be commended for stepping up to learn about the new-millennium talent marketplace, and even more so for stepping up to take control of your career! That's a big step.

You are a rock star already, and we're just getting started. Imagine how powerful you'll be two or three chapters from now!

JANINE'S STORY

Janine is in reinvention. She is burned out on her job and wants to explore new career paths. She is stepping back to think about her life and her learning so far.

Janine has never thought about her life or her career. She never needed to. She didn't know that the topic "My path so far" was worth studying, but it is!

Janine wants to think about her possibilities much more broadly than she has in the past. Throughout her life and career, Janine has believed that whatever career path she started on as a 22-year-old would be her career throughout her life. That's why she never stopped to wonder, "Is this still the best career path for me?"

Now she is revising her opinion! Janine is 45. She's ready for a change. Her current job is destroying her health and her sparky personality.

At first Janine thought, "What good will it do me to think about alternative career paths if I can't get a job in those fields?" Finally Janine realized that creating a vision for her life at a high level—letting no doubts or cynicism get in her way—is an important exercise whether she ends up exactly the way she imagined, or not. She realized that she had been afraid to give herself permission to imagine her perfect career. She thought, "If I dream up my ideal situation and I don't get there, I'll feel like a loser."

Janine's common sense kicked in and she realized, "Wait, does that mean it's better not to have big goals at all than to have them? Of course not! I'm going to dream as big and bold as I want. That's Step One. How I get to my dreams is Step Two—a whole different project!"

To get her creative career-path-envisioning juices flowing, Janine lists six alternative career paths that she'd like to follow, if she could have any career she wanted to have.

Janine writes down the six alternative career paths she'd like to follow if she could snap her fingers and make it happen.

Here are Janine's six alternative career path ideas:

JANINE'S SIX ALTERNATE CAREER PATH IDEAS

Fashion designer

First-grade teacher

Holistic healer

Theatrical costume designer

Makeup artist

Nanny

Right now, Janine works on Wall Street. She works for an international company. She is a Research Associate for a financial consulting firm. Janine works with numbers in her job. She loves her co-workers and she likes using her brain at work, but Janine knows she is not on her path. Her job is boring, stressful, and exhausting.

Janine says, "My job wins the Bad Job Trifecta! I am a stress-case every day. I don't have fun at work, and I pretty much hate my life because of how much I hate my job. That's no way to live!"

Have you ever worked at a job that was boring, stressful, and exhausting all at the same time? That is a tough combination!

Janine wants to start planning now to begin exploring new career possibilities next year. Janine has committed to herself that she'll find a more suitable job within 12 months.

First she has to answer the question, "What do I really want?" Janine doesn't expect her new job to be her dream job necessarily, but she wants to take the time to seek out a new job that will use more of her gifts and talents than her current job does. How else would she start than by envisioning her perfect job?

What kinds of jobs could Janine pursue apart from financial-consulting research jobs? Plenty! She has hundreds of choices. She is a capable businessperson with strong finance skills. It's up to Janine what she wants to do next.

Janine has talents in many nonfinancial areas. Her current job only scratches the surface of her talents.

When Janine writes about her six dream career paths—the career paths she would follow right now if she could snap her fingers and make it happen—she notices that none of them are financial jobs, but all of them have financial aspects.

Janine is logical and practical. Everybody who knows her knows that she has common sense—what our grandparents used to call "horse sense." Whatever kind of job Janine steps into next, her brains and practical problem-solving talents will come in handy.

Janine showed her list of six alternative career paths to her brother Malcolm. "What do you think about my list of six alternative career paths?" she asked him.

Malcolm is not in reinvention. He isn't thinking broadly about Janine's career or his own career right now. So Malcolm's reply to Janine was a bit negative.

"Nanny?" he asked Janine. "Aren't you a little old for that?"

"It just means that I love kids," said Janine. "Hang out with kids all day? That would be a blast. This is a reinvention exercise, Malcolm. The practical side of my job search comes later. First I need to create a vision for a working life that will be more fun and more rewarding than the one I have now."

"If you say so!" said Malcolm. "I don't know anything about reinvention. I always heard that you should do the job that pays you the most money."

 What are your thoughts about Janine and Malcolm's conversation? Are Janine's passions for costumes and theater, kids, and healing less professional or less significant because she has never been paid for pursuing them?

REINVENTION IS NOT AN EQUATION

What can we guess about Janine from her six alternative career ideas? Janine is creative and colorful. She likes theater, dress-up, and children. Could Janine use her wonderful financial skills plus her passions for kids and theater in her next career chapter? How could Janine move in that direction?

Janine has spent her entire career in the world of big business and finance. She doesn't know anything about kids' theater programs, about fashion design, or about holistic healing, except that she recovered from a very bad bicycle accident some years ago with the help of a holistic healer whom she respects very much.

Janine knows that her reinvention is not an X + Y = Z equation. She will not "solve" her reinvention in her head. Reinvention is an exploratory process full of self-reflection.

What are Janine's next steps?

- Janine will begin researching organizations in her city that help kids, create and promote theater, or both.

- She will start attending kids' theater productions and paying attention to people and organizations that are doing interesting things with theater for kids or involving kids.

- She will look into holistic healing and the healers in her area. Janine will tune in and learn as much as she can about the topics that interest her most.

- Janine will research organizations that she could work for in her next career adventure, but she won't limit her exploration to full-time or part-time jobs. Janine could start her own business as a way of advancing her mission. She could start her own company or a not-for-profit organization.

Her mind is wide open! She is in reinvention, learning as much as she can and resisting the temptation to say, "There! Now I know the answer." Janine knows that there is no answer to the question, "What is my life supposed to be about?" The question itself, and Janine's exploration of it, are the most important things!

Big, ambitious missions like Janine's mission to bring herself to her work don't come about through small, incremental steps.

When Janine gave herself permission to think more broadly about her life and to think about her possibilities from a higher altitude than she had before, she felt more confident.

"You know what's crazy?" Janine asked. "I felt that one hundred percent of my competence and credibility was in my job title and my job responsibilities. I thought that my company conferred credibility on me. In a funny way now I feel that I bring my competence and credibility to my company and confer those things on them. I know that I'll be successful in whatever I do next career-wise, because it will be at least one step closer to what I care about. There's nothing wrong with financial consulting, but I don't care about it. I want to bring myself to work more than I do now!"

Why would Janine invest the time and energy that a job search requires, only to get a new job that is just like her old job, only across the street at a different company? Janine would not invest the time and energy that it requires to look at her life and her career from altitude if her goal were only to get a job like her current job. What would all that effort get her? She wants to get closer to her mission, not to get a new job and learn almost nothing new.

What are your thoughts about Janine's realization? Will Janine's visioning and research make her aware of career opportunities she might not have explored otherwise?

WHAT ARE YOUR ALTERNATE CAREER PATHS?

When you trust yourself to let your dreams expand beyond what you may have thought was possible, your perspective will change dramatically.

Whatever annoying, immediate obstacles you saw blocking your path yesterday and last week will look much smaller to you, or they'll melt away entirely, once you step on your path.

Your vision for yourself will fuel your forward motion.

That's what happened for Janine when she let go of the idea, "I have to stay in the same field I've been working in all these years because I am a Finance Person!"

Janine realized that *she* gets to decide who she is. It's not up to anyone else what Janine's career is supposed to be about. Janine is making her own career decisions now, and she knows that she'll always get to decide what's best for her life and career.

No one else can tell Janine what she is—or what she isn't.

Janine is a Finance Person, but that is only one side of her. Janine has many other talents to bring to the world!

What other sides to you have not been reflected in your career so far? Which six alternative career paths would you choose for yourself if you could choose any career path at all? Write them in your Mojo Journal in a table format, like this:

My Six Alternative Career Paths Are...	Why I Chose This Alternative Career Path

PERPETUAL REINVENTION

We are all reinventing ourselves all the time, but some reinvention processes are bigger than others! Some changes in our environment require major course corrections.

Reinvention is an awakening from a time period where we tuned out and stopped noticing the world around us. That's why an important part of reinvention is the simple act of paying attention to the external world around you and listening to your own heart and mind.

Many of us grew up with the idea that our brains call the shots. We believe that our busy minds have the best advice for us. Sometimes that's not true. Sometimes we have to tell our brains to pipe down and be quiet, and we have to listen to our bodies instead!

Our bodies register changes in our environment very well. If we are paying attention, we will make small, constant changes in our lives to respond to changes that are happening inside us and also out in the world. When the weather changes outside, we naturally put on a coat or take off a layer if it gets warmer. When we're driving on a straight road and it gets hilly, we might slow down or pay more attention.

We human beings are good at responding to changes in our environments—but only if we're paying attention! If we aren't paying attention, changes can pile up before we react to them. We might not notice the weather changing if we're distracted. We might set off on a hike one day and only realize too late that it's about to start snowing, when we're a mile into the woods without a jacket.

That's the situation many people find themselves in today, with respect to their careers. The changes in the working world have caught them unprepared. They don't have the right equipment. They don't know how to brand themselves to get the jobs and assignments they want. They don't know how to navigate the new terrain in the careers marketplace.

That's what you are learning to do right now!

Reinvention is a process. Snakes shed their skin every so often. Hermit crabs leave one shell and go find a bigger shell when the old shell gets too small for them. We are no different from those snakes and hermit crabs. (Sorry I couldn't think of a cuter, fuzzier animal to use as an example!)

Every now and then we need a new shell or we need to slip out of our old skin and into a newer, shinier one. That's what reinvention is!

What are your thoughts about stepping out into new territory and trying new things? Write your ideas in your Mojo Journal.

Write in your Mojo Journal about your greatest triumphs in life so far. Write about your accomplishments at work and elsewhere, like these:

- Write about a time when you helped out a friend in need.
- Write about a time you learned to do something completely by yourself.
- Write about a time you taught someone how to do something.
- Write about a time you were proud of yourself.

RECLAIMING YOUR PATH

It is tempting for us to say, "I don't like to be uncertain about anything, especially my own career direction. I'm going to choose a new career path NOW!"

We might take a test in a magazine or go to a counseling center and be told, "This is the perfect career for you!"

There are certain to be people around you who are dying to tell you what you should do about your career. Some of them will say, "Take the first job you can get!" Some of them will tell you to play it safe and do the same kind of work you've always done before, even if you're sick of it. A lot of people believe that we don't get to choose our own paths. They believe that we have to take the most conservative course of action, or else something terrible might happen.

In my experience the exact opposite is true. The more you step out into new territory by trying new things, the bigger your muscles get. As you learn to try new things all the time, the more confident, marketable, and flexible you become!

An important step in reinvention is to reclaim your path.

TELL YOUR STORY

Reclaiming your path means thinking about and talking or writing about where you've come from. It means writing or talking about your life so far, going all the way back to your childhood and even before you were born.

You have a story. Your story is unique. No one alive on earth right now and no one who's ever lived can tell your story. It's completely yours! You have done a lot, met a lot of people, seen a lot, and accomplished a lot in your life, whether you are very young or whether you're old and wise! Either way, you have a powerful life story, and you will gain power by telling your story.

Now it's time to reinvent yourself and take charge of your own life and career. Looking back at your path is an important and wonderful piece of that journey!

In this chapter you'll think about and answer questions about your path in life so far. Write your answer to each question in your Mojo Journal.

Think about the situations you've encountered in your life so far and the struggles you have faced. You are a survivor. You've conquered everything in your path so far!

Here are questions about your life. Think about each question and answer it in your Mojo Journal. Then, write about your life story there.

Your Birth

- What is the story of your birth?
- Were you the first, second, or a later child in your family? Write about your family's situation when you were born, or the circumstances surrounding your birth. If you were adopted, write the story of your adoption.
- Write about your wonderful arrival on our planet. That's the beginning of your movie.

Your Early Childhood

- Where did you grow up? What was it like growing up where you did?
- What kinds of things did you like to do when you were a child?
- What are some of your favorite childhood memories?

The People in Your Early Life

- Who did you play with when you were little? What games did you play?
- Who influenced you as a child? Write about your family or the people you grew up with, and what you remember about them.

- If you have siblings or cousins you were close to as a child, write about the things you did together.
- What did your parents do for a living when you were little? How did your parents' occupations influence your ideas about your own career?

Your School Experiences

- What was your first school experience? Was it scary, fun, or something else? Write about that here.
- What subjects did you enjoy most in school?
- What other things (apart from school subjects) were you interested in or did you like to do during your grade school years?
- What were your school experiences like? Did you enjoy school, or not? What was interesting and stimulating for you and what was hard, or boring?

Your Career Plans and Dreams

- When you were a child and someone asked you, "What do you want to be when you grow up?" how did you answer?
- Which career paths did you think might be interesting or fun to try?
- Did you get advice or support from adults in your life, people who encouraged you in your dreams? Write about those people.

Your Early Career

- What did you do when you finished your schooling? Write about that here.
- What was your first job? Write about it here.
- What events or circumstances led you to your first career direction? Write about that here.
- Have you changed careers yet in your life? If so, write about what led to that career change.

If your hand gets cramped from writing, you can take a break. Most of us don't write very much. Writing is a great exercise. It brings out ideas so we can look at them.

What "Aha!"s or realizations came to you while you were writing about your life and career? Write them in your Mojo Journal.

YOUR PATH HAS POWER IN IT

In our culture we talk and think about the future all the time. We seldom talk about or think about the past. That's a shame, because your life story is incredibly important. There is tremendous learning available to you in the story of your path in life so far.

To get that learning, think about the stages in your life so far. Think about your childhood, your teenage years, or your young-adult years. Your path is a gold mine for insight about your future, but only if you reflect on it!

The Retracing Your Steps Table has questions to prompt you to think about and comment on what you've learned by retracing your steps. To complete this exercise, grab your Mojo Journal. Write the answer to each question in your Mojo Journal, using a table format as shown here.

RETRACING YOUR STEPS TABLE

Question	Your Answer
What did you love to do most, as a child?	
What did you know you were good at when you were little?	
What did you think your career would be about when you were a child?	
What talents did you show as a child that you haven't yet had the chance to develop as an adult?	
What did people around you tell you were your talents and gifts as a child?	
What activities have you given up in adulthood that you'd like to pick up again?	
What do you love to do, whether you can earn money from it or not?	

What else did your Retracing Your Steps exercise tell you about your path?

Pay attention to your dreams. Your dreams are important. Old memories will resurface as you reclaim your path and think about your life thus far and your path ahead. Those memories have messages for you! What have you been dreaming about lately? Write your dreams and thoughts in your Mojo Journal.

Pay attention to other signals, too. Anything can be a sign worth paying attention to—a blade of grass that catches your eye, a commercial on TV, or a billboard or sign on the highway. Pay attention to signs that catch your attention. They may have significance for you. Think about signs and symbols you've encountered lately and answer these questions in your Mojo Journal.

Consider:

- Which ideas and themes have you been thinking about more often lately than you did before? Write about them.
- What have you been dreaming about lately?
- What have you noticed in the weather or in nature recently?
- Which songs have you been thinking about or singing or humming lately?
- Which books, movies, or TV shows have you been thinking about lately?
- Which slogans or quotations have been on your mind lately?
- Which people from your past (or inspiring people you don't know personally) have been in your thoughts lately?
- What other signs or symbols have been nudging their way into your consciousness lately? Write about them in your Mojo Journal.

WE'RE RESPONSIBLE FOR OUR CAREERS

Remember, Job Security Is Gone

Job security is something that went away with the traditional working world, the world of long-term, stable employment. Those days are gone. Now, we are all entrepreneurs and business owners, whether we work for ourselves or for an employer. We are responsible for our own careers.

Any job could disappear at any moment. We don't have the job security anymore that working people used to rely on. Long-term employment is not coming back in our lifetimes. We have to manage our careers like businesses now.

When we are working at one job, we have to keep our eyes open. We have to be aware of the other organizations that could hire us if our job were to disappear one day. We won't have job security on any job, but we will have "income security," meaning that we will be able to work and get paid whether our current job sticks around or evaporates one day.

If you want to make big changes in your life, you have to start by looking back at your path so far and answering the question, "How did I get to this place, where I stand right now?" You have to look in the mirror to make changes in your life and career. You have to ask, "What's in my way right now, and how can I move that obstacle out of my path?"

Don't Blame Others

It's very easy to make a mean boss or a stupid recruiter the biggest obstacle in our careers, and to say, "My life would be perfect if that awful person wasn't holding me back!" Most of us have fallen into this trap at least once. We make somebody around us the bad guy. We wouldn't want to be the bad guy ourselves, so we assign that role to someone else!

Other people, even people who are driving you crazy (like an annoying boss or a mean interviewer), have nothing to do with your path. We make them more significant than they are, because doing that gives us an "out."

We don't have to ask, "Why can't I surmount this obstacle?" when we make the obstacle so large and so terrifying that no one could get over it!

Other people don't hold you back, but sometimes it may seem as though they do. We control our own futures, and the most important step in your reinvention is to see your own part in your story. You are the star of your movie, after all!

Have you ever made someone else the bad guy in your movie? Write about that in your Mojo Journal.

Be Willing to Make Personal Changes

The most important thing to know about getting the life and career you want is this: To get the life and career you want, you have to be willing to make personal changes, rather than waiting for other people to change. You have to step into new territory, even if it feels scary to do that. The only way to grow new muscles is to try new things!

Grab your Mojo Journal and write your thoughts about your path and your starring role in your movie. Write your answers to these questions about taking control of your life and career:

- When you were a child, were you encouraged to explore a lot of different topics and activities and choose your favorites?

- When you were little, were you ever discouraged from doing something you enjoyed on the basis that it could never be a viable career path?

- Were you ever discouraged from doing things you liked to do because other kids were better than you were? Did you ever stop participating in an activity primarily because you weren't one of the best kids participating in that activity?

- Have your career choices so far been based mostly on your own preferences, or on other people's opinions or guidance?

- Do you feel that you get to choose your own career path—or do you feel that many career paths are unavailable to you because of your age, your past experience, your education, or some other obstacle?

- As a child, were you taught to pick a "safe" career path?

When long-term employment was the norm, there were some career paths that were "safer" than others. These days, there are no "safe" career paths. The only job security that exists today is the kind you build in yourself and carry around with you!

YOUR ASSIGNMENT

Complete the Path Exercise shown on the next page by thinking about and writing about your path in life so far. Think about each stage of your life so far and write in your Mojo Journal about what you were doing, thinking

continued ...

PART ONE

about, and wondering about at each point on your path. Use the legend at the bottom of the Path Exercise to note the biggest events and "Aha!"s in your life and career so far.

To complete the Path Exercise, pick a quiet place and a time when you can sit (or stand or lie down) and think about your life so far. Choose a pen that you like and grab your Mojo Journal!

THE PATH EXERCISE

Look at the Path diagram on the next page. Think and write about each stage of your life and about the big changes and events that took place while you were growing up. Think about the big changes and steps you've taken on your path so far. Draw a similar Path diagram in your Mojo Journal and then mark places in your life using the three symbols or others.

The legend at the bottom of the Path diagram shows three symbols: an exclamation point, a question mark, and a lightning bolt:

The exclamation point symbol marks a "nudge" from the universe. Losing your job or living situation is a big nudge! A nudge is a shift that you didn't choose. Somebody in a high place (God, Mother Nature, or the laws of physics if you like) wanted you to learn something. As you write about your life so far, you can use the exclamation point to highlight those times when you were nudged or violently shoved out of one situation in your life and into a new one. You can draw or paint about your path if you like. When was the last time you picked up a marker or a colored pencil? Drawing and painting are amazing mojo-builders!

The question mark designates a time when you weren't sure how to proceed. Maybe you feel that way now. Who hasn't been confused about how to get forward? I feel sorry for anyone who has never had the opportunity to stop and look and wonder, and then make choices about his or her life.

The lightning bolt symbol denotes a time when you got a shock or a big "Aha!" Maybe you realized you were in the wrong job and changed jobs, or maybe you suddenly realized that you wanted to go back to school.

You can invent your own symbols to illustrate and illuminate your path. Have fun thinking, writing, or drawing about your incredible life so far. Where have you traveled, and what have you learned along the way?

GETTING ALTITUDE ON YOUR CAREER

Throughout this part of the book we've been looking at getting altitude, or having perspective on your life and career. We're going to dive more into the topic of career altitude in this chapter.

What is altitude? It's height above the ground! Look at the drawing below. The drawing shows three levels of altitude—the Cloud, the Hilltop, and the Ground.

THREE LEVELS OF ALTITUDE

The Cloud

The highest level of altitude is the Cloud level.

It's the level of altitude where you look down at your entire life and career—your entire path stretching back to your birth and forward to everything that lies before you.

At the Cloud level you ask the question, "What am I trying to do here on planet earth? What's my mission?"

The Cloud level of altitude is where you'll set your vision for your life and career.

The Hilltop

Below the Cloud level is the Hilltop level of altitude. If you climb a hill and look down from the height of the hilltop, you can see how to move left, right, or forward. You can see how to overcome obstacles on your path.

The Hilltop level is the level for strategy and planning. It's very exciting to see a new way to surmount an annoying obstacle.

You are not only the visionary creator of your life and career, but you are also the chief engineer and principal strategist. You are the person who will create your vision, and also the person who will plan from the hilltop how to get over, under, around, or through whatever obstacles appear in your way.

The Ground

The lowest level of altitude is the Ground level. That's where most of us spend most of our time. There is always something else to do on the to-do list—a load of laundry to deal with, a bill to pay, or something arresting to watch on a screen. We have a lot to get done every day and most of us are also easily distracted.

You'll step into your reinvention and through it on the ground, step by step. In fact, all the thinking and planning in the world won't give you control of your career and your life. The control comes through your actions—you have to take steps.

You have to try things, especially if they seem a bit daunting or scary. You have to push yourself over the border, out of your comfort zone.

Let's zoom up to the Cloud level and understand its place in your reinvention.

GIVE YOURSELF PERMISSION TO GET ALTITUDE

If you were sitting on a cloud, you could look down and see your whole neighborhood or even your whole town. You can see a long way from that altitude!

The Cloud level of altitude is the level where you will think about your life and your mission here on earth. You'll think about why you are here, and what you can accomplish in your lifetime.

Some people don't think about their mission on earth, because they think, "Who am I to have a mission?" I will turn around that question and ask you, "Who are you *not* to have a mission?" Why shouldn't you do what you want to do and what you believe you were born here on earth to do? Why shouldn't you achieve your dreams? Why shouldn't everyone at least try to do that?

Envision Your Future

You can accomplish your dreams, but it probably won't happen by accident. You'll accomplish the things you want to do in your lifetime by taking steps every day to make your dreams real.

You'll start by envisioning what you want to do and to be in your lifetime.

That's the kind of activity you'll spend your time and energy on when you are looking at your life and career from the Cloud level.

The Cloud level is where you create a vision for your life. That vision can include where you want to live, what sort of work you want to do, what kind of family and friends you want to have, and lots more. You can decide what sort of house or dwelling you want to live in, whether it's near the woods or the ocean or the mountains, and what you want to do with your time.

What do we have to invest that's more precious than our time, after all? You can design your life the way you want it to be.

You won't get your perfect life in a few minutes by snapping your fingers, unless you know something I don't know! You can get your perfect life, or get much closer to it, by taking steps all the time to accomplish your goals and live your mission.

What do you want from your life and career? How do you envision the perfect life? Write about your perfect life in your Mojo Journal, and answer these questions:

1 In your vision for your life, where will you live?

2 Who will live with you or be closest to you?

3 How will you spend your time?

4 What is your mission in life?

5 What do you feel you were put on this planet to make happen?

Most of us cannot quickly or easily answer the question, "What is your mission in life?" and that's okay. It's important to keep asking the question, because your answer to the question, "What is your mission in life?" is central to every big decision you make.

Where you live, who you live and spend time with, how you invest your precious brain and heart energy, and how you earn money are all tied up with your mission—or they can be! You get to decide when and how to bring your mission into your "regular" life.

When you decide which brand of toothpaste to buy at the drugstore, you probably won't have to ponder the question, "What's my mission in life?" We can make small, ordinary decisions without having to confront the big question, "What's my mission?" over and over again many times a day. Still, when we're in reinvention the question can easily stay uppermost in our minds and even begin to drive us crazy!

The key is to stay open to possibilities. Sometimes people think, "I can just imagine myself taking the time to design the perfect life and then not getting there. Partly that's because my mojo is depleted right now. I've been hit in the gut by life a few times recently and I'm wary. I feel vulnerable. Even if I don't tell a soul about the perfect life and career that I've decided I'm worthy of—assuming that I can reach that point—I'll still know that I set that lofty goal.

"I'll still know if I don't get anywhere near reaching my goal. Then I might feel worse!"

That's true. You will know about the perfect life and career you've designed.

Roadblocks to Overcome

If you run into a roadblock or a bump in the road, as you undoubtedly will, that doesn't mean you've failed. It just means that you've run into an obstacle on your path. We all run into them all the time.

There isn't any way to fail in your quest to live the life you want. The only way to fail is not to try at all. If you can stay open to possibilities and remind yourself that nothing you've set as a goal for yourself is out of reach or impossible, you can put one foot in front of the other and keep moving forward.

Who could ask any more of you than that? Even you, who can sometimes be impatient with yourself about all kinds of things, can't ask more than that!

You're on a Journey

The key to stepping through your reinvention to step into your next chapter is to let go of the idea that you can succeed or fail in your reinvention. Those words don't apply. You are on a journey.

You're on your path. Every time you learn something new, your muscles are growing. You are getting stronger.

It's hard not to judge yourself. Most of us have criticized and judged ourselves for years. Instead of judging ourselves and finding fault with our blemishes and defects, we can keep asking these two questions:

"What do I want to make happen while I'm alive, and how can I move in the direction of carrying out my mission?"

How would you answer those two questions?
Write your answers in your Mojo Journal.

Only the people who keep asking hard questions and keep exploring their options see ways to live the lives they envision. Other people won't see those opportunities, because they have already stopped looking. They believe that they can't make things better in their life. They don't try, because they believe their efforts will be wasted. They believe that all the important decisions have already been made for them.

Do you believe you can change your life circumstances?
Write your answers to these questions in your
Mojo Journal:

- Which parts of your life are within your control, and which parts are outside your control?
- What could you do to change your answer to the last question, and get control over more aspects of your life? What steps could you take to regain control over parts of your life that you don't feel you control right now?

It can take time to become a believer in your own power to change your life and career.

DREAM BIG

Many of us have been taught since early childhood that it's not a good idea to dream too big. We've been taught to keep our aspirations modest. If we don't, somebody might think we're getting too big for our britches! Who are you, after all, to think you can design the career and life you want?

I had an angry first-grade teacher ask me, "Who do you think you are?" one day when she put me in the bad-kid corner for drawing in the margins of my worksheets or for some other infraction. I sat on the bad-kid stool in the corner and thought about it.

Who did I think I was? I didn't think I was anyone in particular, but I figured I was still someone. I was six. I had a life like everyone else. Why would my teacher ask me, "Who do you think you are?" I couldn't understand what she meant.

Later I realized that she meant, "Don't think you're anything! Don't hold a high opinion of yourself." What a mean thing to say to a kid. It's almost like my first-grade teacher wanted the kids in her class to know that they weren't anyone special. It hit me as I sat on the bad-kid stool in the corner that the teacher was trying to make me and the other kids afraid to speak up and be ourselves. She tried to control us by telling us that only bad kids think anything of themselves. That's a horrible message to send to a kid, but many or most of us got similar messages when we were little.

We can guess that my teacher got the same message when she was a little kid. People in pain tend to lash out at other people. People who feel bad try to make themselves feel better, and sometimes they do that by making other people feel worse. Now I feel sorry for my first-grade teacher and whatever she had to deal with as a kid, herself.

Here is a journaling exercise. Grab your Mojo Journal and answer these questions in it:

- Did you get negative and limiting messages when you were a child?
- Did some grown-ups caution you and the kids around you not to dream too big or believe in yourself?

With luck, as a kid you had people on your side who grew your flame and told you that you are awesome. Who were those people—do you remember? A wonderful way to grow your muscles and mojo is to mentor someone. Could you mentor a young person you know, or a friend of a friend who needs advice in their life and career?

KNOW YOUR PASSION

When you know what you are passionate about, you can include your passions in your mission.

MARISSA'S STORY

Marissa is passionate about children. She is a single woman without kids, but she loves kids and is very grateful to several adults who were wonderful guides and mentors to her when she was young.

A few months ago, Marissa got laid off. She got a little bit of severance pay to tide her over until she finds a new job. "This is my chance to start a new career, aligned with my passion," Marissa said.

She knew that she wanted to work with kids. Marissa had had a very tough time growing up and she wanted to invest her precious mojo to help other kids get a better start in life. She wanted to be the supportive adult that she had found so important in building her self-esteem when she was young and struggling. She wanted to make the welfare of children her personal mission.

Marissa is a CPA—a financial person. She had never spent time around kids before, but she knew that she wanted to make the welfare of children her personal mission in her life.

She knew that if she got caught up in the details—"How will I transition from my financial career into a career involving helping kids?"—she would never move forward; the problem of how to surmount her total lack of paid experience (and in her own mind, credibility) in her new field would overwhelm her.

It would suck all Marissa's mojo away to try to solve the problem called "How to Bring My Passion into My Work" in her head.

Marissa decided not to try to solve her problem in her head—at least not right away. She did something else. She stopped trying to puzzle out her problem and envisioned the life and career she wanted, instead. Marissa got a journal and started writing in it. She found that her friend Abigail was also interested in thinking about and talking about her life plans and goals, so Marissa and Abigail teamed up.

They started to meet once a month for coffee. After a few months, the coffee meeting turned into a dinner meeting. One month Abigail would have dinner at Marissa's apartment and the next month they would eat at Abigail's place.

They spent those dinner meetings catching up and helping each other with their life and career plans. Everybody needs a support group, especially when they're going through big changes!

Marissa envisioned the life and career she wanted. At first her vision was very murky, but little by little it began to come into focus. Marissa knows that she's very good at numbers. She figures that she can help children somehow using what she knows about finance. Abigail helped Marissa to see that there are tons of ways to help kids using Marissa's tremendous financial background.

Marissa could start a foundation or a not-for-profit organization to help kids in an important way, right in her town. She could link up with a larger, national, or international organization that already exists. To learn about the not-for-profit world, she could first become a volunteer or a board member. Or, instead of nonprofit, Marissa could work for a for-profit company that helps kids, or start her own company.

She had felt so limited at first—like her plan to help kids somehow was just a pipe dream, and something she should forget. Marissa had had several important people in her life, including her aunt and her sister, tell her, "Just stick to what you know, Marissa. You're thirty-five. You're too old to change careers."

Marissa had to shake off that advice and listen to her own heart and brain. She had to push through the obstacle called "Who do you think you are?"

Write in your Mojo Journal about your reactions to Marissa's story. Then, write the answers to these questions in your Mojo Journal:

- Who did Marissa think she was to change careers at age 35 and strike out on a path she'd never walked before?
- Who are you to try to shoot higher, and find work that has meaning for you beyond a paycheck?
- What makes you think you are special?

You *are* special. You are mighty! Everyone has the capacity to rise up and do more, see more, touch more, experience more, and learn more in life than many other people choose to do.

You get to decide how to spend your time on earth. Your career is a big part of your life.

Doesn't it make sense, as long as you have to work to find a new job anyway, to invest the time and energy it will take to get the best job possible? What is the best job? Is it a job that speaks to you rather than one that just keeps a roof over your head?

What would you want and expect in a job or career apart from a paycheck? Write your ideas in your Mojo Journal. What is your ideal job? Write about your ideal job, and be sure to include your answers to these elements of the job:

- The setting—what kind of workplace will you work in, or will you work from home?
- The work—what kind of work will you be doing?
- The mission—how will your work support your personal mission, and vice versa?
- The people—think and write about the people you will work with.

Will envisioning your ideal job help you to get that job or bring your ideal job into reality? In my experience the answer is a resounding "Yes!" The more clearly you first envision and then articulate your dream scenario, the future life and career you are designing for yourself, the more easily you'll spot opportunities to move closer and closer to that vision. Keep working on your vision. Don't lose sight of it as you deal with the real issues we all have to surmount in day-to-day life. Keep your vision clear in your mind!

Write in your Mojo Journal about your mission. What could your mission in life be? If you're not sure what your mission is, that's okay! You are exploring the question, "What was I born to do?" and the exploration is more important than the answer! Write about your mission in your Mojo Journal and then treat yourself to something nice—maybe a scoop of gelato!

CHAPTER SEVEN

THE FIVE STAGES OF REINVENTION

Reinvention is a process. You won't wake up one morning and say, "Wow! I guess I got reinvented overnight!" That isn't likely to happen.

Reinvention is gradual. If you've ever looked back at an old photograph of yourself and thought, "Gee, I was so different back then! I thought about things differently. I saw the world differently," then you already know something about reinvention.

Reinvention works in the background, while you are going about your life and even while you're sleeping.

The cells in your body are always changing. Your ideas and perceptions are changing. Reinvention can sneak up on you! You might not realize you are always changing, but you are.

Sometimes you might think, "My life is pretty good right now. I don't really want anything to change," and then WHAM! Out of the blue, something changes in your life.

Evidently the universe or whatever higher power you believe in thought you did need some new problems to tackle in your life, after all! Later on you may look back and say, "I hated that change and I resisted it, but it turned out to be a great thing for me."

Have you ever had a terrible experience (in the moment) that turned out to be a great thing over time? Write about that experience in your Mojo Journal.

When you are job-hunting or just thinking about changing jobs, you are already in reinvention. You wouldn't change jobs unless one of two things is true:

- You need to get a new job because your old job went away, or

- You want to get a new job because you feel you can get a better job than the one you have now.

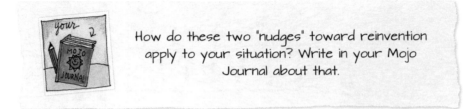

How do these two "nudges" toward reinvention apply to your situation? Write in your Mojo Journal about that.

Maybe you aren't thinking about getting a new job right now. Maybe you're content in your current job or your current working situation. Maybe you're wondering what the rest of your career will be like. That's a good thing to wonder about!

You're in reinvention whenever you are making changes or contemplating making them.

You might have goals for your life and career that you won't easily reach by following your current path. You might feel that you need to make a course correction in order to accomplish your goals and have the life and career you want.

Reinvention happens when you allow yourself to expand into greater possibilities.

ARNAUD'S STORY

I was a housepainter. I liked that job. I didn't go to college and I never thought of having a so-called career job, but I'll tell you what. You don't get hired as a housepainter unless you are extremely responsible. I worked for my friend Ike, who owned a painting business.

I made good money painting houses. I loved it. I never would have thought of doing anything else except that I had a cycling accident. I messed up my arm and shoulder, and I've had three surgeries. There was no way I could keep painting houses.

I was really down when I realized that my career path was over. I guess I'm lucky because I busted my left hand and I'm right-handed. I started painting on paper—fine art.

I've always liked to draw and paint, but I had never taken an art class. I felt kind of silly making paintings when I didn't have a job and I needed to get one, but it was good therapy for my arm and also for me.

I took a graphic design course at community college. I was 34. I had never been to college before. I loved graphic design.

Now I'm a graphic designer. I work in an office. The environment is very different from my old life as a housepainter, but there are so many things in my current job that remind me of my old house-painting job.

You wouldn't think that there would be a lot of crossover between those two jobs, but there is. I guess I've reinvented myself. I had no choice, but it was a great change for me! I'm glad it happened.

When I was down on the pavement in agony with a busted elbow after hitting a rock riding my bike, I felt like the unluckiest person in the world. Now I'm glad I had the accident. It got me into my new career path. Isn't that crazy?

What are your thoughts about Arnaud's story?
Write your reactions in your Mojo Journal.

Any change can be scary. Making a career move or shifting into a new career field can be a frightening experience. You could easily doubt yourself. You could wonder, "Why will hiring managers find me credible in a field where I've never worked?" Your feelings of self-doubt will recede and diminish the more you reflect on the many challenges you've already overcome in your life and career.

You'll remember that jobs are not so different from one another and that confidence and competence in one field easily translates into many other career paths. To build your mojo, think of your career accomplishments.

What is the one career accomplishment you're proud of? Write about it in your Mojo Journal. Also answer these questions about your favorite career accomplishment so far:

· What was going on when you accomplished your biggest career triumph so far? Was it an emergency that you took care of? Was it a project that you were responsible for, or did you help someone who needed a hand?

· What is it about your favorite career accomplishment so far that makes you feel proud? What qualities in you did your favorite career accomplishment call forth?

· What does your favorite career accomplishment tell you about your path going into the future? What does it signal to you about the kind of work you should be doing?

THE FIVE STAGES OF REINVENTION

Here are five common stages in a career change—either a small career change or a huge, monumental one. You may move through the stages in the order they're described below, or in a different order. Your movement through the five stages of reinvention may happen smoothly or in bursts. Reinvention is a physical process. Mother Nature is in charge of your reinvention. Reinvention doesn't follow anybody's rules!

Here are the five stages of reinvention:

1. Reclaiming Your Path

2. Getting Altitude

3. Wandering in the Desert

4. Choosing a Place to Put Your Canoe in the Water

5. Taking a Step, Reflecting, and Stepping Again

What do these stages mean? Here's an explanation:

Reclaiming Your Path

Reclaiming your path means looking back at your life and career and taking time to think about where you've traveled on your journey so far. Reclaiming your path means capturing the learning you've accumulated so far in your life.

This is a very important step to take when you're contemplating making changes.

It's important to stop and look and see where you've come from and where you're going. Looking back at your life so far is a powerful way to learn about yourself. Once you understand where you've traveled so far in your life, you can look ahead. You can get altitude to see where your path in life could lead from here.

After all, you will take every step on your path. No one else will decide for you where you should travel! Before you take another step, take some time to reflect on where you want to go. If you don't have a direction in mind, how will you know which way to step first, after all?

What events in your life do you feel have had the most significance in putting you on the career and life path you're on now? Write about them in your Mojo Journal. Answer these questions about the events in your life that have had the most impact on your career path so far:

· Which events have influenced your career path the most? (Did you choose a college major that influenced your career path? If so, why? Did you follow in your parents' or another relative's footsteps in choosing your career? Did fate choose your career path for you? Did you change careers when something in your life shifted?)

· Did the events that shaped your career path put you on your path, the path that feels right to you and that aligns with your passions, or did some of the events take you off your path? Write your thoughts about this question.

· Now that you are getting altitude on your career and your life, where would you like your career to go?

Looking back at your path is a powerful experience full of "Aha!"s or realizations about your talents, the situations you are meant to be in (and other situations that aren't a good fit for you!), and what your next, best career step might be.

Getting Altitude

As you think about your life and career so far, you will get altitude on your path. You'll look at your past, your present, and your future in a connected line and make a vision for your future.

The first question most of us ask any tourist or traveler is "Where did you come from, and where are you going?" but most of us don't know the answer to those questions as they apply to our own lives.

That is the big question for each of us to answer, though: Where have you come from, and where are you going? Write your answer to these two questions in your Mojo Journal. How has your view on this question shifted from when you reflected on it in chapter five?

The Desert

The Desert is the middle, exploratory phase of your reinvention. This part of your transformation out of your old self and into your new self can feel disorienting and can wear you out. It can feel like you're wandering in an actual desert, without a destination and without any clear idea of which way to walk.

The Desert can be a tiring place, but it's also the part of your reinvention where most of the powerful learning happens!

It's in the Desert while you're investigating possible career paths, meeting new people, trying new things, and catching up on all the exciting things you missed while you were asleep on your career that some of your greatest "Aha!"s can hit you.

They may not hit you right at the moment you take them in. Sometimes the most powerful learning takes weeks or months to seep into our conscious brains. That's okay! As long as you are open to learning from your environment and the people around you, you'll do fine.

As you wander around in the Desert of Reinvention, certain things will become clear to you. You'll see new opportunities for yourself that you wouldn't have recognized as opportunities before. You'll take bigger steps and try new things less cautiously than you may have done before—if only because you want to get out of the desert!

You'll grow new muscles in the Desert. You'll see that being on your path is more important than getting the first job you can get or putting up with a bad situation just so you don't have to deal with it. You'll realize that you are worth the time and energy your reinvention requires. Gradually, as you wander in what feels like the Desert during the exploratory phase of your reinvention, plants will appear.

Tiny trickling streams will appear, too, and those streams will join together to form bigger streams where more plants and flowers grow. The Desert will begin to bloom. Gradually you will feel stronger and more confident.

You'll realize that you always had the power to change your life and career, but you never knew you also had permission to change them! Have you felt the effects of the Desert of Reinvention in your career so far?

Take out your Mojo Journal. Write about your confusion or uncertainty over your career decisions or career steps.

A Place to Put Your Canoe in the Water

Gradually, as you step through the Desert of Reinvention, you will see ways to plug in to your new career and bring more of yourself to your work. You will step out of the Desert and into a clear spot—a spot near the water where you can begin your new journey!

We call this place a Place to Put Your Canoe in the Water. It's a career path you choose for yourself, rather than one that someone else chooses for you.

You'll choose your Place to Put Your Canoe in the Water based on your reflection on your path so far in life, your dreams for your career, and your time here on earth and your understanding of the problems you solve for your employers and clients.

Your Place to Put Your Canoe in the Water is not your dream job necessarily, but it is a next step that moves you down your path and closer to your mission.

It's a job that really exists or that you can create here in the real world. It's a job or a business idea that will pay you enough money to live on and that will use your talents and the things you love to do.

That's a great place to start your interactions with the real-world talent market! That's why your reinvention "sweet spot" is called a Place to Put Your Canoe in the Water.

What are your ideas right now about possible Places to Put Your Canoe in the Water in your career? Write about them in your Mojo Journal!

Take a Step, Reflect, and Step Again

The last stage in career change is the step called Take a Step, Reflect, and Step Again.

You won't stop thinking about and reflecting on your path and your reinvention in this stage, but this stage is all about forward motion.

You'll research prospective employers and clients, send out Pain Letters and your Human-Voiced Resume to organizations that you suspect could use your help, and you'll network with everyone you know. You'll take control of your job search and your career—because who could be better qualified to oversee them than you, the star of your movie?

What are some of the steps you can take to learn more about possible new career directions than you know right now? Write your ideas in your Mojo Journal. What are your thoughts about the five stages of reinvention? Write about them in your Mojo Journal, as well. Why is a career change more complicated than just choosing a new career direction and applying for jobs? Why are there emotional and even physical aspects to career change? Write your thoughts in your Mojo Journal.

10 STEPS TO MAKE YOUR REINVENTION ROADMAP JOURNEY WORK FOR YOU

You can probably read this book quickly and retain a few ideas from it. You might remember a few of the ideas you found in this book a month from now, but how would that help you or change your life for the better?

There is a better way to follow the Reinvention Roadmap path. Here are 10 steps to make your Reinvention Roadmap journey successful and impactful for you, so that your ideas about your career and your job search, your actions, and your perspective are different when you finish your Reinvention Roadmap journey than they are now.

1. Give It Time

Reinvention has its own timetable. Racing through this book from start to finish won't help you nearly as much as taking your time with it, working on the exercises and writing in your Mojo Journal often. One of the most persistent, false ideas that most of us grew up with is the idea that any problem can be reduced to an equation or a simple, linear process. If you want to eat a boiled egg, you just get an egg, boil the egg in water, and eat the egg. Boom! You're set. That simple process works every time.

Reinvention doesn't work that way. It has its own timetable. Mother Nature is in charge, and your job is to notice the changes happening around you and align with them. That is a new activity for many of us to learn. We want to know the answer to the question, "Now that my old identity is gone, what's my new identity?" Your new identity will emerge slowly.

You will learn the most and grow the most by experiencing your reinvention and noticing the changes going on inside and outside your body, not by rushing to be "done" reinventing yourself.

Give this project time in your heart and brain, and in your schedule. The time you spend reading and thinking about your Reinvention Roadmap journey and about your life and career will have benefits for you in the clarity of your new direction, your self-image, and your self-confidence.

2. Allow

As kids we were always learning new things. We were always exploring. As adults we tend to shut off the sources of learning around us. We like to do familiar things. We like to do things we already know how to do. It can be hard to "not know." We want to know what's going on! We want to be in control. In your reinvention process, you are not in control.

I got a lesson about being in control the first time I gave birth. It hit me very strongly as my labor progressed that I was not calling the shots. Mother Nature was running the show. I was used to being in charge of my body, but that day was different! I was awed by the visceral reminder of how powerful nature is, as much as we try to pretend that we humans run everything.

When you allow your reinvention to proceed without feeling that you have to control it, you'll be able to relax. You won't feel like a failure because you haven't figured out exactly what the rest of your life will be like. Maybe you thought you knew how your life would turn out. Maybe Mother Nature had her own ideas.

You can practice allowing things to unfold without judging them. You can practice allowing yourself to feel however you feel and accepting your shifting emotions as perfectly wonderful things. You can observe your emotions. You can say, "Ah, look at that, I feel like crying now." You don't need a reason to feel emotions. You can say, "Look, I feel excited and creative right now." You can write in your Mojo Journal about your emotions. Your body is going through a lot. Allow your body to process the big changes you're experiencing.

3. Notice Your Reactions

Most of us want to be in control of our lives. We feel more powerful and secure when we know what's happening and feel that we have power over events. During reinvention we may feel like we have less control over our futures than we would like.

Pay attention to your reactions to the ideas presented in this book. Some ideas might evoke the reaction, "That's exactly how I feel—right on!" Other ideas might leave you cold or make you angry. In this Reinvention Roadmap program I talk about taking steps toward the life and career you choose. That is not always a comfortable idea to take in. It can feel like pressure on you, when you already have enough on your shoulders!

When you accept that you make your own reality and that your path is completely up to you, you won't feel angry or frustrated about the new latitude you've given yourself. You'll feel just the opposite—like the proverbial kid in a candy store. When you get to decide what's important to you and then to pursue it, your power over your life is almost unlimited. You still have to deal with reality, of course, but you'll accept real obstacles instead of pretending they don't exist or using them as excuses not to work toward your vision for yourself.

4. Use Your Mojo Journal

Your Mojo Journal is a powerful tool, but only if you use it. If you can write in your Mojo Journal every day, that's ideal. If you can write in your Mojo Journal three times a week, that's fine. If you like, you can type on a keyboard instead of writing in a journal. You can draw or paint or sculpt your ideas and feelings about your reinvention, too. Get into the process of processing what you're reading and thinking about. The information you need is in you—the purpose of this book is to draw it out!

5. Talk About It

Talk about what you're experiencing in reinvention. Get together with a friend who's also in transition or get together with a group of friends who support you and vice versa. Share your ideas, the crazy ones and the practical ones, with people who get you. Listen to their ideas, too, both the out-there ones and the logical ones. Both kinds of ideas are important when you're thinking about your life and career. Let the ideas fly. Nourish and reinforce them!

6. Try It

Everything you will learn and understand about yourself and the world through your Reinvention Roadmap journey relies on taking steps. You can't reinvent yourself in your head. You have to interact with the real world and with other people to learn how the Reinvention Roadmap worldview and techniques intersect with your mission, your personality, and your situation. Try the techniques you're learning about in this Reinvention Roadmap project. Take baby steps at first. Get the learning. Don't be afraid to fall down and get back up again. That's the only way to grow new muscles!

7. Get the Learning

When you try something and it doesn't work, don't get angry at yourself, or at me! It is a common reaction to say, "That doesn't work. Liz Ryan ripped me off. Her ideas are stupid!"

We revert to our six-year-old selves at times when we are frustrated. You won't get any learning from your steps outside your comfort zone if your response to a roadblock or a scraped knee is to say, "That's stupid! I felt awkward. I'm never trying that again!"

You'll get learning when you say, "Okay, that was an amazing experience in feeling completely out of my depth. I'm going to think about that and see what I can learn from it. I'm used to feeling totally competent, but that's not the best way for me to learn. I have to feel *in*-competent in order to pay enough attention to get better at something new. That's what I'm doing now!"

8. Get Out of School Mode

There are no tests in this Reinvention Roadmap program. It is a self-discovery and muscle-growing project for you. You are the athlete—I am the coach. I have a whistle and a clipboard, and you have to do all the work. That's okay—you will grow the muscles and no one can take them away from you. Your reinvention is not something to pass or fail. You can only keep learning and growing. There is no one to impress. You have graduated from school and are kickin' it in the real world. Welcome!

9. Don't Judge Yourself or Others

It is hard not to judge yourself. You can start by listening to the critical voice in your brain when it pipes up and starts telling you what you're doing wrong. You can talk back to it. You can say, "No one cares what you think. I'm listening to my body and trusting my heart now. I know you'll always be there ready to tell me when I goof up, but I don't mind goofing up now. That's how I learn!"

Try not to judge other people—even if they're judging you. Some of them won't understand your reinvention. They won't understand why you don't just get a job fast and stop talking about your life. Some people can be harsh. They can tell you to stop having big dreams and come down to earth. They might not want you to step out of boxes. Can you get altitude on their situation and see their fear? If you can, you can soften and say, "I understand this isn't necessarily easy for you. Thanks for supporting me the best you can—I appreciate it!"

PART ONE

10. Relax into the Process

If you can spend a little time every day physically and mentally relaxing when you aren't about to fall asleep, that's wonderful. You could try yoga or stretching or just sitting quietly. You could try meditation or listening to music. You are in reinvention. You deserve to relax. Your brain is always busy. You need a break from the tumult. Can you give yourself that gift? You certainly deserve it!

Now, write in your Mojo Journal about your reactions to these 10 Steps and your ideas for incorporating some or all of them into your Reinvention Roadmap journey.

Write about, draw about, sing about, or talk to a friend about the five stages of career change. You could think of your own way to express your reactions to the five stages. You could make a sculpture or bake a cake. However you do it, your assignment is to reflect on the five stages and how they relate to your own situation.

CHECKING IN: GETTING ALTITUDE

You have finished Part One of the Reinvention Roadmap, Getting Altitude! Talk to a good friend about your Reinvention Roadmap journey so far, and write in your Mojo Journal about how you're getting altitude on your life and career.

You've made it one-quarter of the way!

PART 2

FINDING Your PATH

Part Two of the Reinvention Roadmap is called Finding Your Path. You've looked at your life and career from several perspectives—you've gotten altitude—and you've thought about the learning you've picked up along your path so far.

Now, where does your path lead you from here? That's what you will explore in Part Two.

Enjoy the discovery!

WHAT DOES IT MEAN TO BE ON YOUR PATH?

"I didn't like my job, but I wish I still had it!"

Big changes can be hard. Maybe you had a job you really didn't like, and then one day your department was shut down and you got laid off.

Maybe you didn't like your job, but at least you had a job. Now you have a big new headache to deal with—how to pay the bills! You have to get a new job. You might feel panicky—most people would. You might think, "I just need any kind of job. This is a crisis!"

Losing your job can stink in the moment. It can cause you sleepless nights, anxiety, self-doubt, and all kinds of awful feelings. Still, sometimes something wonderful can happen in the middle of all that pain and disruption. The minute your boss told you, "Our department is closing, and you guys are all laid off," new possibilities opened up for you. You were suddenly free of the job you didn't really like anyway.

SEEING THE POSSIBILITIES

If you view your job-search project as an emergency effort to get the first job you can, you won't see your own potential to take a step on your path. Maybe it will turn out to be a good thing that you lost your job. Maybe you'll get a much better job now and grow new muscles in the process.

Your career change or job search is a great time to grow personally and professionally, and that will only happen if you trust yourself enough to allow some reinvention in. If you don't trust yourself, you're likely to say, "Forget the reinvention! I just need to get a job right now!"

Did you realize at the time that although you got one new problem that day (you needed a new job), you solved another big problem, too? All of a sudden you can do lots more things than whatever you were doing before. That can be scary, but also a wonderful feeling—sometimes Mother Nature knows what we need better than we know it ourselves!

Have you ever had an unwelcome change turn out to be a good thing later on? Write about that in your Mojo Journal!

Every job search includes some reinvention. You aren't limited to pursuing jobs like the jobs you've held before. You can branch out! That can be an exhilarating feeling, but it can also feel scary.

The world is so big. How will you know what kind of work is right for you? Any time you are job-hunting, you're going to ask questions of yourself—questions like these:

- Do I want a new job like the old job I had? Maybe I should try something new!

- I know what jobs I can get most easily—but are those still the best jobs for me to go after?

- What do I really want to do next? Should I pursue a "safe" job, or one that will challenge me?

- Am I doing the kind of work that I like the most?

- Is my career making the most of my talents?

- Am I being paid appropriately for my work?

Have you ever wondered, "What is the best kind of work for me?" Reflect on that and the questions above and write your answers in your Mojo Journal.

AM I ON MY PATH?

Every time we get the chance to ask questions about our path, we should take it.

What is your path?

Your path is the road that you will follow as you live your life. Everybody has a path. Your job is to find your path and follow it. Finding your path means listening to your heart and mind, not just doing what other people tell you to do. It means deciding for yourself what you're meant to be doing in your life and career, rather than staying in a rut because it seems easier. You'll know you are on your path when you feel great about what you are doing. Your path is connected to your purpose here on earth. It isn't random that you were born. You were born with a mission to complete on this planet. The more you give yourself permission to ask big questions like "What do I want to do with my time on earth?" and the clearer you allow your mission to become, the easier it will be for you to take steps toward realizing it.

 What do you think that mission might be? Write about your mission in your Mojo Journal.

TAKING RESPONSIBILITY

When you are on your path, you'll know why you've made the choices you have made. You won't say, "Well, I was forced to take this stupid job and live in this dumb apartment that I don't really like."

When you're on your path, you'll take responsibility for every choice you've made, including the sort of work you do, where you live, who you live with and spend time with, the car you drive, and the clothes you wear.

You'll be happy to take responsibility for those things. They are all representations and facets of you—and we already know you are insanely cool and talented!

It's easy to push off responsibility on other people, and blame the world for our problems. It's very tempting to do that. The trick is that when we take complete responsibility for where we are at every point in our lives, we also see that we can change our situation at any point. Then we really feel powerful!

 Grab your Mojo Journal and write about a time when you changed something that wasn't working in your life.

OTIS'S STORY

I think about my career in two chapters. In the first chapter I was really happy. I got a job right out of high school, working in a warehouse. That job suited me. I really liked the place. I liked my co-workers. I learned to drive a forklift, use a lot of different machinery, and run inventory reports.

In that job, I felt responsible and competent in a way I never had felt as a kid in school. I had a hard time concentrating in school. If I were a kid these days, I might get diagnosed with something like ADHD, which my son has.

I felt stupid most of the time in school, so I goofed off. Until I got my warehouse job, I wasn't really sure I was good at anything. Once I got that warehouse job, I started to feel more confident. The boss gave me a lot of compliments and gave me a nickname: "O-Man." About ten times a day somebody would come on the PA system at work and say, "O-Man to the front office!" Pretty soon everybody in my company called me "O-Man." I didn't mind when I heard my name over the PA system. That meant the boss needed my help.

I got married and bought a house working at that job, and my wife and I had our two kids, a boy and a girl. I really thought my life was perfect. I played on the company softball team and I had a good retirement plan going.

Then the company went out of business, eight years ago.

That's when my second chapter started. It's been very hard on me for the past eight years.

I've had six different jobs in that time. I started to get frustrated when every job seemed to put me into a dead-end situation or didn't work out the way the company told me it would. I felt mistreated at work, and lied to.

I started to get very cynical. I was mad at my bosses, and mad at everyone. I was even mad at home. I guess I was not the easiest person to be around.

I got fed up. I walked off my last job. I just left. That's not like me, but it was something I had to do, because my boss lied to me for about the tenth time about something important. I just left the job and went home.

I walked home, about two miles, because I had taken the bus to work and I didn't feel like waiting for the bus to get home. Also, it was a beautiful day and I felt like walking.

On the walk home I had a kind of knock to the head. I guess you would call it an "Aha!" It hit me that it wasn't working very well for me to be mad at everybody and blame my bosses and other people for my problems.

It was easy to do it, but how did blaming those people help me? My problem was still just as big when I was blaming people as it was when I wasn't blaming anyone.

I decided to make big changes. I went home and made lunch for my daughter, who was surprised to see me. She was home from school for lunch.

She was eating a bowl of cereal for lunch because she didn't feel like making a sandwich. I made her a ham-and-cheese omelet and we talked. "I really think you would be happier if you weren't fighting with your boss all the time," she said.

I didn't tell my daughter that I had quit my job, but I told my wife when she got home from work and then all four of us, my wife and our two kids and I, talked about it.

My wife said, "Take some pressure off. Take a little time to figure out what you want." We didn't have a lot of money saved up, but I knew my wife was right.

I could get another warehouse job pretty quickly, but I just couldn't take a seventh job and go through the same headaches I'd already been through six different times.

I took a job at the grocery store in my neighborhood just to pay the bills while I figured out what to do next. Here's the crazy thing—I like working at the grocery store.

It pays less than my previous jobs, but my wife and I are making it work, at least for a while. I can catch my breath. I don't have to go apply for a job that I can tell right on the interview I'm going to hate.

Finally I feel like I'm getting some control of my life back. I don't know what kind of work I'll do next. Now that I look back at the bad jobs I had—six of them in a row—I can see that it wasn't the job description that caused me problems.

I like working in a warehouse. All six jobs were bad-energy workplaces. I could tell even on the six job interviews that something in the culture or the air in the place was

broken. Six different times I ignored the signals my gut was sending me. Six times, I took the job that I could get the fastest. I'd go for an interview, and they'd say, "Can you start on Monday?" and I'd say, "Sure!" I didn't check out the company at all because I was desperate for work. I'm not making that mistake a seventh time.

I feel more like my old self now. I'm glad I quit that sixth job! I'm glad the job was so lousy that I felt I had to walk out. Otherwise I'd still be there, feeling miserable! I don't know what I'm going to do next. I feel nervous on the one hand but also excited about my future.

What are your reactions to Otis's story? Have you ever thought about your career in chapters, the way Otis does? What characteristics of a person in reinvention do you see in Otis's story? Write your thoughts in your Mojo Journal.

WHO CONTROLS YOUR CAREER?

In Part One, we looked at how jobs used to be much more secure than they are now.

Since the 1980s, millions of people have seen their working situation shift dramatically, and not always in welcome ways. We live in a time of massive shifts in the world economy. Industries that are riding high suddenly plummet. Jobs go away. Jobs that were solid for years are suddenly sent far away or replaced by technology.

New industries spring up—sometimes industries we don't understand at all. How could we understand them? We never learned about them when we were younger, and we're still not learning about them now!

These days it's unusual for a working person to stay in a job for more than a few years. On top of that, it's not necessarily a great thing to keep a job for a very long time. When you stay in the same job for years on end, you stop learning at a rapid pace. It's hard to make the case that you've grown and developed your skills as rapidly on a job that you've held for years—whereas when you have a new job every few years, you're obviously stepping into a new situation every time.

How can you or anyone else manage a career in this crazy work environment? Just staying employed feels like a huge challenge for many people nowadays. It's easy to feel like your career is out of your hands. You may feel as though you have to do whatever other people tell you to do, just to keep a roof over your head.

Having a job that you might enjoy, that would grow your flame and teach you something new, can feel like a fanciful, unrealistic goal. It's easy to think, "I don't get to choose my path. I have to do the practical thing in every situation just to feed myself and my family!"

Things have changed! We need a new approach to managing our careers. We can't depend on staying employed with any one employer for a long time. We have to look out for ourselves. We also can't depend on our employers to manage our careers for us. We have to manage them ourselves.

Before you started your Reinvention Roadmap journey, the idea of managing your career may have been new to you. We are out of practice in managing our own careers. Most of us have forgotten how to take charge of our own careers. We didn't think we needed to manage anything in our careers. We thought that getting out of bed and going to work every day was enough!

It turns out that going to work to do your job is not enough. We have to take a much more active role in our careers than just performing whatever jobs we've got.

Doing your job every workday is only a part of managing your career. If you only do your job, how will you respond and recover when something changes? We've got to take steps to manage our careers as businesses, beyond just performing whatever job we've been hired to do.

Have you had the feeling that your career is in someone else's hands? Write about that and your current working situation (or your job search) in your Mojo Journal.

It's appropriate and responsible of you as a citizen or resident of your community to look out for yourself and the people who depend on you. That doesn't mean getting a "secure" job with one company and hoping for the best. That was a great career strategy in 1963, but not now!

The good news is that we can start building our muscles at any age, after any length of time spent sleeping with respect to our careers.

You can take charge of your own career and get better jobs and assignments whether you work for yourself or someone else. We are all entrepreneurs now. You might get paid as a consultant or you might be paid on a payroll twice a month. That makes no difference. You have the same responsibility in each case to look out over the horizon and plan your steps.

We can look out over the horizon and make plans for our careers. We can decide what we want out of our careers and take steps to get it.

 How would you answer the question, "What do you want from your career?" right now? Write your answer in your Mojo Journal.

HOW YOU GET PAID IS NOT IMPORTANT

Many people think that it's very important to get a full-time, salaried position. They are stuck in an old mental model, or frame. That makes sense, because most of us grew up with the idea that a full-time job is more stable than working for ourselves. Folks who grew up with the notion that only a full-time job is acceptable will hesitate or outright resist taking a temporary, contract, or consulting job. They are used to getting a paycheck, so how can we blame them for wanting to stick with what they know?

The fact is that these days, a contract or temporary assignment could be a better choice for your next career adventure than a full-time job would be. If the short-term engagement gains you powerful resume fodder (new information to include on your resume) and/or contacts, and if it grows your flame (or powerful feeling inside), then it's a good thing!

We used to think that job security was the bee's knees. We thought that the best kind of job to get would always be a full-time job, because we thought that full-time jobs were more secure than part-time, temporary, or contract jobs.

Many of us grew up with the idea that working for yourself is the least-secure way to go.

That was undoubtedly true at one time—but not today!

Here's the problem with that old way of thinking:

No job is secure these days! No one can promise you job security. Don't believe anyone who says they can promise you job security. You carry your job security around with you. It's not job security in the sense that you'll stay in one job forever—no one can give you that.

When you broaden your career plans to include all kinds of employment, including self-employment, contract work, and full-time work, you will gain something more valuable than a job that you hope to keep for years on end. You'll grow muscles and gain professional credibility that will serve you for as long as you continue working.

You are growing get-hired-and-get-paid security. That security comes through in your ability to market your services and get hired by clients and employers to solve their problems, whether you end up taking a job or a consulting project or starting your own business.

All that any job can be in this new-millennium workplace is a lily pad. That's not an insult to any job or any employer you might run into. Lily pads are important!

What is a lily pad? It's a floating plant that sits on top of a pond. Frogs sit on lily pads sometimes.

Lily pads are attached by a stem to another part of the same plant that sits on the bottom of the pond, but the stem isn't made of steel. It's a plant. The lily pad could die or float away at any point. That's okay!

The frog sitting on the lily pad doesn't put a lot of weight on the lily pad. He or she just rests on the lily pad for a little while, then hops away to find his or her fame and fortune elsewhere in the pond.

Any job you get is a lily pad—a resting place to gather your strength and think about what you want next in your life and career.

We are learning not to get too upset when a job goes away, or when we can see that we're reaching the end of the usefulness of a particular job (or lily pad, to stick with our analogy).

When it's time to leave, we'll start a new job search and go to work somewhere else. Our muscles will keep growing. We'll have more and more stories to tell as we move from place to place.

Staying in one spot doesn't teach you how to deal with change, yet change is the one element of the new-millennium workplace that is guaranteed to keep coming!

As you move from lily pad to lily pad and learn more and more about your own talents, how to spot and talk about the problems you solve, and how to value yourself so that other people will value you, you'll have more and more great resume fodder.

Resume fodder is made up of stories. The more new experiences you have at work and the more your muscles grow, the more exciting stories you'll have to share with prospective employers or clients.

You'll have more and more new reasons for your next employer or client to hire you.

Not every job you get will be your dream job, but that's okay—as long as you are learning something new, supporting yourself and the people who depend on you, and looking ahead to plan and control your own future, you're in great shape!

Write in your Mojo Journal about your experiences with "lily pad" jobs that taught you something new, no matter how long or short a period you worked at them, and answer these questions:

· What did you learn on a short-term job (whether the learning was positive or negative)?

· How have your "lily pad" experiences influenced your thinking or your views about yourself and your career?

I hope through this program to get you out of the mental frame of "There is a huge difference between a full-time job and any other kind of employment." There isn't—they are both ways of solving other people's problems, growing your muscles, and getting paid. We'll look more at our mental frames in chapter nine.

I don't want you to focus on the question, "Am I going to be a full-time employee or a contractor?" so intently that you block out all other aspects of your job search. There might be a better opportunity for you in a consulting engagement than in a full-time job. You are broadening your field of vision, and considering a wider range of opportunities than you may have before.

What are your thoughts about where your path lies?
Write about that in your Mojo Journal!

Try something you've never done before—something that feels a bit scary. Maybe it's going to a job-search networking group. Maybe it's signing up for a 5K or 10K running race. Maybe it's sharing your feelings about your reinvention or another topic that it isn't easy to talk about. Take a step—that's how your muscles grow!

FRAME-SHIFTING AND THE REACTION-O-METER

Most of us were taught very specific ideas about work and employment when we were young. Look at the following traditional ideas about work and careers:

TRADITIONAL IDEAS ABOUT WORK AND CAREERS

The longer you can keep a job, the better.

Full-time employment is always better than other kinds of employment.

If you get a job, keep it—it's risky to change jobs.

If your employer has a plan for your career, follow their plan!

Your job is to please your boss at work every day.

If you have to take a different job at your employer, or take a pay cut,
do it—it's still better than changing jobs.

People who own their own businesses are risk-takers, very different from the rest of us.

The more secure a job you can find, the better.

It doesn't really matter what kind of work you do, as long as you
can pay your bills. Your job is just a way to make money. It's not supposed
to be fun—that's why they call it work!

How many of those traditional ideas about work and careers have you always considered to be true? Write your comments about each of those traditional ideas in your Mojo Journal.

WORKING PERSON, JOB-SEEKER, CONSULTANT—WE'RE ALL IN THE SAME BOAT

Whether you work for a big company, a small company, a university, a government agency, a not-for-profit organization, or yourself, you still have the same issues to surmount. We all have the same hill to climb. We have to pay the bills somehow and stay afloat financially, manage our careers and our lives, and take care of the people who rely on us.

That sounds simple enough, doesn't it? It sounds like it should be easy.

It sounds easy, but it's not. It is very complicated to be an adult. There are a lot of moving pieces to manage. All grown-ups know that being an adult is not that easy. It really isn't. There are headaches and roadblocks everywhere. We keep a brave face on, but it's just not that easy to put all the pieces together in our complicated lives, or keep them together once we've got them where we want them.

 What do you find to be the most challenging aspects of adulthood? Write about them in your Mojo Journal.

Whether you work for yourself or for someone else, you have to run your career like a business. You have to think like a business owner.

Think Like a Business Owner

Let's look at the way business owners think about their work compared to the way employees typically think about their work priorities, income, long-term plans, and working hours. The following chart compares how employees think versus how business owners think in four key areas:

TOPIC	WHAT EMPLOYEES THINK	WHAT BUSINESS OWNERS THINK
Priorities	I have to please my boss. As long as my boss is happy, I'm fine.	I have to listen to my customers, along with the people who don't buy from me. I have to watch my marketplace constantly, because things keep changing.
Income	I have a steady paycheck, so I don't have to think about my income, thank goodness—I only have to watch my spending.	I have to think about my income constantly, but that's good—it keeps me on my toes!
Long-term plans	I just hope I keep this job for a long time. It's a pain to job-hunt.	I am always planning for my business—I have to! I have a long-term plan, but I have to stay flexible, too. Things never work out exactly the way we think they will.
Working hours	I work a lot of hours, but when I leave the office, I'm done with work (unless my boss calls me or I have to finish a project at home).	I work a lot of hours, but it's my company. I get to decide what products and services to offer, how much to charge for them, what to spend money on, and where to take the business—it's mine!

PART TWO

What are your thoughts about the table above? Do you identify more closely with the traditional "employee" mindset or the business owner's mindset? Write your thoughts in your Mojo Journal.

If you aren't working and you're job-hunting, you can drop your "job-seeker" persona and adopt a new persona—a consulting persona!

Why Not Start Your Own Consulting Business?

Every muscle we need to manage our careers in the new-millennium workplace is a muscle that consultants grow. If you can land and cultivate just one client, that relationship will keep you tied to the outside world in a way that very few if any full-time jobs can.

You will have fun designing your consulting persona. You will decide what kind of consulting work you want to do and what kinds of clients to work for. You will design the consulting business you want, and then (all at once or gradually) step into it.

Creating your consulting persona is one concrete way of taking control of your career. You don't have to quit your full-time job or abandon your job search to become a full-time consultant. You can consult part-time, or only when you want to. Even if you know for sure that you don't want to be a consultant at all, even for two hours per week, it's still worthwhile to walk through the steps to design your consulting persona.

Plus, I'm sure you can find those two hours a week in your schedule! Once you have your consulting business cards, you can start giving them out to people. Who knows . . . you may discover a new and insanely powerful side of yourself through consulting! The power in developing your consulting business is the power that comes from knowledge of yourself and your environment.

When you develop your consulting persona, you will answer important questions that you'll also need to answer to get altitude on your job search. Here are questions you will explore:

- What am I especially good at doing? What kinds of problems can I solve for my consulting clients?

- What kinds of Business Pain can I solve for my clients, such that they'll be happy to pay my consulting fee to make their problems go away? (Not sure what Business Pain is? We'll discuss what Business Pain is in chapter fifteen.)

- What kind of consulting work do I want to do?

- How can I tell stories in my branding materials that will make it clear to consulting clients that I can help to solve their problems?

What are your thoughts about these questions, and your answers to them? Write them in your Mojo Journal.

MUSCLES & MOJO

If Anybody's Going to Save You, It Will Be You!

When you're between jobs or feeling stuck in your career, it's very easy to start to feel hopeless. It's very easy to think, "Won't one of these managers just take pity on me and hire me?" or "Won't somebody just solve my problem and tell me what kind of work I should be doing, once and for all?"

It's understandable that you would feel that way. You could easily start to feel desperate and panicky. You might think, "I just need one helpful employer to swoop in and rescue me from unemployment." You might think, "I just need to stop taking short-term, dead-end jobs and get on a solid career path."

Many job-seekers and working people feel exactly that way. It is a hopeless feeling—that you must wait for someone else to see you and notice you, then take pity on you and hire you, or to guide you into the career path that's right for you. The problem is that the "Please save me" mentality will keep you from getting a new job or discovering your path.

The discovery—your personal experience of it—is the key to finding your path. There is no employer who can save you from the challenge of learning who you are and stepping into your power.

If the phrases "learning who you are" and "stepping into your power" sound airy-fairy and New Age-y to you, I understand. I used to think those terms were too touchy-feely to be useful to me, but they aren't. The reality is that the working world has fundamentally changed, and it's not about to change back. We have to step into it, so why not step in with confidence, equipped and prepared for the new-millennium workplace? We have to grow muscles in this workplace, and nobody can grow those muscles for you.

You'll grow them yourself by trying new things and listening to your instincts. We seldom talk about our instincts in relation to our careers, but your instinct is a much better guide than your busy, problem-solving brain!

You may have experienced going on a job interview and feeling panicky and desperate to get the job. You may have shot yourself in the foot on the job interview by coming across as too needy. Most of us have done that at least once.

People do a good job of reading the energy that comes off the people around them. When you feel desperate, you give off a desperate energy and other people can pick up on it. You already know about energy and desperation if you've ever been on a date. Most of us are attracted to people who are confident and comfortable in their own skin. We aren't attracted to people who are cocky and who seem to think that they are God's gift to men or women. We also aren't attracted to people who are desperate and needy. Would you be attracted to a person who went on a first date with you and said, "Oh my gosh, you're so amazing! You're so far out of my league, I can't believe you're having a date with me! It would be so great to date you again. Would you please take pity on me and date me? I'd be honored!"

Most of us wouldn't be all that attracted to a person who begged us for a second date. Employers and clients are the same way. They want to hire someone who knows what he or she brings to the talent equation and is confident in his or her abilities.

When you are feeling fearful, your judgment is impaired. Your decision-making ability will suffer enormously when you are feeling desperate and panicky. If you have ever taken the wrong job—a really bad job—because you felt desperate, you know how off-kilter your senses can become when you just need a job!

Have you ever felt so panicky about a job search that you knew your judgment was impaired? Write about it in your Mojo Journal! Have you ever taken the wrong job and instantly regretted it? Write about that topic in our Mojo Journal, too.

Mojo-Sucking Jobs

If you have ever taken a horrible job just because you were desperate to get a job, you know that there are some jobs that are worse than another few months of unemployment. The wrong job will suck your mojo away. Then you won't have energy to hunt for a better job, or even to remember that you are awesome and powerful. Your mojo will get depleted even further.

 How is your mojo now? Write about your mojo level in your Mojo Journal. Answer these questions about your mojo level in your Mojo Journal:

- When your mojo is depleted, how do you build your fuel tank up again?
- Which activities at home and elsewhere build up our mojo level?
- Which activities deplete your mojo?

What steps can you take to manage your mojo level throughout the day and the week?

You Are Qualified

Most people don't believe they're qualified to move outside a very small career niche. They say, "This is the kind of work I've always done, and this is the kind of work I can get hired for easily." They make the mistake of believing that their professional credibility resides in the job titles they've held, or in their certifications or degrees. That isn't true!

You carry your professional credibility around with you. When you decide to change careers, your credibility comes with you. It's portable—but only if you believe that it is!

 How are you feeling about your career, and about your job or your job search? How do you feel about your ability to move to a new career path if you want to? Write your answer in your Mojo Journal.

Growing Those Muscles

When you learn how to do something new (how to ride a bicycle or make lasagna, for instance), you get a little stronger. Your muscles grow. When you learn to ride a bike or bake lasagna, it's not the same as reading about something and then saying, "I read about that topic—I understand it now."

When you learn something by doing it, you change a little. Your muscles can get bigger. You are more competent than you were before you learned to ride the bike or make the lasagna.

You are more confident, too, because once you've learned to do something for yourself, you have confidence that you can do it again when you need to.

It's the same way with the work you are doing in this Reinvention Roadmap program. You're becoming stronger when you try the suggestions in this book and work on the exercises with intention.

What does the term "with intention" mean? It means that you can't race through this book skimming the pages and hope to see big, positive changes result. You have to take the time to think about your own life as you go. You have to look at your place in the movie for which you are the star and the director. You have to stop and think about your life and your goals to get the value of the Reinvention Roadmap process. You have to slow down and ask questions you may not have asked yourself for a long time, or perhaps at all.

The benefits of following the Reinvention Roadmap won't come to you because you read the words written here and look at the pictures. You have to do the work!

PART TWO

WHAT IS FRAME-SHIFTING?

To shift a frame means to look at something differently—maybe something you haven't thought about for a long time, or ever. You are stepping out of old frames, or mental models, about your career right now. You might be seeing your career in a new light.

MY NEW FRAME

Think about a time in your life when you thought you understood a topic one way, perhaps because you'd always been told, "Here's the way this works." Then, you shifted your view and stepped out of an old frame and into a new understanding. You had an "Aha!" that said, "There is another way to look at this topic!" Write about that frame-shifting experience in your Mojo Journal.

New Ideas, New Frames

You might feel comfortable with some new ideas right away. You might say, "That makes perfect sense to me!" or even feel, "This is such a great idea, I'm going to try it right away!"

Other new ideas might be harder to take in. Why are some new ideas harder to get comfortable with than others? If a new idea rocks your understanding of the world, you might resist it.

We grow up with mental models that we have learned since early childhood. These mental models are called "frames." We grow up setting frames in place to shape our understanding of the world. We accumulate a lot of beliefs and ideas about the world. We may hold very strong beliefs about the way things work, but our beliefs may rest on thin evidence or none.

We learn a lot about the world from the people around us. If people we look up to tell us, "This is how the world works," we may accept what we're told and never question it again.

When you hear about or read about a different point of view—one that runs counter to what you always believed to be true—the experience can rock you a bit. It can knock you back on your heels and force you to ask, "Do I really know how I feel about that topic? Maybe I just accepted what I had always heard."

That's what most of us do.

It can shake your frame—the way you've always looked at things—and it can be jarring. It can be upsetting. To hear someone share a new idea that sounds foreign to you can even make you mad.

Write your answers to these two questions about frame-shifting in your Mojo Journal:

1. Have you had the experience of being offended or put off by a new idea you were hearing for the first time?

2. Have you seen someone you know have a strong negative reaction to a new idea that you shared with them?

If you are feeling stuck and desperate for a job, you can reframe your situation in your mind. You can tell yourself, "This painful period is the nudge I needed to stop trying to get any job I could get, and to stop begging and contorting myself into pretzel shapes to please people who will never get me anyway.

"This painful stretch is just what I needed to set my sights higher and to remember that only the people who get me, deserve me!"

What are your thoughts about reframing a desperate career situation to see your difficult period as a nudge that gets you back on your path? Write your thoughts in your Mojo Journal.

The Reaction-o-meter

I taught job-search, career, and leadership workshops for years. I thought the curriculum I designed was fun and useful. Every day people told me, "That technique you taught us in class last week was awesome!"

There was something important about my teaching that I didn't understand at first. I didn't see that without mojo to power your learning, you won't learn anything.

That's because you won't try new things unless your Mojo Fuel Tank is full. If you don't feel confident enough to take a step, you'll stay stuck.

When your Mojo Fuel Tank is depleted, you won't step out of your tiny comfort zone. Instead, you'll come up with reasons why you can't try new things. When your mojo is depleted, you won't learn much. You'll fall back on the script, "This is too hard to learn."

You'll say, "I'm tired. I don't want to learn a new way to job-hunt. This Liz Ryan doesn't understand how hard I've got it!" You'll say, "This is stupid. I don't want to try it."

I understand that reaction, because almost all of us have had that reaction when we encountered a new idea. We see that reaction so often at Human Workplace that we created a diagram to explain it. We call this diagram the Reaction-o-meter.

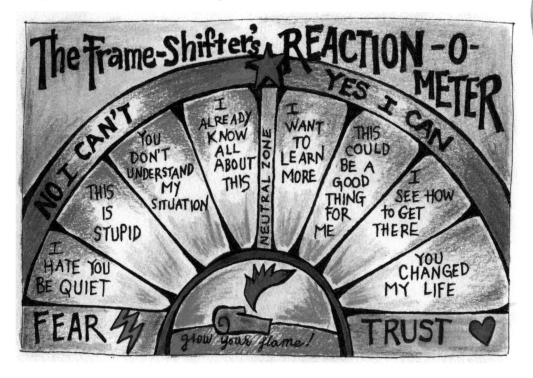

The Reaction-o-meter is a helpful tool. When you are taking in and getting comfortable with a new idea, you can experience the full range of reactions shown on the Reaction-o-meter diagram.

Notice that the area on the left side of the Reaction-o-meter shows the reactions you will get to any new idea that throws a particular person into a fearful state. The reactions on the left side of the Reaction-o-meter are fear reactions.

PART TWO

The reactions on the right side are the reactions of a person who feels more trust than fear toward you and/or the new idea you share with them.

When people feel really fearful about stepping out of a mental frame and thinking about a topic a new way, they may tell you to shut up and go away. They won't want to hear what you have to say if it jars them out of their frame when they don't want to budge.

Test your own reactions against the Reaction-o-meter Exercise.

Reaction-o-meter Exercise

Here is a list of new ideas you are learning in this Reinvention Roadmap program:

NEW IDEA

I get to run my own career—and I must run it!

I can choose a new career at any age. It's up to me.

Reinvention can be a scary place, but there's tremendous learning in it, too.

No one is responsible for my career apart from me.

My belief in myself is the most important element in my career and life success.

My experience and education are less important in my career than my own goals and my commitment to them.

I don't have to bury my personality or beg to get a good job.

When I see my own value to employers and clients, they will see it, too.

Maintaining my Mojo Fuel Tank is the most important thing I can do for myself.

I don't have to run my career or look for a job using the old rules. It's a new millennium and new rules apply.

Only the people who get me, deserve me. Anyone who doesn't care for me or value my talents is not someone I need in my life.

For each new idea listed, think about your reaction to it. Write about your reactions in your Mojo Journal. Indicate in your journal whether you feel fear, not much feeling at all (neutral zone), or trust toward each idea. Write about which ideas sound scary or silly or unrealistic and which ones sound exciting and appealing. If you like, you can set it up in your journal as a table for each idea, like this:

NEW IDEA	FEAR	NEUTRAL ZONE	TRUST
I get to run my own career—and I must run it!			

WHERE HAVE I COME FROM AND WHERE AM I GOING?

Throughout your Reinvention Roadmap journey you've been getting altitude on your life and career. You're allowing yourself to float up to Cloud level and ask, "Where have I come from in my life, and where am I headed?"

You can see how your path has brought you to this point and you can see the road ahead, too. You can see that the only obstacles in your way forward are the ones that look very big when you're down on the ground, but look tiny and insignificant from your Cloud-level vantage point.

When you're down on the ground, you can't see very much of the landscape. When you climb a hill and look down at your neighborhood, you can see how the streets and blocks fit together. You can see much more terrain from a higher elevation, or altitude.

If you could get up to the level of a cloud, you could see even more of the landscape down on the ground. That's what you are doing as you follow this Reinvention Roadmap program.

Getting altitude on your career and your life is the purpose of this book, apart from teaching the Reinvention Roadmap methodology. My mission in this book is to help you get enough altitude to see that there is nothing in your way—nothing so significant that you can't sail over it, tunnel under it, or zip around it.

Down on the ground, our obstacles look huge. They seem to be insurmountable. Once you give yourself permission to look down on your life and career from the Cloud level—from the perspective of your whole life, with your mission for your life in mind—you'll see that any obstacles between you and the life you envision are tiny and insignificant.

You might give yourself the gift of allowing yourself to envision a career that is more interesting, more rewarding, and more financially appealing than the work you may feel you are forced by circumstances to perform now.

You can give yourself that permission even if you're unemployed and feeling desperate right now. No one knows your current state of mind or the state of your career unless you tell them.

What obstacles feel like your biggest hurdles to surmount right now? Write about them in your Mojo Journal. Also, answer these questions:

- What is your biggest frustration at this moment?
- What would you change, remove, or fix if you could wave your magic wand right now?
- What steps have you taken so far to surmount or get around the obstacle you are thinking about?

COMMON OBSTACLES JOB-SEEKERS AND CAREER-CHANGERS PUT IN THEIR OWN WAY

You will need those obstacle-surmounting muscles for the new-millennium talent market, the one we've been talking about. It's not a place filled with high-rise glass and chrome buildings and massive complexes on rolling green hills—impenetrable, monolithic corporate and institutional fortresses that mere mortals can't possibly enter. It's not a scary, evil kingdom, one that you could never gain entrance to. The working world is becoming more human every day—but only for those people who themselves insist on being human and bringing themselves to work.

HOW DO YOU BRING YOURSELF TO WORK?

When you bring yourself to work all the way, you speak with your own voice at work. You bring your ideas and your opinions to work. You don't fall into character and do and say the things you think you're expected to say—instead, you say what you mean.

Say No to Bad Work

Once you gain altitude on your career and see that you get to decide what sort of work to do and who to work for and with, you'll see that you don't have to stay in a bad work situation. You can leave. You can look for something better. That's your choice and, some would say, your responsibility as well.

The minute you get the thump to the head that says, "Gee, I have put up with a lot of garbage! I have tolerated a lot of nonsense. I'm not going to tolerate bad treatment at work anymore. I'm going to find my own Human Workplace and run my own career, no matter what it takes!" your situation will start improving.

For those people who are willing to step into new territory and bring themselves completely to their work, the working world has already become much friendlier and more human.

Why is that? It's because people who take control of their own careers don't stay in abusive or mojo-crushing work situations. They would rather make a change in their life or career than send a message to the universe that their own needs don't matter.

Most of us have fallen into a doormat state at least once. We've let people walk on us. Why do we do that?

Sometimes we don't want to enter into conflict, no matter how bad we're feeling about the terrible way we're being treated. Sometimes we just don't want to rock the boat. We're afraid that if we speak up and say, "You can't treat me like that!" something terrible might happen.

When you decide that you deserve better treatment than you've been getting, your situation will begin to improve.

When you decide that your old state (in our example, your old doormat state) doesn't work for you anymore and that you're going to take concrete steps to improve your situation, watch and see how Mother Nature, God, or the universe supports your decision!

You might speak up about your feelings, or you might stay quiet, but start looking for a new job or a better situation. You'll have a new power source fueling you. That power source is your own clarity about what you want and need in your life. Your clarity fills up your Mojo Fuel Tank!

Have you ever inadvertently sent a message to the universe that your needs don't matter? Have you ever spoken up or made another change when you were being treated badly at work or somewhere else? Write about these experiences in your Mojo Journal.

People who take control of their careers don't tolerate bad behavior on the part of people around them. They don't have time to put up with bad treatment. They have a path to follow!

They don't believe they have to tolerate bad treatment on the job search or on the job, so they don't.

If they are ignored or disrespected during a recruiting process, they will drop out of it. They have confidence that when they say "No!" to the wrong thing, their trust in themselves will invite the right thing in.

You might think, "Those people who believe they can say 'NO!' to the wrong things are brave but foolish. They'll starve!"

Yet people who take control of their careers don't starve. They rise up to a higher level of altitude, where their expectation to have the work and life they want powers them.

That's why we tell people in our workshops, "There is a different way to work—at a higher altitude. You have to step into it."

Little by little, they do! Every one of us can do it.

 Do you believe that when you slam the door on a situation that would dim your flame, a better situation will show up for you? Grab your Mojo Journal and answer this question in it.

GRAZIELA'S STORY

I have a good job, I know it—I lead a marketing team, but I'm not on my path. I haven't had two seconds to think about my path over thirty years of work. I'm an executive—I make a bunch of money and my life is really complicated. This job is not my life's work, but I mean—am I allowed to shoot for the brass ring? I feel as though I don't have the right to ask for more than I have now. I was brought up not to be greedy. I feel I should be grateful for what I've accomplished and what I've been given, but I want something else from my life. Is that bad?

 Have you ever felt about your job the way Graziela feels about hers? Capture your feelings in your Mojo Journal.

TAKING THE LONG VIEW

It doesn't matter what your career background is. It doesn't matter what your education is. You can have the career and life you want, not in a flash or through some get-rich-quick scheme, but by simply stepping back and looking at what you want out of your life.

It's very simple, but we generally don't do it. We have distractions. We have daily problems and fires to fight. Grown-up life is very taxing. There are tremendous demands on us. Getting through the week feels like a huge victory. The question is, "What do I owe myself out of this lifetime?"

If we look at things from that perspective, we may see our job search or problems on the job differently. We might decide to take the long view and say, "Dang! Whatever age I am now, I don't have time to lose. I'm alive and I want to make the most of it. I want to figure out what I'm supposed to be doing here on earth and do it loudly and proudly.

"I'll figure out how to earn money in connection with figuring out what my mission is. That project is worthy of my effort because I am worthy of having a career and a life that support who I am and what I believe in."

We could say, "That's fanciful. You don't get to make those decisions about your life." We can say that but then we have to ask, "If I buy your premise that we don't get to make those decisions, who does?"

Who gets to tell us how to live? The government? Our employers? No one can tell us how to live our lives. We get to—and have to—carve out the life we want, the life that speaks for us.

It may seem impossible to move your life in the direction you want it to go, but that's largely because we have so many Ground-level (day-to-day) and Hilltop level (planning and strategy) questions to consume our time.

We are overwhelmed with questions and situations to resolve. It's exhausting.

Naturally the big question, the one always hanging around in the rear of our consciousness, gets neglected. We forget about it. The big question is, "Why am I alive? What do I want to leave behind me when I step off this train at the next station?" That's a big question.

One of the ways we keep this big question at bay is to create a value system that puts things like big houses, fancy cars, and lavish vacations at the top of our lists.

Who could blame us for wanting to have nice things and go on nice trips? We deserve those things. There is nothing wrong with indulging ourselves and taking care of ourselves, but if our pursuit of nice things takes us off our path, we're going to feel the dissonance.

This is one reason my colleagues and I started the Human Workplace movement. We heard from people around the world who would be viewed as successful by almost anyone. They have great jobs but they aren't happy, because their job is so philosophically or emotionally detached from who they are. If you're in that position, you can take control of your career and make a change.

YOUR ASSIGNMENT

MOJO FUEL TANK EXERCISE

In the Mojo Fuel Tank exercise, you see a drawing of your Mojo Fuel Tank, an "Up" arrow, and a "Down" arrow. You'll think about the activities, people, and situations that deplete your Mojo Fuel Tank (the "Down" arrow) and those that fill up your Mojo Fuel Tank (the "Up" arrow). To complete the exercise, create a list of the activities, people, and situations that deplete your Mojo Fuel Tank, and a separate list of the activities, people, and situations that fill up your Mojo Fuel Tank. Notice the differences between the two lists.

We all know which activities, people, and situations bring us up and which bring us down, but we seldom think about managing our mojo supply. Now you are focusing on the goal of keeping your Mojo Fuel Tank full. You are in charge of your time. How will you manage your time and activities to keep your Mojo Fuel Tank as full as it can be?

Maybe paying bills depletes your mojo supply, but working in your garden fills up your Mojo Fuel Tank. Can you organize your schedule to reward yourself for paying bills by making time to work in your garden immediately after the bills are paid?

Some of the people you spend time with increase your mojo supply and other people bring you down. Can you arrange your social time to spend more time with the people who lift you up and less time with the people who suck your mojo away?

As you walk the Reinvention Roadmap path, you are learning to protect your precious mojo supply. You get to decide who to spend time with, and when. You can say, "Sorry, I can't get together this week—how about next week?" even to people you love. You can set boundaries around your personal time.

The more you get a handle on the activities, people, and situations that grow your mojo supply and the ones that deplete it, the more easily you'll be able to schedule your time so that you're managing your mojo supply carefully.

Your mojo is the only fuel you've got to power your reinvention and your life. Don't take your mojo supply for granted!

THE LAST JOB CANDIDATE STANDING

I was an HR leader for a long time. I hired a lot of people and helped to hire many thousands more.

We hired people who were smart and capable, but there was something else noteworthy about them, too. The people who got hired were people who knew themselves. They knew that they brought something valuable to the job.

We didn't hire people who seemed to need the job desperately. Would you? We hired people we felt confident could step into the assignment and do a great job. That didn't mean they had already performed the exact same kind of job before. It meant that they were confident people. They knew they could learn the job if they hadn't performed a similar job before.

You won't get a new job, much less a great job that deserves you, by being the most desperate or the most grovelly (willing to beg) job-seeker you can be.

You won't get the job you want, a job that really deserves you, by putting up with bad treatment as a job-seeker and giving in to whatever unrealistic demands an employer makes of you.

If you are a consultant, you won't grow your flame and get better at what you do by begging your clients to hire you and putting up with bad treatment.

It's just the opposite. You'll get hired more quickly for better jobs and better assignments when you have confidence—when you know what value you bring to an employer or a client!

Some job-seekers think, "I will be the nicest, most agreeable, and most compliant little job-seeker the world has ever seen! The organization I want to work for will hire me because I will do everything they ask me to do—quickly and politely!"

This is a losing job-search strategy because it will bring in the wrong people—people who won't see your value and who will expect you to bow down to them and beg for a job.

Your ability to find a job (or a set of clients) that deserves you rests on your own understanding of your value—and your ability to speak up for your value when the situation requires it.

You don't want to get a job because every other job candidate (job applicant) has left the process, disgusted. You don't want to be the Last Candidate Standing—the person who is still sitting by the phone waiting for a callback, weeks after a job interview, hoping that he or she is the only person who wants the job.

That is no way to grow your flame, or to follow your path!

What are your thoughts about standing up for your value as a job-seeker? Write them in your Mojo Journal!

ABIGAIL'S STORY

I went on two job interviews two weeks ago, and I didn't hear anything back from the first company. The second company called me back. They asked me to come back for a second interview. I was excited and nervous at the same time.

At the first interview, the interviewer had told me that the department manager didn't want to pay more than $40,000 for her new hire. I'm not sure she was supposed to tell me that, but she did. That number worked for me. I just didn't want to make much less than $40,000. I didn't want to take myself off the job market for an annual salary less than $40,000.

I felt strongly that my background and abilities are worth at least $40,000.

When I went to the second interview, I met the department manager, Ella. She asked me a lot of questions about my previous job. I could see that she was impressed by my background and by my answers to the questions she asked me. I asked Ella a number of questions about the job, too.

At the end of my second interview, Ella said, "Your background is great. I'd like to offer you the position if we can agree on your salary. I can pay you thirty-five thousand dollars in this job."

My heart sank. I didn't want the job for $35,000. I knew my background was worth more than that. I didn't want to lose the opportunity, but I knew that I could contribute more value to Ella's department than that.

Ella and I had been talking at some depth about problems with her company's largest accounts. I wouldn't be selling anything to those large accounts if I took the job working for Ella, but I'd certainly be a big part of keeping those clients happy. Ella's big accounts brought in a lot of revenue—at least $10,000 per month, per client, and she had a number of them, because she rattled off their names in the interview.

I was asking for $40,000 a year in salary—a little more than $3,000 a month. If Ella couldn't justify paying that salary, then I could find someone who had more pain than Ella did.

I said, "Thanks for sharing that information. Your opportunity is very interesting, but I'm not sure we have a match. My minimum salary requirement is forty thousand dollars per year."

I shocked myself by speaking up like that. I wasn't working, but I just knew that I had to stand up for myself.

Ella thought for a moment and asked me, "Are you talking to other firms about other job opportunities?"

I wasn't expecting that question, but I could see that Ella was trying to see whether I could afford to hold out for my $40,000 salary target because I had already received or was expecting a competing job offer.

She wanted to know if she was about to lose me to another employer, or if I might feel forced to take her job offer at $35,000 because I had no other choice.

I said, "I'm certain that your conversations with other job candidates are confidential, and my conversations with other employers of course are confidential, too."

I wanted Ella to know that I was very interested in joining her team, if we could agree on my salary. So I asked her a question: "Should we talk by phone in a few days, once you've had a chance to think about what you need most in this position, and see whether we can bridge the five-thousand-dollar gap?"

Ella said, "No, that's okay. We can do it. I can offer you forty thousand dollars a year to start."

When I got home, I told my roommate, Bev, about the job offer. She asked me, "Why didn't you tell Ella that the recruiter had already told you that the company could afford to pay forty thousand for this position?"

I told Bev, "If I had said that, I think Ella would just have said, 'Well, our budget has changed since then.' I didn't want to make the five-thousand-dollar gap the recruiter's problem. It's Ella's problem. She is the department manager. She is the person who is living with her problems. If she doesn't value me at forty thousand dollars, then she has to live with her pain a little longer."

 What are your thoughts about Abigail's job interview and her job offer? Write them in your Mojo Journal.

You will have more fun at work, earn more money, and have more control over where you work and who you work for when you take control of your own career and stand up for yourself. Abigail did it, and other job-seekers and working people do the same thing every day.

They feel the same fear that you feel when your financial security is at risk. They feel the same anxious feelings that anybody feels when they aren't sure how they're going to pay the rent next month. They feel those scared feelings, but they still say, "I'm going to trust myself to follow my path, instead of getting sucked into a bad situation only because I want to be employed. That's a bad move."

RUNNING YOUR OWN CAREER

We are talking about running your own career. Most people have never done that, so they aren't sure what the term "running your own career" means.

You might think, "I'm already running my own career!" Most people think they're running their own careers, but they're not. They're in a bad situation then. No one is running their career, because they aren't running it and their employer certainly isn't. They go to work every day they're scheduled to work. That's their career plan. They say, "I'm running my own career!" because they get in their car or on the bus and go to work and do the work they are told to do. That's not a career plan! That's a plan for one day—not for your whole career, or your whole life!

If your job went away tomorrow, what would you do to survive economically? Would you move to a new employer—and if so, which organizations would you approach? Write your ideas in your Mojo Journal.

You can give yourself the gift of allowing yourself to envision a career that is more interesting, more rewarding, and more financially appealing than the work you may feel you are forced by circumstances to perform now. You can give yourself that permission even if you're unemployed and feeling desperate right now. No one knows your current state of mind or the state of your career unless you tell them.

GROW YOUR FLAME

Your goal as a person on your path is not to get the fastest job offer that you can possibly get. If you must get a job quickly to pay the bills, you can keep job-hunting or you can take a breather and start job-hunting again when you know what kind of work you really want to do.

You don't have to stay in the wrong job just because it's inconvenient to job-hunt.

If you are job-hunting, you can take a survival job to pay the bills while you think about the rest of your career.

You can stay on your path and continue growing your muscles and growing your flame.

What is your flame? It's the spark inside you. Your flame is what makes you "you." Your

flame grows when you perform work that makes you feel successful and whole. Your flame grows when you can bring yourself to work, all the way. Your flame grows when you work among people who value and appreciate you. Your flame grows when you speak with your own voice and say what you believe. Your flame dims when you have to play a part at work, or believe that you can't be yourself there. Your flame grows when you are paid what your talents are worth. Your flame also grows when you are acknowledged by other people for your work.

What kind of work have you done so far that grew your flame? How has your flame been fanned and/or dimmed at work in your career so far? Capture your thoughts in your Mojo Journal. Also write about a time when you got acknowledgment for your contribution at work. How did it feel when that happened?

TRYING SOMETHING NEW

You are not bound or obligated to get a new job that's similar to jobs you've already held. You can easily brand yourself for a new job, one that you haven't held before.

You might try a very new career path and decide that it isn't your cup of tea. That would be great learning. That adventure would grow your muscles. It would not represent a waste of time or energy! You could try a new career path and love it.

In your Mojo Journal, list one job title that you might focus on in your job search if you are job-hunting now, or that you might focus on the next time you are job-hunting.

Now, answer each question with that job title in mind.

- Does this type of work use your talents and abilities?
- Does this kind of job make you feel powerful and successful?
- Does this type of work pay you what you are worth (or close)?

When you get clear on what you're passionate about doing and bring that passion into your work, then it will be your life's work.

You'll sail over the obstacles that stand between you and the career and the life you want. You'll be powered by your own belief in yourself and your passion for the topic you want to pursue. That combination of energy sources is powerful. It's rocket fuel!

What are some topics you are passionate about? Don't censor yourself by saying, "That topic could never intersect with my paid employment." That doesn't matter for this exercise.

Don't put up your own obstacles! Just write about the topics, themes, causes, people, activities, trends, problems, and issues that speak to you most. Write your thoughts in your Mojo Journal.

You are qualified for a lot more jobs than you may think you are!

SETTING BIG GOALS

In this book you are learning new approaches to running your job search and your career, but the intention of this book and the Reinvention Roadmap program is to give you something more valuable than "how-to" advice. My mission in this book is to shift the way you look at yourself, and to remind you of the power that you have to run your own life and career.

You are much smarter, more capable, smarter, creative, and more powerful than you think. You can accomplish the ambitious goals you will set for yourself the minute you give yourself permission to set your sights on the life you really want.

In fact, setting big goals and committing to pursue them no matter what anyone else thinks is the single best way to reach your goals! You're going to have to work hard to get to the life and career you want, but that's okay—your work to get there is exactly the cost of the vision for your life that you are creating.

Why work that hard for a slight improvement in some minor area or aspect of your life? Why not give yourself permission to dream really big?

Many of us hesitate to set ambitious goals because we fear that the people closest to us will say, "Who do you think you are to set such lofty goals?" You don't have to tell anyone that you're thinking about making big changes in your life. You don't have to set yourself up to have the people around you poke fun at you for daring to envision a different life than the one you have now. You don't need that pressure.

You can keep your dreams to yourself for now. The key is to envision them, and then to commit to them!

When you can look at where you are now, at this moment, and where you want to go in your life and your career, you will gain a huge amount of power.

YOUR ASSIGNMENT

Your assignment is to write in your Mojo Journal about the things, people, and ideas that grow your flame. How can you grow your flame a little bit more today? Write about it, and then do it!

LIFE AFTER THE CORPORATE LADDER

THE CORPORATE LADDER

Years ago we used to talk about the "corporate ladder." Are you familiar with that term? What does (or did) the term "corporate ladder" mean? If it is not familiar to you, you can put this book down, look up the term, and then write your answer in your Mojo Journal.

The corporate ladder was the system that let working people begin a job at a young age and then get promoted to more responsible jobs over time. We talked about that system using a ladder as an analogy. On a painter's ladder or any ladder, you climb up the ladder rung by rung, from the bottom to the top.

From about the end of World War II right up to the end of the last century (and millennium), the corporate ladder system was in place at many or most large corporations and institutions.

A lot of people started their careers at the bottom of the ladder and then gradually moved up. Many of us got used to being promoted at work every few years. We expected it—after all, we worked hard!

Did you grow up when the corporate ladder system was still firmly in place? How did the corporate ladder system affect

your career? If you don't remember the corporate ladder, talk to an older person. Ask them about the corporate ladder, and then write a summary of what you learned in your Mojo Journal.

The corporate ladder system had good and bad points. A lot of people climbed the corporate ladder and had great careers. They had a tremendous amount of job security. At the same time, they didn't have as much opportunity to try new things and to grow muscles as we have today. We have no choice—we have to grow muscles!

The corporate ladder system has almost completely disintegrated. As we say at Human Workplace, the corporate ladder is now sawdust under our feet. (The ladder was made of wood, but termites ate it and turned it into sawdust.)

The corporate ladder system through which working people worked hard and climbed the ranks has nearly disappeared. We can't rely on it anymore. We have to create our own career ladder or, to use a more apt analogy, our own career roadmap!

"Moving up" in an organization the way we worked so hard to do in the corporate ladder days is not necessarily the best path for you.

"Moving up" to higher- and higher-level management jobs only means that your goals become more and more entwined with the corporation's goals, and that your financial and emotional well-being become more and more dependent on whatever organization you work for.

That isn't an ideal situation!

In the ideal situation, your goals are your own. One employer may take you far down your path or just a short distance.

When you are on your path, it won't matter to you whether you stay with one employer for a long time or take an exit ramp and go in another direction to perform work that you prefer. It's your career—you get to choose when to get on and off each highway you encounter. You are behind the wheel in your career. You are driving—not your employer!

What are your thoughts about the disappearance of the corporate ladder system and your own responsibility for driving your career? Capture your thoughts in your Mojo Journal.

Many jobs today offer little or no opportunity for upward advancement. They have no career path associated with them. You could do a great job for years and your employer would be happy about that, but there would be no guarantee that you'd ever get promoted or get paid more money on the job.

Have you run into a disappointing situation on your current job or a past job—a situation where you thought the job was going to progress one way but it actually went a different way? Write about that here in your Mojo Journal.

Can there still be value to you in working at a job that has little or no career advancement opportunity? There can be—if that "dead end" job takes you down your path and gives you valuable experience and stories that will grow your muscles, mojo, and marketability for your next career adventure!

You are not looking for one job that will take you all the way from today to retirement. You are looking for a job (or a consulting project) that will grow your muscles and make you more marketable the next time you look for a job—while growing your flame!

Open your Mojo Journal and write your thoughts about gathering the good things you can from one job and adding them to your portfolio as you continue down your path. Also write about something valuable you gained while working at a job that was not a good long-term career job for you.

You can still gather valuable contacts, great learning, and wonderful Dragon-Slaying Stories (we'll cover these in chapter fourteen) at a job that has no upward career path. You can stay at the job long enough to gather the valuable things that the job has to offer, and then hop to a new lily pad!

The working world has changed. The talent market where job-seekers pursue new jobs and employers hire them has changed.

What do these changes mean for us? It means that we have to be as good at getting a job as we are at doing a job once we're hired.

These days knowing how to get a new job is a critical career skill! It doesn't do us any good to be great at our work unless we can find new work when we want to, or when our old work goes away. We have to see our own careers as businesses. Your career is your business!

Every person who runs his or her own business knows these three things:

- You can be incredibly good at what you do, but you won't grow your business (or even keep it running successfully) unless you're not only good at performing the work but also good at getting work in the first place.

- Your knowledge of your market is the key to running your own business. You have to keep your eyes and ears open for changes in your marketplace!

- If you listen to your customers and pay close attention, you won't struggle to find work. Changes in the wind won't escape your notice. You'll be alert and on the lookout for new pain you can solve!

How do these three elements intersect with your career situation? Write your thoughts in your Mojo Journal.

LUCIE'S STORY

I'm a Librarian. I went to school for library science many years ago. A Librarian is a long-term career job for many or most librarians. Graduate school is expensive. It takes years to pay off your loans. I've been a Librarian for more than 20 years. Now I'm wondering if there are more creative ways to use my talents.

I like my Librarian job, but it is very structured. There isn't much room for me to customize the job around my talents and passions. I work for a school district. My job is very closely defined. I can't put my individual stamp on it as well as I would like to do.

I have some choices to make. I can apply at another school district. In that case, I would lose all my seniority in this district. That is a scary idea; but then again, it's my life! I have to ask myself, "What do I really want?"

I could leave my library profession altogether. I could try something completely new. I know that my experience as a Librarian won't be wasted, no matter what I decide to do.

 What advice would you give to Lucie? Write your ideas in your Mojo Journal!

STAYING ON TOP OF YOUR CAREER

When it hits you that you are the Chief Executive Officer (CEO) of your career and your life, you'll pay closer attention to the question, "Does my job or work situation support my life goals?" You'll take steps to manage your career the same way any business owner manages his or her business. You'll pay attention to your career, way past the question, "Am I working now?"

Having a job right now is the booby prize if your flame and your muscles aren't growing. That is the big change that has taken place in the talent marketplace.

Just because you have a job today doesn't mean you will have a job tomorrow. How will your work-home-sleep-work-home-sleep routine prepare you to find a job when you need one, much less to find work that is satisfying and worth your talents?

When you live in a house or an apartment, you try to take care of it. You don't want your roof to leak when it rains or snows. You don't want leaves and twigs to clog up your gutter or you might have problems down the road.

Your career is the same way. You have to stay on top of it, the way every business owner pays close attention to his or her business and the changing market landscape around him or her.

Many people choose career paths for chance reasons. Sometimes they "fall into" a career path and then they stick with it because it's all they know.

 How did you get into your career path? Write the story in your Mojo Journal.

Over time, people begin to believe that their credibility as a working person, and their ability to get a new job, come from their experience in their particular career path.

That's false! Your credibility comes from inside. It comes from your belief in yourself and your knowledge of what kind of work you're meant to be doing.

What do I mean by "meant to be doing"?

Meant to be doing means being true to yourself and your dreams. Everybody has dreams and plans. We often don't give ourselves the chance to dream, especially if our dreams seem really big and ambitious. We might think, "Who am I to have a big, ambitious dream?" Then again, who is anybody to have a dream—and who are you NOT to have a big dream?

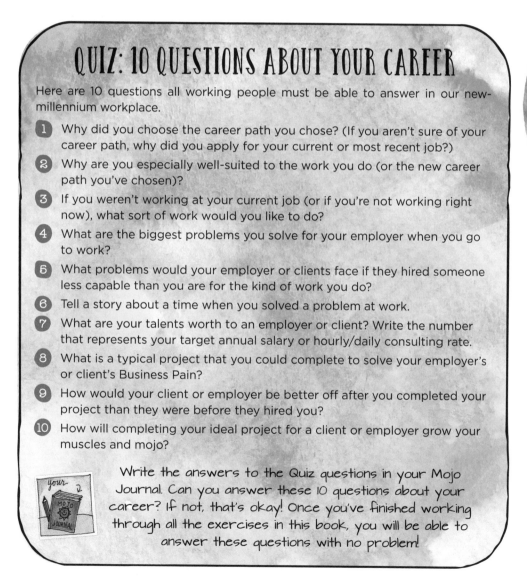

QUIZ: 10 QUESTIONS ABOUT YOUR CAREER

Here are 10 questions all working people must be able to answer in our new-millennium workplace.

1. Why did you choose the career path you chose? (If you aren't sure of your career path, why did you apply for your current or most recent job?)

2. Why are you especially well-suited to the work you do (or the new career path you've chosen)?

3. If you weren't working at your current job (or if you're not working right now), what sort of work would you like to do?

4. What are the biggest problems you solve for your employer when you go to work?

5. What problems would your employer or clients face if they hired someone less capable than you are for the kind of work you do?

6. Tell a story about a time when you solved a problem at work.

7. What are your talents worth to an employer or client? Write the number that represents your target annual salary or hourly/daily consulting rate.

8. What is a typical project that you could complete to solve your employer's or client's Business Pain?

9. How would your client or employer be better off after you completed your project than they were before they hired you?

10. How will completing your ideal project for a client or employer grow your muscles and mojo?

Write the answers to the Quiz questions in your Mojo Journal. Can you answer these 10 questions about your career? If not, that's okay! Once you've finished working through all the exercises in this book, you will be able to answer these questions with no problem!

CASEY'S LESSON ABOUT BIG GOALS

I worked for a fellow named Casey. He was the CEO of our company and he was my boss. I learned a lot about business from him.

We worked in a renovated Art Deco building. In the lobby was a big reception desk and a broad staircase going up to the second floor. One day I was talking with my friend Donna at the front desk. We talked every day, or many times a day. Donna was our receptionist and the nerve center of the human energy in the company.

On this particular day, our CEO, Casey, was walking down the stairs. I was standing near the reception desk chatting with Donna. Donna had to answer an incoming call. Casey asked me, "Have you got a second?"

"Sure!" I said.

"Good," he said. "I want to tell you about my plan for the business."

"Awesome!" I said. "I want to hear about it."

Here's how our conversation went.

CASEY: So, obviously, our company is growing fast.

LIZ: For sure. It's fantastic.

CASEY: It is, and now we're going to set a big new goal—an ambitious goal. Everybody who works here will be a big part of reaching the goal, and that's why I'm talking with you about it now. When you started here two years ago, our sales were about fifteen million dollars a year.

LIZ: Yes, and last year sales were about thirty-eight million, and this year they might be fifty million—right?

CASEY: Or a little more. Now we need a really ambitious plan to keep growing.

LIZ: Growing at about the same rate?

CASEY: No, not the same rate. We're going to grow a lot faster. That's more fun and more exciting for everyone. Everyone has to be in on it. It has to the biggest thing we focus on, and something we talk about all the time. It will be our focal point.

LIZ: Okay! What is the plan?

CASEY: Our plan will be to grow ten times over in sales during the next five years. The plan will start this year, 1990, and we'll hit our goal in 1995. We're going to hit five hundred million dollars in sales that year—five years from now. We can do it.

LIZ: That sounds great, but how?

CASEY: We don't know that yet. There's no way to know the details at this early point. Committing to our big, ambitious goal is the first step. The specific path to get there will emerge as we get closer. The bigger issue is for everyone to be excited about this enormous goal. The rest of it will sort itself out.

LIZ: What if we don't hit the big, ambitious goal?

CASEY: That's not a big deal. We'll still learn more and get further shooting for a big goal than we would by making little goals that no one cares about.

We made T-shirts that said "Five by Five" on them. "Five by Five" meant that we were going to grow the company to sell five hundred million dollars in modems and data communications equipment by 1995, which was five years in the future.

Of course, we didn't just make T-shirts. We talked about the goal. We got everybody on the team to see his or her part in it. Everybody got excited.

We started to think about the new products, new customers, and new ideas we would explore on our way to hitting our five-hundred-million-dollar sales goal.

The goal was real once we committed to it. Then there was no question that we would reach our goal, and everything we did was right in step with that mission.

We hit the goal with room to spare but even more importantly, it was a fun and exciting environment to work in.

When everyone is energized around the same goal, you can feel the electricity in the air. When I felt that way at U.S. Robotics, I remembered that feeling from musical theater productions in high school. Most of us have felt the great feeling you get when you're working on something important with other people.

 Open your Mojo Journal and write about a time when you took on a big goal with other people and accomplished it. How did it feel when you and your teammates reached the ambitious goal? Write about that here.

You are the CEO of your career, the same way Casey was the CEO and founder of U.S. Robotics. What will you call your company—which is also your career? Here are the names that three Reinvention Roadmap followers used for their businesses—which is to say, their careers:

- Jason's Career, Inc.

- Allyson's Adventures

- Srinivas Industries

What will you call your career (which is your own company)? You are President and CEO. You are the sole owner of your company and your career. You get to choose its name!

Write your name ideas in your Mojo Journal.
Then, answer these questions:

- Can you give yourself permission to set ambitious goals for your career?
- Can you give yourself permission to dream as big a dream as your mind and heart can create?
- What would your ideal career situation be?

When you take the time to figure out what you can do professionally apart from the jobs you've held already, you are taking a big step. You are telling yourself and the universe, "Yes, I am worthy of more than I have right now. I have a right to live the life I want."

That's a huge step to take! It's the first and most important step toward taking charge of your own career.

You won't say, "I've been a bartender all my working life so far, so I guess I'll always be a bartender!" It's up to you whether you want to remain a bartender (or an accountant, a database analyst, or a preschool teacher) or to try something new.

Most of us have not been taught that we get to choose a new career path when we want to. We've been taught, "You have to stick with what you know!"

Have you ever thought, "I guess I'm stuck in this career path, because it's all I know"? Think about and then write down other professions, career directions, or professional paths that you would follow if you felt that you could choose your own career. Write these alternate career paths in your Mojo Journal.

MADELYN'S STORY

I didn't feel that I could choose my career path because I got my degree in a very specific subject. I got a BS in Psychology. In college I got the strong message that a BS in Psychology was mainly a starting point for a Master's Degree and maybe a PhD in Psychology. We didn't talk about other career paths. I was completely adrift when I graduated from college.

I took a job as a Senior Support Analyst at a large teaching hospital. A Senior Support Analyst is basically a higher-level customer service person for employees in the hospital who run into any problems with operational things—booking conference rooms, replacing ID badges, and dealing with paperwork and supplies. Our department doesn't get involved with the medical treatment side of things.

I was surprised that I liked the job. I felt like a failure, though, because I wasn't using my degree. I had the idea that if I wasn't pursuing a job in the field of Psychology, that made me a failure and a loser.

I stayed in the Senior Support Analyst job for 18 months. I applied for another job in the hospital. In that job, I was the Department Administrator for several of our pediatric departments. I love kids, so that was a lot of fun, too.

Then I applied for a job outside the hospital. I got hired as a Business Manager for a medical practice. At that point I was 30 years old and it hit me that I get to choose my career path. I liked my three first jobs, but the world is big.

I thought about other topics I'm interested in apart from health care operations. I didn't have the confidence to make a huge career leap, but I wanted to at least step away from running or helping to run a hospital or health care facility.

The reason I majored in Psychology is that I like to talk with people and help them solve problems. I did some of that in all three of my first jobs, but I didn't do enough of it for my taste.

It struck me that I need to do more one-on-one problem-solving. I'm not qualified to be a Psychologist, but that's okay with me. My Psychology degree wasn't a waste of time!

My family didn't understand why I wanted to look beyond my steady job. They gave me a hard time about my career exploration. But my exploration was valuable to me. I learned a huge amount about myself and the world. I don't want to do Clinical Psychology alone in an office with one person at a time. I like to work with groups.

I applied for a job as a Practice Leader in a health care consulting firm. The Practice Leader doesn't work directly with clients but makes sure that consulting projects are going smoothly. The Practice Leader works for a partner. I got the job and I love it. I have a great working relationship with the partner in our firm, who is my boss. Our styles work well together.

I'm so happy about my job. I work with a group of consultants who travel all over the world. I keep them up to date, equipped with information they need, and feeling supported.

I do so much day-to-day problem-solving now and I love talking through challenges with my teammates and with my boss. I went from the health care business into the consulting business, but there are so many things that cross over from one industry to the other, I can't really say that I've changed careers.

At the same time I realize that when you're qualified to do one thing, you're qualified to do a ton of different things!

I don't know how long I'll stay in this job or what I'll do next. I'm having a lot of fun and learning a lot but I'm not afraid of changing careers anymore.

I see that the career change that looked so big and scary to me from one side of the imaginary wall looks like a tiny step from the other side of the wall. That's the gift that my zigzag career has given me!

What are your thoughts about Madelyn's story?
Write them in your Mojo Journal.

Give yourself permission to set a big, ambitious goal
for your life and career. You don't have to tell anyone
about your goal if you don't want to. The first step in
getting the career and life you want is to give yourself
permission to dream big. Write in your Mojo Journal about
your ambitious dream.

Now that I am formally instructing you to
create a huge, ambitious vision for yourself,
I hope you will give yourself permission to
do it! Nobody ever accomplished anything
ambitious without a big dream to power
their effort.

CHAPTER TWELVE

DECIDE WHAT YOU WANT
AND GO GET IT

I was a Human Resources leader for a long time. I saw people changing jobs in order to get a better salary or a more interesting position, or for other reasons.

I didn't blame them for making changes to improve their situation. Who doesn't want to improve his or her situation? Almost all of us do! We should aim to improve our working situations. That's what upward mobility is all about!

However, one person's definition of "improve my working situation" might be different from another person's definition.

For Erica, moving up at work might mean getting promoted to a higher-level position.

For Stanley, moving up might mean getting more time off at work or gaining the ability to work from home. That would improve Stanley's quality of life dramatically. Stanley doesn't want to get promoted. He wants to work from home and do his work in relative quiet. That's how he works best!

How do you work best? Write your thoughts in your Mojo Journal.

MARSHALL'S STORY

I'm a go-with-the-flow guy. I work hard in my job, but I've never really thought about my work situation before—not unless I'm actually at work. I've never stepped back and asked, "Is this the exact job or working situation I want?"

I'm really involved with a group of friends I've known since I was a teenager. We're all married now. We get together and hang out every few weeks. We have a great time. I feel very lucky to have such a solid group of friends who support me, and of course my wife, Brianna, is in my corner. I have a decent job, too. My boss is a great guy and I know I'm important on our team.

I was at a barbecue with this group of friends I mentioned, all the families and little kids running around. I was talking with Maeve, who is married to my friend Roger. Maeve said, "I work from home half the time." We talked about her job working from home. That sounds exotic to me. Almost everyone I know goes to work in a building somewhere.

Maeve loves working from home and she also loves going into her office. The whole ride home from the party, I was thinking about Maeve's life working from home half the time and going to work in an office the other half. I think that would work perfectly for me.

I said to Brianna, "Why did I start talking to Maeve? Now I'm determined to get a job like that, where I can work half the time from home and the other half in the office."

Brianna said, "It's good that you talked to her! You deserve to have that kind of job, Marshall. You work hard and you're good at what you do."

Between Maeve and my Brianna, I got a mojo boost to shift my job so that I can work from home at least part of the time. If my company wouldn't go for that kind of arrangement, I know I can get another job.

Maybe a new job would be good for me. I'm not going to prejudge the situation or work out all the scenarios in my head. I'm just going to talk to my manager, Fil, about gradually starting to work from home some of the time. I can get more done at home than I can in our office, and Fil knows that's true.

I'm looking forward to my conversation with Fil, because it isn't a win-or-lose thing from my perspective. It's a real problem-solving exercise. I respect Fil and vice versa. It's time I found my voice and used it to bring up an issue that I care about.

That has not been my style at work, but now I'm feeling like, "Why not ask Fil about working from home? What's the worst thing that could happen?"

I'm going to think more and speak more about what I need and want, not because I'm ungrateful for what I have, but because it's my life. I'm grateful to have Brianna in my corner. I want her to have the life she envisions, too!

What are your thoughts and ideas about Marshall's story? Write them in your Mojo Journal. Also, think about and answer these questions:

- How would you like to improve your working situation?
- Are you looking for a job right now, or thinking about getting a different job than the one you have?
- What is the next step you want to take to improve your career situation?
- What would your improved career situation look like?

WHERE SHOULD I WORK?

Years ago, employers made a deal with their employees. It wasn't a deal on paper. It wasn't an agreement that anyone talked about. It was just understood. The agreement was unstated, but it was well understood by both parties to the agreement—the employer on one side of the desk, and the person who came to work for that employer on the other side.

They both agreed on the old deal that many of us grew up with. That deal said, "Come to work every day and work hard. You'll be guaranteed a job and you might get promoted, too."

That was a good deal! My dad took that deal and so did millions of other working people. That deal was in place since at least the end of World War II up until the 1990s or a little bit later.

When I was a young HR person, we were told that the old deal had a name. It was called the Social Contract. Now the Social Contract lies in tatters.

It's history. The Social Contract is gone.

That deal is dead! It's not available anymore.

We know that life is all about change, but this change was a tough one for many people to accept, and many folks are not quite ready to accept it yet!

There is no job security anymore except one kind—the kind of job security that we build in ourselves. Where does that job security come from? It comes from our knowledge of what we do well. It comes from our understanding of the reasons why employers hire people in the first place. It comes from our understanding of the problems we solve for our employers and the stress and money those problems cost organizations until they are solved.

Our built-in and portable job security comes from our understanding of the kind of work we do and the talent market in which we operate. That means we need to know which people and organizations typically need services like the kinds of services we provide.

How could you learn which organizations might need the kinds of services you provide?

You could read published job ads.

You could read your local newspaper (in print or online) to see which organizations in your area are building new facilities, moving into larger work spaces, or launching big projects.

You could create a Target Employer List and follow the employers on your list. You can follow them on Twitter and on LinkedIn and read their press releases.

How to Create Your Target Employer List

How will you decide which employers to target in your job search? Most business publications (like the Business section of your local newspaper) publish annual lists of the largest employers in your area. You could add some of these employers to your list—but why stick to large employers?

Small employers are great places to grow your flame! Your local business publication probably also publishes an annual list of the fastest-growing small businesses. You could choose some of those organizations to add to your Target Employer List, too!

You can visit your local Chamber of Commerce website to learn about other organizations. You can ask your friends and family members which organizations are great to work for. Many publications publish annual lists of the Best Companies to Work For, but if I were you I wouldn't base my Target Employer List project on a list like that.

Some or all of those companies may be great to work for, but they don't get on the Best Companies to Work For list published by your local paper unless they fill out an application to be included on the list. That's a Public Relations project.

A company's reputation among working people and job-seekers is a more reliable measurement of whether they're actually a great place to work than their inclusion on a published list of Best Companies to Work For!

To create your Target Employer List, open a spreadsheet or create your list on paper. Include the organization's name and location (the one where you would go to work if you end up working for them), their website address, and the reason you've included them on your Target Employer List.

Maybe it's because you've used their products and liked them or because your sister used to work there and she enjoyed her time there. You can populate your Target Employer List any way you want.

How many organizations should I include on my Target Employer List?

That's up to you! You could start with just 10 or 20 organizations, or with 50. Just remember that your next step will be to research each of the organizations on your list!

How will I research my Target Employers?

You'll visit each organization's website and read about them. You'll visit their LinkedIn Company Page (if they have one) and their Facebook page (if they have one). You'll also use LinkedIn to read the profiles of their managers, including (especially!) the person who will be your boss if you go to work at that organization.

You can add to and subtract from your Target Employer List any time you want. You can attend business networking events and learn from your fellow attendees which organizations are doing interesting things.

What other steps could you take to stay in touch with your local talent marketplace? Write your ideas in your Mojo Journal, and answer these questions:

1. You need to know which organizations and people are likely to run into the problems you know how to solve. How could you figure that out?

2. How could you learn more about the Business Pain your target hiring managers are likely to be experiencing?

GLENN'S STORY

I've been a cable installer for a long time, but there's not as much need for cable installers now as there used to be. I'm investigating other career opportunities. I've had to back up and decide what kind of problems I solve in my work. I know a lot about technology, and of course I know how to find addresses and help people with problems in their houses once I get there.

I don't know anything about heating or air conditioning, but I applied for a job with a heating and air conditioning company anyway. In my Pain Letter I wrote that I learned cable installation in two months and I know I could learn heating and air conditioning pretty fast, at least enough to be useful to the company right away.

I heard back from them. They said they always need sharp people on their team. They said they could start me on the phone in customer service and move me up as I understand more and more about their business.

Since I told them I'm a fast learner, now is my chance to prove it! I'm taking the job on the phone in customer service because I see it as a foot in the door. I'm going to show these folks that I can soak up their business details, and believe me, I'm going to be asking a lot of questions! I knew I could solve problems other than just cable TV problems. I knew my 26 years of experience couldn't be for nothing!

What are your thoughts about Glenn's story? Write them in your Mojo Journal.

What Jobs Have in Common

Most jobs have much more in common with other jobs than we would expect. Once you hold a few different jobs in very different settings, you realize that there are fundamental elements that almost all jobs have in common.

You have to think and solve problems, interact with other people, and use your noggin, as they used to say, at work. If you can perform one job, you can perform hundreds of them—not every single job, but a huge number and variety of them!

Once you've learned the basics of holding a job, solving problems, communicating with other people, and managing your time and energy, you can perform an incredible array of different jobs. To make a career change that might feel ambitious or daring you have to do three things:

1. You have to decide what you want to do next in your career, and what sort of work would grow your flame. That exploration is a very different exercise from asking, "What kinds of jobs would I be qualified for? What kinds of jobs would employers accept me for?"

2. You have to brand yourself differently for your new career direction. First you must clearly see yourself in your new role. When you see the connections and crossovers between your old career path and your new one, you'll communicate them in a way that anyone could understand.

3. Finally, you have to stop focusing on the qualifications or credentials you wish you had for your new career and remind yourself that you have tremendous work and life experience that can help employers. Not every organization will appreciate what you bring, but who cares about that? Only the people who get you, deserve you!

Many things you've done on past jobs will be valuable and useful in your new career path.

What are some of the tasks and activities you've performed at your past jobs? Write them in your Mojo Journal. Don't censor yourself! Write everything you can remember! Here are some tasks and activities people perform at work—to spark your thinking!

Answering the telephone   Helping customers   Writing email correspondence

Creating reports   Writing software code   Organizing projects

Working a machine or equipment   Solving problems   Analyzing data

Making sales calls   Interviewing people   Driving

Maintaining or building a database   Drawing or illustrating   Graphic design

Creating newsletters or other publications   Improving processes   Marketing

Human Resources   Information Technology   Operations   Sales

Purchasing   Accounting   Finance   Distribution   Recruiting

Quality Control   Program Management   Leadership

Forecasting   Budget preparation   Bookkeeping

IS MY CREDIBILITY TRANSFERABLE?

Most of us worry about the question, "How will hiring managers find me credible or qualified for a job I haven't performed before?"

It is easy for all of us to forget about the power of framing! You can set a new frame around your background to let a hiring manager know that you already understand his or her challenges at work and that you're ready to dive in and help.

The words you choose to describe yourself tell any reader, including a hiring manager, a lot of important things about you.

Human-Voiced Resume

The words you choose to describe yourself in your Human-Voiced Resume tell the reader how you chose your career path, and why.

When you write your Human-Voiced Resume, you'll pay special attention to the Summary at the top of the resume. Your Human-Voiced Resume Summary comes right after your name and contact information at the top of the first page.

Your Human-Voiced Resume Summary may be the most important part of your Human-Voiced Resume. It sets a frame, or mental model, for your reader. Your Summary tells the reader how you view yourself. That's far more important than your past job titles, job descriptions, or your education.

Your Human-Voiced Resume Summary brands you in the way you want your reader to understand you and your background. You can change your Human-Voiced Resume Summary every time you decide to send your Human-Voiced Resume to someone new.

PART TWO

BERNICE'S STORY

Bernice has been working as a Marketing Coordinator, but now she's switching career directions. Bernice may end up with two or three versions of her Human-Voiced Resume. Each version of her resume will brand her perfectly for one type of job.

For this version of Bernice's Human-Voiced Resume, she is emphasizing her experience working with clients.

Bernice worked closely with the clients of her old employer, an advertising firm. Bernice is applying for a job as the Employer Liaison at her local community college. The Employer Liaison is the person who works directly with employers, helping them to meet, interview, and hire students and alumni of the community college.

Bernice knows she can do a fantastic job in that position if she can get the hiring manager at the community college to see past her advertising-agency experience to view Bernice as a skilled account manager and problem-solver.

Relationship Manager/Employer Liaison

I'm focused on building and maintaining close, supportive relationships with my clients and helping them understand the range of our services. At Angel Advertising Agency I created customized programs for each of our corporate clients and built strong relationships up, down, and across my client organizations.

Bernice only needs a job interview! She can get the job, she is sure, if she can get inside the organization to meet with the person who is doing the hiring (her hiring manager).

Bernice wrote her Human-Voiced Resume Summary to highlight the fact that she worked closely with a number of different people inside each of her client organizations back at the advertising agency.

Bernice's dealing with her clients at the ad agency had nothing to do with hiring. If Bernice goes to work as an Employer Liaison at the community college, she'll be working with numerous people who work for several large and medium-sized employers in her town.

She'll help those folks hire community college students and graduates, many of whom are job-hunting.

In Bernice's Human-Voiced Resume Summary, she has emphasized the parts of her old job that have the most overlap with the job she wants. She figures that the manager of the Career Services department at the community college—her possible next boss—needs someone in the Employer Liaison job who can reach out to local employers and forge strong relationships, as well as keep the community college's job-seeking students and alums clear on the radar screen for those employers.

 What are your reactions to Bernice's Human-Voiced Resume Summary? Write them in your Mojo Journal.

Bernice knows that if she can increase the number of new hires that local employers make directly from the community college, she'll make it easier for the college to recruit new students. Nearly everyone who comes to study at a community college is thinking about his or her career.

Bernice's goal is not just to get the Employer Liaison job at her local community college, but also to help the college get a lot more of its students and graduates hired by local employers!

Bernice wants to know as much as possible about the impact she can have on the community college's success before she starts writing her Pain Letter to her hiring manager.

She goes online and researches placement rates for new graduates from other community colleges. Bernice wants to talk about those numbers in her Pain Letter.

What is Bernice doing in her research? She is connecting the dots! She wants to know as much as possible about how she can help a new employer before she reaches out to them!

What Do You Do?

To get built-in job security, you have to know how to rebrand yourself for new opportunities. When one career door closes, another one can open!

You have to practice describing yourself in words, both on paper (or on the screen) and in words you'll speak when someone asks you, "What do you do?"

You have to know the value of your own services. When you're running your own career, you know within a narrow range what your services are worth to a potential client or employer, no matter what they tell you!

How could you negotiate if you weren't equipped with the knowledge of what your talents are worth to an organization?

You have to be ready and willing to start conversations with people you don't know—conversations that start through the mail, email, LinkedIn, or the telephone, or maybe a conversation that started when a friend of yours made an introduction to a person you haven't met before.

Networking comes naturally to some people and not to others. You will get better at networking and grow new muscles as you follow the Reinvention Roadmap path!

This book is about learning these things and many more so that you can run your own career rather than constantly worrying about being made redundant or getting laid off.

PART TWO

YOUR ASSIGNMENT

You have two assignments following chapter twelve.

Your first assignment is to create your Target Employer List.

Your second assignment is to establish your talent market value for each of the career directions you are interested in. How can you establish your market value? Start by visiting salary.com and payscale.com to research the salary levels associated with the job titles that interest you most. Next, think about the cost of the Business Pain you'll solve in your next assignment. What did your research tell you is the market salary range for one of the job titles you're interested in? Write that information in your Mojo Journal, and answer these questions:

- What kind(s) of Business Pain will you solve for your next employer?

- What does it cost an organization to suffer from the kind of Business Pain you identified on the lines above? Estimate the cost and explain your logic in your Mojo Journal.

HOW TO FIND
AND APPLY FOR JOBS

When you're thinking about reinvention, career change, or a job search, browse some published job ads whether you are ready to respond to job ads or not.

Visit your favorite careers site (I won't play favorites, but you can Google search the term "job ads + [your city]" or "careers site + [your city]" to find the largest ones). Read the job ads carefully and if the employer name is shared in the job ad, jump to the employer's own website and read a few pages of it, too.

If the employer's name isn't shared in the job ad, then you can ignore it. So-called "blind" job ads are placed by employers who don't want job applicants like you to know who they are.

Sometimes "blind" job ads are placed by recruiting firms in order to recruit new employees for their clients (organizations that are trying to hire people).

The trouble with "blind" job ads is that you can hardly learn anything useful about an employer or a job opportunity from a "blind" ad. All you typically get in a "blind" job ad is a list of the qualifications the employer is looking for. That's why I advise job-seekers to ignore "blind" job ads or "un-blind" them as described below.

HOW TO UN-BLIND A "BLIND" JOB AD

A "blind" job ad is a job ad that doesn't include the hiring employer's name. Sometimes you can figure out the employer's name and visit their website to learn more about them, as well as to find your hiring manager's name so that you can reach out to him or her with a Pain Letter.

To "un-blind" a "blind" job ad, follow these steps:

Read the job ad carefully, looking for any phrase that identifies the employer or that describes the job in a way that doesn't use the standard, boring corporate or institutional language. Here's an example:

"Our client is the leading publisher of magazines and websites for the automotive market." Take that distinctive phrase and put quotes around it (the way I've done in my example above). Copy the whole phrase, including the quotation marks, and paste it into a Google search box. Because this language is probably the language the employer always uses to describe itself, there's a good chance that your Google search will take you right to the employer's website—or to another job ad (one that isn't "blind") where the employer name is included.

USING LINKEDIN

If you are not working right now, you can use your LinkedIn "headline," which is the line just underneath your name in your LinkedIn profile, to let the world know you are job-hunting.

Your LinkedIn headline is an important part of your branding. If you're working now and you're conducting a stealth job search, then you won't be able to put your job-seeking status in your LinkedIn headline (unless the people you work with already know you're job-hunting—for example, if you've been told that you're going to be laid off or made redundant).

Here are six LinkedIn headlines to give you an idea how six job-seekers branded themselves for the benefit of other LinkedIn users (including recruiters and hiring managers) who might find their LinkedIn profiles:

- Customer Service/Office Support Person Seeking a New Challenge

- Office Manager/Business Air-Traffic Controller Looking for a Busy Office to Organize

- UI/UX Designer with e-Commerce Expertise ISO Next Assignment

- Development Director with Corporate Sponsorship and Grant-Writing Focus Seeking New Adventure

- Warehouse/Inventory Control Team Leader Available

- Public Relations Manager ISO Regional Brand Ready to Grow Its Audience ("ISO" stands for "In Search Of.")

WHAT IS LINKEDIN?

If you're not familiar with LinkedIn, here's an introduction. LinkedIn is a professional tool that has helped a lot of job-seekers, consultants, and working people. It's a free website that lets you create an online profile and interact with other people online in many different ways. If you haven't used LinkedIn before, now is a great time to start! You can join LinkedIn for free at www.linkedin.com.

Recruiters and hiring managers often spend a lot of time on LinkedIn. They use LinkedIn as a place to hunt for job applicants when they need to hire someone as an employee or a consultant. Your LinkedIn headline is an important way for hiring managers and recruiters to learn who you are and what you do professionally.

AM I QUALIFIED?

Most people are qualified for dozens or hundreds of different jobs, but they don't pursue them, because they are turned off by the job ads that employers publish.

We can't blame them for that! Most published job ads are horrendous.

Brilliant and talented people read job ads and think, "I can't apply for any of these jobs. I'm not qualified for any of them!" Of course you are qualified—you are qualified for any number of jobs, including positions you've held already and positions you haven't held. You are smart and capable. Don't let badly written job ads suck away your mojo!

Job ads are delusional and ridiculous. The so-called Essential Requirements or Critical Qualifications for the vast majority of published job ads are ludicrous. They are goofy.

I was an HR leader for eons and I got used to comforting the wonderful hiring managers on my team. "We are going to lose half of these Essential Requirements," I said, "and hire someone amazing who is going to knock your socks off and make a fantastic addition to your team."

Job ads are badly written, but the job itself behind the lousy job ad might be fantastic.

To find out whether a particular job opening is a good fit for you or isn't, you have to get over the wall between you and whichever organization has posted the job opening. Once you get over the wall to talk to a live human being about a job, you can determine whether you'd like the job if you got it, and whether the job would grow your flame and move you down your path.

You have to get into a job interview so that you can see whether the job is interesting to you or not.

The hardest part of working these days isn't performing a job, but getting the job in the first place!

HOW MUCH TIME SHOULD I SPEND ON PUBLISHED JOB ADS?

Remember that when you respond to a posted job ad, tons of other people are applying for the same job.

By all means apply for a posted job ad if you want to, being sure to send your Pain Letter and Human-Voiced Resume rather than completing an online application (we'll talk about this in Part Three), but don't put all your job-search eggs in the basket called "Responding to Posted Job Ads."

There are two other ways to get a new job, apart from responding to posted job ads. One way is to reach out to employers who don't have job ads posted (or they may have job ads posted but you haven't seen them). You can write to any hiring manager who works for any company or employer. We used to think that these organizations were hidden behind a very high and forbidding wall. The good news is that they are not! You can write to anyone you want—any hiring manager working for any organization you might consider working for.

Reaching out to hiring managers who don't have job ads posted (or if they do, you haven't seen those ads!) is the second way to job-hunt. The first way is to respond to posted job ads.

The third way to job-hunt is to use your network. Your network means the people you know. You've known some people for years and you've undoubtedly met more people recently. Networking is a critical part of your job search and your ownership of your career. Your network connects you to the local business and professional scene—the talent marketplace. Your network also gives you moral support for your journey. You give your friends and acquaintances moral support, too!

Open your Mojo Journal and write about your network. Write the names of people you know—friends, relatives, neighbors, co-workers, and past co-workers. Could your network help you in your reinvention and career, or in your job search?

Here is a diagram that shows my recommended allocation of your precious job-search time and mojo:

PART TWO

PAIN LETTERS

When you find a job you're interested in learning more about, you can begin researching and then composing a Pain Letter to send directly to your hiring manager inside the organization that posted the job ad.

You can skip the automated application form. That process is broken. You can go to the "side entrance" and reach your hiring manager directly at his or her desk.

You'll send your hiring manager—that is, your possible next boss—your Pain Letter together with your Human-Voiced Resume, in one envelope. You'll send the two documents stapled together, through the postal service. We'll look more at job-search tactics in Part Three when we dig into the how-tos of using your Pain Letter and your Human-Voiced Resume.

Create a LinkedIn account if you don't have one already. It's easy to do. Just visit www.linkedin.com and create an account for free.

You can take time building your LinkedIn profile. You can work on your profile for a few minutes each day for a week or so. You can update your LinkedIn profile any time you want to.

Make sure and upload a fantastic photo of yourself for your LinkedIn profile photo. You can ask a friend to take a photo of you using their phone. Choose a LinkedIn profile photo that shows your face clearly rather than one that's taken from far away.

CHECKING IN: FINDING YOUR PATH

Amazing job completing Part Two! You are a superhero! (What is your superhero name? You certainly deserve one!)

Part Two was called "Finding Your Path." What are your thoughts about your path-finding process so far? What have you learned about the work you are best-suited to do and the work that will grow your flame? Write about it in your Mojo Journal.

How will you celebrate having completed Part Two and the first half of your Reinvention Roadmap journey? I suggest a gelato with a friend!

You've progressed halfway through the Reinvention Roadmap!

PART 3

TAKING STEPS

Part Three of the Reinvention Roadmap
is called "Taking Steps." By now you know
that your reinvention is not something you
can sit on the sidelines and observe. You're
participating in your reinvention and stepping
out of an old frame into a new one!

Let's move forward!

DRAGON-SLAYING STORIES

A frame is a mental model. We see the world through the mental models our brains construct. Our brains start building mental models when we are tiny babies. Our mental models, or frames, help us make sense of the world.

Once a frame is set in our minds, it can be hard to change it. It can be tough to take in new ideas. They might sound foreign and off-putting to us at first.

Now that we are well into the new millennium and seeing the massive changes happening around us in the working world, we need to change our thinking about our careers. Still, that can feel like a scary thing to do!

We've learned a lot of ideas about work and careers. We've heard these old ideas so many times that we believe they are carved in stone and unchangeable. When you begin to take control of your career, one of your first steps is to question the ideas that you've learned and perhaps have taught other people concerning work and careers.

Now you are questioning the frames that you have put around the topic "my career." You may have had the same frame around the topic "my career" for decades. Now you are rethinking things you always assumed to be true about work and careers!

We are entrepreneurs now.

You are a business owner, sometimes called an entrepreneur, whether you work for yourself or work for someone else. We are all entrepreneurs. We have to be!

We don't know what outside influences or internal issues could affect our job security at any moment. Just because you've had a job for a long time doesn't mean that you will keep your job for another year, or even another month. We have to be ready to make a change and get a new job (or start a business of our own) no matter how secure our job may have been in the past.

That way, you'll be prepared if something changes and your job goes away. Also, when you stop and think about your life and career the way you have been doing throughout this Reinvention Roadmap process, you make important choices about the things you want to do in your career and other things you don't want to do.

It's your choice! You get to choose your career path every day, and by the same token, you have to choose! "Not choosing" and continuing to do what you've always done is a choice in itself.

We have discussed how the working world is changing under our feet, and how we cannot run our careers using the old ideas and old rules anymore. We will limit ourselves terribly if we try. We will dim our own precious flames if we buy into the old, bad idea that we are only worth what somebody else tells us we are worth—that our own opinion has nothing to do with our value or our success!

Most of us have grown up with the idea that other people tell us whether we're good or bad at what we do. Other people confer titles and salary increases on us. We've grown up with the idea that we have to please higher-ups at work—that pleasing people above you at work is the way to get ahead.

YOUR POWER AND CREDIBILITY

Your power and credibility as a working person now are in your ability to help other people solve their problems. You have to know which problems you solve. You have to know what those problems cost the people who have those problems!

That's what business owners do. They don't say to their clients, "Pay me whatever you think is fair." They can't afford to do that, and why should they? They know the value of their services, because their eyes are wide open. They know what other people charge for similar services, and they know when they can charge more than the average price because their services are higher quality.

These are things every businessperson—including you!—needs to know.

Your value to an employer or client has very little to do with your years of experience, your educational credentials, or the certifications you've earned. Those things won't matter if you can't solve real problems employers and clients face. If you can solve those problems, you'll quickly see that no one will care about your years of experience, your degrees, or your certifications. People in pain can't afford to care about those things—or your age, ethnicity, gender, or nonstandard political views, either!

When you know your real value to employers and clients, something wonderful happens. You can stand in your value. You can bring yourself to work, because you've earned the right to do that by understanding your value to the people who pay you.

Who you are and how you operate at work are far more important to your career than where you went to school or which job titles you've held before. Your track record will speak for itself when you know how to convey the power of your accomplishments and your understanding of the problems you solve for your employers and clients.

You might be thinking: *Wait! I'm a new graduate. I don't have tons of accomplishments. I don't know what problems I solve for employers. I have no idea. I'm 22 years old. I only know that I have a new degree and I'm eager to get a job. How can I show my value to anyone?*

Young people often believe that they have to beg for a job even more than other people do. They believe that because they haven't worked very much yet or perhaps haven't worked for money at all, they don't have anything to offer.

That's ridiculous! Twenty-two years is a long time. You have accumulated life experience and learning during that time. You have stories to share—stories about times when you saved the day or took steps that made a positive difference to people at work, at school, or somewhere else. Your college degree is a great thing, but it's not what makes you valuable to other people. Your personality, your point of view, your crazy sense of humor, your ideas, and your values make you the amazing person you are.

All of those things also contribute to your value to the people who hire you to work with them or engage you to consult with them. You are much more than your resume! You have stories to tell whether you're right out of school or you've been working for a long time, whether you've worked for wages before or not.

Many of us were taught that the higher-level a position you can attain in life, the more significant a person you are. Now we know that's not true and has never been true.

Open your Mojo Journal and write your thoughts about your value and your understanding of the ways your work helps your employers and clients. Consider also how the world is changing too fast for our comfort level. Do you feel that way sometimes? In your Mojo Journal, write your feelings about the super-fast changes going on around you.

TELLING YOUR STORIES

Your Story Is Your Brand

If your education, work experience, and professional credentials aren't the most significant things about you, then what is?

It's your story.

Your story is your power, your strongest branding choice, and the best representation of who you are and where you've traveled.

The conventional working world, the world of employment, has not traditionally valued a job-seeker's story, but now things are changing. More and more employers are realizing that the best aspects of the people they meet won't show up on a traditional, boring, zombie-style resume. Your value to employers and clients is your ability to solve their problems. You can get your problem-solving accomplishments across far more easily and powerfully in a story than in any other way!

Is there anything worse than a resume that lists a job-seeker's "skills" with no context by which to evaluate them? Those resumes give lists of Skills and Abilities, like this:

- Operations

- Customer Service

- Problem-Solving

- Negotiation

- Administrative Skills

What useful information can a hiring manager get from a long list of skills that anyone could claim, and that almost everyone does claim? This is the worst way to write your resume, because it is so weak.

You can list terms like Negotiation Skills and Administrative Skills, but what do those terms really mean?

We don't have well-understood, shared definitions for terms like Negotiation Skills or Administrative Skills. When you say that you have Negotiation Skills, we won't know what you mean unless you tell us a story to illustrate.

We won't know whether you negotiated peace accords between nations at war or got your office coffee vendor to throw in a couple of extra creamers with the coffee order. We'll have no idea of the scope or scale of your negotiation triumphs unless you tell us about them—in the form of a story.

The same is true for all the traditional skills that job-seekers list on their resumes. If you have technical skills in the sense that you've used software applications, development platforms, and various kinds of hardware, you should list those on your resume.

If your skills are nontechnical, standard-issue business and professional skills like Negotiation Skills or Communication Skills, don't list them on your resume. Tell us stories about the times when you pulled those talents off the shelf and used them to make something awesome happen. You can tell us about your talents using Dragon-Slaying Stories. Dragon-Slaying Stories are quick stories about times in your career or life so far when you stepped in to make something good happen.

Writing Down Your Dragon-Slaying Stories

Writing down some of your Dragon-Slaying Stories will remind you how many problems you've solved already in your life, whether or not you got paid to solve them.

In your Mojo Journal, add your own notes to remind yourself of a Dragon-Slaying Story from your wonderful career. You can use quick notes like, "The Johnson account," or "That thing with Tisha and the angry dude on the phone."

Below are 15 Dragon-Slaying Story prompts to help you remember the awesome times when you came, saw, and conquered on your past jobs. Next to each of the first two prompts is a sample story that fits the category. Copy this chart into your Mojo Journal and write your own Dragon-Slaying Story for each category. You can use Dragon-Slaying Stories from your school days and your volunteer activities, too. You can compose fast, high-impact Dragon-Slaying Stories the same way these job-seekers did!

DRAGON-SLAYING STORY PROMPTS

DRAGON-SLAYING STORY CATEGORY	YOUR DRAGON-SLAYING STORY
A story about a time when you helped an angry customer	*In my boss's absence, I sorted out a thorny $10,000 billing issue and saved our biggest customer's account*
A story about a time when you helped close a sale	*I provided the product information and backup to our Regional Sales Manager to help close a new $300,000 customer*
A story about a time when you came up with a great idea	
A story about a time when you taught somebody something	
A story about a time when you invented a better process	
A story about a time when you pushed for something important to happen, and it did	

PART THREE

A story about a time when you represented your employer well	
A story about a time when you created a manual or educational tool	
A story about a time when you went above and beyond	
A story about a time when you helped your employer save money	
A story about a time when you jumped into action to solve a problem	
A story about a time when you helped people work together who had had conflict before	
A story about a time when you put a plan together (whether your managers acted on your plan, or not)	
A story about a time when you acted without supervision and saved the day	
A story about a time when you found a creative way to solve a problem	

Using Your Dragon-Slaying Stories

You'll use Dragon-Slaying Stories in your job search and in your career in four ways:

- You'll use Dragon-Slaying Stories in your Human-Voiced Resume, in the Summary at the top of your Human-Voiced Resume, and in your descriptions of the jobs you've held so far;

- You'll use Dragon-Slaying Stories in your LinkedIn profile;

- You'll use one Dragon-Slaying Story in each Pain Letter you write; and

- You'll use Dragon-Slaying Stories on your job interviews.

When you are talking with potential clients about consulting projects, you'll use Dragon-Slaying Stories, too!

You will never see the statement in a help-wanted ad, "Here is our problem—please come over and help us solve it!" Your ability to get a great job, a job that deserves you in a field of your choice, depends on your ability to zero in and spot the most likely kinds of Business Pain cropping up for your hiring manager.

Pain Hypothesis

Your job is to formulate a Pain Hypothesis about your hiring manager's pain. You'll zero in on that hiring manager's pain and understand it well. That manager's pain is important to you. It's the source of your power in the hiring equation!

Once you've identified the specific kind of Business Pain that you want to address in your career (or at least in the next step down your path), you'll do something else. You'll recall and collect powerful stories about times in the past when you've solved Business Pain that is similar to the kind of Pain your target hiring manager is dealing with!

Sarah just got a new job by thinking about the Business Pain she solves for her clients. Let's see what we can learn from Sarah's story!

SARAH'S STORY

I worked at a dry cleaner while I studied for my Associate's degree. When I graduated with my AA degree I wasn't sure what I wanted to do next. My boss at the dry cleaning store was a very good boss, but there was no place to go beyond the job I already had.

I decided that I was interested in education. I thought I might want to become a teacher one day, or be involved in education in a different way. I decided to focus my job search on jobs that were somehow connected to education.

I had never held an office job. I didn't know how to do office work, but I know how to talk on the phone, and from my experience at the dry cleaning store I know how to deal with customers and how to work with money.

I started to focus my job search on educational institutions and education-related companies. I made a Target Employer List. I used a spreadsheet to make my list and maintain it. I chose 12 employers to include on my Target Employer List to start my job search. I listed each organization's name, its website, its location, and a short description of the organization to jog my memory.

The community college I just graduated from was on my Target Employer List, and so was our local four-year college, an educational consulting firm in my city, a not-for-profit foundation that supports educational programs, and several firms that make educational software.

Since all my target employers were involved in the field of education, I only had to create one version of my Human-Voiced Resume. I had only held two jobs in my career so far. One of them was the job at the dry cleaner. The other one was a job I held in high school. In that job I worked at a fast-food restaurant.

I branded myself for the jobs I wanted. The jobs I wanted were in the education industry. I wrote the headline just above my Summary at the top of my Human-Voiced Resume this way:

Education Coordinator

I had never seen a job opening for an "Education Coordinator" and I'm not sure that a job with that title even exists, but I chose the headline "Education Coordinator" for my Human-Voiced Resume because the word "Education" in my headline would signal right away to anyone who saw my Human-Voiced Resume that I'm interested in education.

Every single employer on my Target Employer List was involved with education. I wanted them to know right away within one or two seconds of seeing my Human-Voiced Resume that I'm passionate about education, the same way they are.

I figured that most of the other people who might apply for jobs with my Target Employers wouldn't brand themselves the way I did.

Here's what I wrote in my Human-Voiced Resume Summary:

> Education Coordinator
>
> *I've just graduated from Middle Fork Community College, where I discovered my passion for education and making educational opportunities available to everyone. I'm experienced in customer service, daily firefighting, and keeping fast-moving teammates in the loop and equipped to do their jobs effectively. I'm looking to help an education-focused organization grow.*

I felt that I had to keep my Human-Voiced Resume Summary fairly general because of the range of different missions, types of organizations, and sizes of organizations in my Target Employer List.

At first I felt very insecure about wanting a job in an educational firm or institution when my only work experience was in a dry cleaner and a fast-food restaurant, but my Summary helped with that problem a lot.

Whenever I sent out a Pain Letter together with my Human-Voiced Resume, I either heard nothing back (suggesting to me that either no one saw my letter and resume, or they were too busy to get back to me) or I got a positive reaction—a phone call or an email message.

I never got a negative reaction, so I figured, "Why not just keep sending out Pain Letters until I get a job?"

In my Summary, I emphasized the parts of my dry cleaning job that would carry over to my new office job when I finally got it. I highlighted my customer service, problem-solving, and keeping people in the loop activities.

I had plenty of stories to tell about those situations, from the dry cleaner, the fast-food restaurant, and even from my community college experiences.

I had to develop a Pain Hypothesis for each of the 12 organizations I contacted in my job search. Some of the Pain Hypotheses were easy to develop. Community colleges, for example, have too much work to do and not enough people to do all the work. They also don't have a lot of extra money lying around! They need people who can wear a lot of hats and get a lot done in a short period of time. I knew I could do that! I did that at the dry cleaner.

One of my first Pain Letters went to the Director of Community Education at my old community college. Community Education is the department that puts on courses for regular citizens to attend—people who are not working toward a community college degree.

The Director of Community Education at my community college didn't have a job opening listed. I just wanted to send him a Pain Letter because I thought it would be a lot of fun and great learning to work for him, organizing classes for citizens who wanted to learn something new.

Here's what I wrote in my Pain Letter to the Director of Community Education:

> *Dear Dr. Anderssen,*
>
> *I was thrilled to come across your presentation on the Middle Fork Community College website and to learn about the incredible programs you've added to MFCC's offerings for community members.*
>
> *It's wonderful to see the fantastic reception you are getting for your programs! I can only imagine that running over 20 classes and events per month must keep you and your team incredibly busy.*
>
> *When I was finishing my AA degree at Middle Fork this past spring, I organized a Community Opportunities Day that involved 14 local employers, three not-for-profit agencies looking for Board members and volunteers, and the Middle Fork area Workforce Development Center.*
>
> *I was happy that over 300 students participated and shared wonderful feedback about the event. If you're in need of more help to continue growing participation for MFCC Community Education projects, I'd love to start a conversation.*
>
> *All the best to you,*
>
> *Sarah Phan*

I didn't use any stories from the dry cleaner in my Pain Letter to the Director of Community Education because I had a great story available to me from just last spring. I volunteered to organize the Community Opportunities Day and it was a huge hit, so why not use that story?

I thought that Dr. Anderssen might even have heard about the Community Opportunities Day event I organized, but it turns out that he hadn't heard about it. That's okay, because he sent me an email message and invited me to come over to campus and meet with him.

We had a great chat. He didn't have any budget to hire anyone, but he invited me to sit on a panel that he was hosting. I had never been on a panel before! At Dr. Anderssen's panel event, there were representatives from several local employers. One of them was another organization on my Target Employer List, an educational software firm. After my panel presentation, which went okay, I introduced myself to the man who worked for the educational software firm. "I have just graduated from this school," I told him. "I wonder whether your firm might be hiring right now?"

"I don't know," he said, "but I can introduce you to our VP of HR." He made that introduction by email. I have a meeting with the VP of HR next week. It all came about because I sent a Pain Letter to Dr. Anderssen at my old college.

Of course, I will keep in touch with Dr. Anderssen, and I've already sent him a thank-you note for inviting me to speak on the panel. I even got a video of my panel presentation. I'm going to put it on my LinkedIn profile. I am starting to see how my actions have longer-lasting good effects than just a chance at a particular job. I am growing my Pain-Spotting muscles, for one thing.

I'm making new contacts and becoming a better writer, too. Now I've spoken on a panel. I'm learning how to network and how to spot Business Pain in my environment.

I'm learning how to reframe my background for different hiring managers. I'm learning how to recall and tell my Dragon-Slaying Stories, and how to choose the most relevant stories for each type of Business Pain. My muscles are growing fast!

 What are your thoughts about Sarah's story? Write them in your Mojo Journal.

Here is one of Sarah's Dragon-Slaying Stories:

Sarah's Dragon-Slaying Story: Miracle Worker at the Dry Cleaners

When I worked at the dry cleaner there was a fire at one of our facilities. It wasn't a fire in our building; it was in the adjoining building, but we still had to shut down our store and move everything out of it.

I got a call from our owner when I was getting out of the bathtub on a Friday night. I was at home, getting ready to go to bed. Our owner was out of the country. He told me that he got a call from the store manager at our dry cleaning location next to the burning building. The firefighters had already put out the fire, but they wanted us to get in and clear out the dry cleaning store so the landlord could come in and make repairs to the two adjoining buildings.

I called a service to board up the plate glass window that the firefighters had to break while they were doing their job. Between the store manager and me, we called the staff members and told them to go to a different location the next day. Also, with one of our delivery trucks, we moved all of the dry cleaning orders to our alternate location. None of the dry cleaning orders were damaged—we got lucky!

We got hold of 56 customers and told them where to pick up their dry cleaning, at our alternate location. We gave them a 50 percent discount on their orders because of the disruption. This is one reason our clients are so loyal to us!

We got the refurbished dry cleaning location up and running again in two weeks. Our owner was back in the country by then and he said, "Sarah, you are a miracle worker." I was really proud about that.

As Sarah's Dragon-Slaying Story shows, Sarah is obviously not afraid to jump in and help out in a crisis. How can Sarah use this Dragon-Slaying Story in her job search?

Here is how Sarah condensed her Dragon-Slaying Story for use in a Pain Letter:

When our owner was out of the country and one of our locations was involved in a fire, I organized the relocation of the store, contacted 50+ customers, and arranged for repairs and reopening within two weeks to minimize our customers' inconvenience.

Sarah sets the stage for her reader with "When our owner was out of the country." Now we know that Sarah was on her own to solve a big problem! We can see that Sarah takes charge and does whatever she has to do to surmount an obstacle in her way.

Sarah doesn't have to say "I'm a take-charge person" or "I'm a self-starter" in her resume, and she won't! Her stories tell us more about who Sarah is and how she operates than her self-descriptions ever could.

Here is the same Dragon-Slaying Story condensed even further for use in Sarah's Human-Voiced Resume:

In our owner's absence I relocated our downtown store after a fire, contacted 50+ customers, and managed repairs and refurbishment to reopen within 2 weeks.

How will Sarah use this Dragon-Slaying Story in a job interview? Here's how:

INTERVIEWER: Sarah, this job requires a lot of fast decision making. What can you tell me about your ability to think fast and take action when it's called for?

SARAH: Great question! Last year when our company's owner was out of the country with his family, I got a call telling me that one of our locations had been damaged because it adjoins a retail building that caught on fire.

The firefighters put out the fire quickly but our store had to be relocated right away. I worked with the store manager to get all of the dry cleaning orders out of the store so the contractor could make repairs. We moved truckload after truckload of dry cleaning orders to a second location and contacted over 50 customers to tell them about the switch.

I had to act fast to get the store repaired and reopened. I hired the contractor and managed the repairs and we were back open in under two weeks.

What are your thoughts about Sarah's use of her Dragon-Slaying Story in her job search? Write them in your Mojo Journal.

We'll look more at Human-Voiced Resumes in Part Four, but your assignment now is to start writing about how you will compose your Human-Voiced Resume. Your Human-Voiced Resume is more than a boring list of the jobs you've held. As readers, we want to know more about you than just where you worked and what job titles you held! We want to know about your greatest triumphs on the job—your Dragon-Slaying Stories! Start writing your stories in your Mojo Journal.

UNDERSTANDING BUSINESS PAIN AND SOLUTIONS

Let's look at the concept of Business Pain as it relates to your career and your job search. Understanding Business Pain will help you decide which organizations to focus on!

EVERYONE HAS PAIN

We use the word "pain" for lots of things that don't actually, physically hurt us. We talk about the pain of being separated from people we love, and the pain of trying to make a withdrawal from the ATM and finding that it has no cash available.

Every business has pain. You can't be in business without having problems. To be in business means to have problems, but that's not a bad thing. When your business grows, it creates new problems—we call them Growing Pains. Any sort of organization has problems.

When you think about it, organizations and individuals hire people to solve problems for them. Every office and government building hires a cleaning crew to clean up at night. If they didn't, they'd have problems with garbage overflowing their wastebaskets, and maybe mice—ick!

Multinational corporations hire experts in various aspects of business, from IT Security to event planning, on a consulting basis. They do that because they don't have people inside the company who can do those things or because they don't want to pay someone a full-time salary to take care of a short-term need.

Maybe an organization's customers are unhappy. Maybe they're waiting on the phone too long before they get to speak with a customer service person. Maybe the products are faulty and they're not selling. These are all types of Business Pain!

PROMOTE YOUR ABILITY TO SOLVE PROBLEMS, NOT YOUR SKILLS

You're not going to brand yourself based on your "skills" anymore. You're going to focus on the question, "What kinds of Business Pain do I solve?" instead!

Anybody can talk about their "skills." What are skills? We can't see them. We don't know if they are real. You might have skills, but do you know how and when to use them? You aren't going to talk about your skills anymore—anyone can do that! You're going to look for Business Pain in your environment instead and focus on reaching out to people who are in pain. You are going to shift your perspective onto yourself and the value you bring to employers and clients. Your value to those people is your ability to solve pain.

Noticing Business Pain

There is Business Pain everywhere, at every level in every organization, and your job as a working person and the CEO of your own career is to spot the Business Pain in your environment. Your ability to spot pain in a business setting, to talk about pain, and to solve the pain employers and clients are facing is your value to those people!

We're all learning this new skill called Pain-Spotting. We're learning to spot Business Pain in our environments. First you have to spot the pain. Then you can reach out to a decision-maker inside the organization who can hire you as an employee or consultant to solve the pain.

What sorts of pain do employers and clients have?

Here are 12 common types of Business Pain most employers have run into—and may be dealing with right now!

Customers are unhappy with our products	Competitors are growing faster than we are	We aren't developing new products fast enough	Our technology is outdated	We can't find good employees
We don't have enough sales leads	Our expenses are too high	We can't hold on to our best employees	Our processes are out of date and slowing us down	Our cash flow isn't strong enough
Our workplace is too small for us	We aren't visible on social media sites	Our health care costs are killing us	Our internet security makes us vulnerable	Our customer support isn't strong enough

 What other types of Business Pain are you familiar with? Write them in your Mojo Journal.

What types of Business Pain have you solved?

In the exercise below you will think about and write about some of the types of Business Pain you've solved at work, at school, or in your social life. The more clearly you can identify the types of Business Pain you solve in your work, the more your muscles will grow!

Read through the types of Business Pain listed in the table below. Think about your experiences with each type of Business Pain listed, and other types of Business Pain that aren't listed in the table.

Our products aren't selling	Our customers aren't happy	Expenses are too high
Systems are out of date	Competitors are winning	We can't find the right employees
We can't keep our employees—we have turnover problems	We don't have a good forecasting process for our future sales	Our company culture is poor
Our processes don't work	Our physical facility isn't keeping up with our needs	Our employees aren't well trained enough for their jobs
Our marketing isn't working	Our products are defective	Our competitors are more well-known than we are
Our suppliers aren't getting us our raw materials on time	Our donations are way down	We're not keeping up with regulatory requirements from government agencies
We don't have a long-term vision	Our employees don't care about their work	Our new products aren't as good as our competitors' products

Understanding the pain you solve is the key to taking control of your career! Through your understanding of the Business Pain you solve—a new and very different way to look at your background and your value—you will step into the new-millennium workplace with confidence.

 What kind(s) of Business Pain do you solve in your work? Write your ideas in your Mojo Journal.

Learning to Spot Business Pain

As a job-seeker or a consultant—and when you are a job-seeker, you are instantly a consultant, also!—you're always on the lookout for Business Pain.

You are looking for pain that you can solve in your local ecosystem (or in a broader economic sphere if you are not limited by geography—for instance, if you perform your work online).

You are looking for pain, because the only place in the employment or consulting equation where you have leverage, which is to say power, is in your ability to solve another person's pain.

When you stop thinking, "I wonder whether XYZ Big Corporation is hiring?" and wonder, instead, "Could the new Marketing Manager at Acme Explosives possibly need help getting his e-commerce website off the ground?" you will have learned to use your Pain-Spotting Glasses!

There is pain everywhere. Everyone has pain they'd like to see go away, and they'd be willing to pay good money to make that happen.

Pain-Spotting Stories

Here are a couple of stories about spotting pain.

Makayla's Story

My young friend Makayla is a pain-spotter. Makayla is out of college now, but when she was in high school, she and my daughter were very good friends.

My daughter is our oldest child, but not by much, because she is a twin. Our youngest is nine years younger than our twins. Makayla sent me a Facebook message about five years ago. In her message she said, "Liz, you must be busy during the day. You have a lot on your plate. Would it be helpful to you for me to go and pick up your nine-year-old at day camp, take him to the pool, and give him swim lessons and then take him for a snack and bring him home?"

I couldn't type fast enough in my reply. "Yes!" I wrote back to Makayla. "That sounds great!"

It was a life-saver for me, and my son loved the time in the water and just the attention from a big high school teenager, since he is the youngest of five kids and can get lost in the shuffle sometimes.

Makayla didn't write to ask me, "Do you need any help with childcare this summer?" If she had, I would have written right back "Thanks, no," because I had a house full of teenagers who could watch our nine-year-old.

Makayla went much deeper than that. She put on her Pain-Spotting Glasses and put together a plan to relieve my pain. She developed a product! It was a great product. Now Makayla is charging ahead in her career, and her afternoon-swim-and-pizza product is off the market. It was a limited-time deal!

When you develop your Pain-Spotting abilities, you will see problems and possible solutions everywhere. You will think the way a consultant does—the way every business owner does. That makes sense, because you are a business owner! Maybe your business is called Jason's Career or The Adventures of Marisol.

 What will you call your business—the business of your career? Write some name ideas in your Mojo Journal.

BRUCE'S STORY

I'm an IT person. It's a weird field because everyone says, "Good IT people are hard to find," and it's true, but it's not always easy to tell the good IT people from the not-so-great ones.

I agree with Liz Ryan that the stilted, formal, traditional resume format is part of the problem, and keyword-searching algorithms are another part of the problem.

I know I'm good at what I do. I have about a dozen managers who worked with me at past jobs who know what I can do. When one of those 10 or 12 managers goes into a new company, if the company needs IT people, it's likely that I'll get a call.

But I can't run my career based on when and whether a bunch of managers I used to work with will call me! I have to make my own market for my talents. I started a part-time consulting business alongside my daytime work.

I say "my daytime work" because sometimes "my day thing" is a full-time job, sometimes it's a contract job, and other times I'm job-hunting. No matter which one of those things I'm doing in the daytime, I'm going to be consulting, too. I always keep my consulting business going because you never know when things can change on the job.

In my consulting, I do a lot of different things. I help people with their computers at home and with their home networks. I help them set up home theater systems, and I come to their offices at night and on the weekends and help them with office IT issues.

When I take a full-time job I always tell them that I have a consulting business. I don't take jobs from companies that compete with whatever company I'm currently working for, but then again I've never had an inquiry from anybody like that. I earn a little money with my consulting and it gives me a lot of tax breaks that are very welcome, too.

The most important thing about my consulting business is that it reminds me that I am a businessperson and a business owner whether I happen to be working in a full-time job at the moment, or not.

 What are your thoughts about Bruce's story? Write them in your Mojo Journal. Could you start a part-time consulting business, the way Bruce did? What sort of consulting could you do? Write your ideas in your Mojo Journal.

The Value of Knowing the Pain You Solve

You may ask, "Why is it important for me to know what kinds of Business Pain I solve? Isn't it enough for me to know that I'm a Bookkeeper, a Quality Control person, or an Office Manager?"

Lots of people are Bookkeepers and Office Managers. If all you know is that you've done a particular kind of job before, then you become one of the many, many people who have similar experience to yours. That isn't a powerful message to send when you're job-hunting! The last thing you want to do is to sound like every other job-seeking banana in the bunch.

When you understand which types of Business Pain you solve and can spot that pain in the business and professional environment around you, you have power. You have leverage (power) in a business conversation then, because there are clients around who have the very sort of Business Pain you solve.

When you know what kind of pain you solve for your clients and employers, you have power in the hiring equation. After all, why do employers hire employees? They only hire people for one reason—because they're dealing with a certain kind of pain. If there were no pain, they wouldn't need to hire anyone.

KNOWING YOUR WORTH

Most of us have been taught to beg and grovel for a job. We've been taught that employers are powerful and mighty, and that job-seekers are like ants. We're a dime a dozen! We have to be grateful to anybody who would give us a job interview, much less hire us to work for them!

That is false. Let's break it down and see why.

When an employer hires you to work for them, they pay you money. We'll call your wages or salary "cash" even though very few of us actually get paid in cash money—most of us get a paycheck that's either given to us in our hand or sent into our bank account every payday.

We get paid cash. Cash is important. Many of us have heard the expression "cash is king," but is cash really the highest or most valuable form of currency? Your work is worth something, too. In fact, your work is worth more than what you get paid to perform the work.

If you work as a cashier for a retail store that pays you eight dollars an hour to work the cash register, your work is worth a lot more to the store than eight bucks an hour. If it weren't, then the company wouldn't be able to pay you that much—they have to make money on your work, or else they'll go out of business!

Your work as a cashier could easily be earning your employer ten, twelve, or even twenty dollars an hour. That's okay—you are willing to trade your valuable effort for less cash than you are worth because you want your employer to thrive. You don't want to work for a month and then see your store go out of business! It's important to keep in mind, though, that you are not an ant or a dime-a-dozen job-seeker, and neither is anyone else.

You Don't Have to Beg for a Job

There is a widespread, fictional belief that employers can be very choosy about whom they hire, and that job-seekers have to do whatever employers ask them to do.

This is completely wrong, and I say that because I was a vice president of Human Resources and I hired thousands of people. It's actually very hard to find smart, creative, capable people to fill any employer's job openings. It's hard, but most employers won't tell job-seekers that. They'll say, "We're being very selective."

Why do you think employers tell job-seekers that they have tons of qualified applicants to choose from, when it isn't true? What advantage could employers get by telling job-seekers, "We're being very selective"?

Write your answers to these questions in your Mojo Journal:

· Do you know anyone who works for those employers (employers who treat job-seekers badly) right now? If not, how could you learn more about those organizations and their Business Pain?

· Would you take a survival job to pay the bills while you're hunting for a better job?

· What kind of survival job might you look for, if you needed to earn money right away?

· Would you go to work for a friend who has a business? What other steps could you take to react and recover if your job disappeared suddenly?

· If your job has already gone away, how are you paying your bills and keeping a place to live right now?

· What kind of work would you look for (or are you looking for, if you're job-hunting now)?

· Which specific organizations (employers) would you seek out if you were made redundant or laid off right now (or are on your target list if you're job-hunting now)?

· If you are job-hunting now or if you suddenly had to job-hunt, which job titles would you be focusing on in your job search? Write them here.

Your direction and your brand are evolving. They won't stay the same, and that's good! You are allowed to shoot higher and aim for jobs you haven't held before.

Positioning Yourself

When you think about the problem or "pain" that you solve on the job, you'll see that you are more than a bundle of skills and experiences. You are a pain-reliever, too!

You have already solved lots of problems on the job, but most of us haven't been taught to think about or capture our pain-relief activities. We've been taught to brand ourselves this way:

Results-oriented professional with a bottom-line orientation. Motivated self-starter who works well with all levels of staff.

Look at the two sentence fragments above. What do they remind you of? They sound like a government document, or a manual! They sound stiff and boring.

They don't sound like things that people say to describe themselves to other people!

When you think about real problems you've solved in your career and life already, no matter what age you are right now, you'll see that you have already made some wonderful things happen.

Here are a few stories to get you thinking more about the way people relieve Business Pain at work.

STORIES ABOUT BUSINESS PAIN

MIRANDA'S STORY

I was a receptionist first, and then I got a new job as an Administrative Assistant to a VP at a property management firm. I answered the phones and took care of customers and I created a lot of reports. What pain did I solve at work?

On my first job, as a receptionist, I solved the pain that companies experience when their customers don't know who to talk to or how to solve their problems. I took wonderful care of the customers.

On the second job, I solved a different kind of pain. I kept the VP I worked for from forgetting important projects and appointments and I helped keep him sane and calm by managing the many requests that came into our office.

I created a kind of wall around him, not by pushing people away but by taking care of whatever they needed so he didn't have to deal with it. That's a big service to a company if you ask me.

RAJIV'S STORY

I work as a design engineer and I know what kind of pain I solve. I solve late-product-release pain, which is a serious thing. When companies are late to market with the right products, they lose a ton of money and they lose something else, too—they lose the goodwill of their customers. As I think about it, they even lose a third thing—market share. Other companies will swoop in with products that hit the market first. Will our customers come back if our product is late to the market? I solve three kinds of pain for my employers.

DECKER'S STORY

I didn't really get this Business Pain idea at first. Then I was at work, where I drive a truck for a plumbing and heating contractor and look after the inventory or parts, and it hit me that I do relieve some pain in my work. Before I got here, there was a guy in my job who I guess was nice but kind of clueless. He was a good guy, but he never had the right parts for the jobs we had to do. He couldn't stay on top of the schedule. So my co-workers know the pain that I solve. I have the right parts at the job site when they're supposed to be there, or I find a replacement and I make it work somehow. What did that pain cost them before I got here and figured out the job? I don't know, but it was a lot of money.

What kinds of Business Pain have you solved in your work so far? Write your solutions to Business Pain in your Mojo Journal.

All organizations have pain, but they won't talk about their Business Pain in their job ads. When companies hire consultants, they may be a little more forthcoming about the pain lurking behind their Request for Proposal (a document that invites consultants to bid on a project), or they might not. As you step into your consulting persona (even as a job-seeker), you will soon see that the lower the trust level is in an organization, the less likely people are to be honest about the Business Pain they are struggling with.

WHAT SCHOOL TAUGHT US

Most of us were not prepared as kids or young adults for the working world we find ourselves in today. Many of us, especially if we are over age 40, grew up in school systems that emphasized characteristics and learning that are better suited to paid employment than to entrepreneurism. We were taught that you only really know something when you can take a test and get a good grade on it by answering questions about a particular subject.

School is the only place where we learn that way. In real life we learn by doing, watching, and asking questions. We learn by trying new things, not by reading chapters and answering reading-comprehension questions afterward.

I am grateful that each of my five kids found serious fault with the methods used in schools. If they had not, I would feel like a bad mom!

The best thing we can teach our kids is to ask, "Why?" My middle son asked me halfway through eighth grade, "Why do they put us in a classroom to focus on one thing for forty-eight minutes and then yank us out and tell us to focus on a completely different subject? It's crazy!"

It's good for kids to question, and for all of us to ask hard questions, too. We can ask, "Why don't schools teach kids to start their own businesses, instead of getting a job and taking a paycheck from someone else?"

Now, a lot of people are asking whether our very old-fashioned educational system is really educating kids for the new-millennium workplace they will enter. That's not just grade schools and high schools, but colleges, also! We all have to seriously ask the question, "Will this degree program equip my child to go out into the world as a responsible and well-educated adult, or just rack up a lot of debt that my poor child will take a lifetime to repay?"

Watch how many ads for college degrees and certificates, especially graduate school ads, emphasize, "We give the diplomas employers want!" That's twisted. That's completely unhealthy. We should be sending kids the opposite message: "You don't need anybody's gold star or a stamp of approval to have the life and career you want. You don't need to please employers to have the life and career you want. It's up to you how to spend your precious time and even more precious mojo!"

 How do you feel about your education and your preparation to enter the grown-up world? Did your education equip you and make it easier for you to make it out here in the working world, or not? Write about that in your Mojo Journal.

Whatever your educational experience, the good news is you can choose from a great many career paths, especially if you are willing to shake off the idea that you must have a full-time job with benefits.

WORKING FOR YOURSELF

Most of us were taught that working for yourself or starting a company is hard and scary. We grew up believing that it is easier and safer to work for someone else. But is that true? Is it logical? When you have a full-time job and you lose it for any reason, it is a massively disruptive event in your life. When you lose your job, you lose your income, your identity, and other things—your social sphere and a place to go in the morning, for instance. It's traumatic for many people to lose their jobs.

When you lose your job, the process of getting a new job can be very time consuming and can be hard on your mojo. Meanwhile, your finances are dwindling. It's a stressful time.

When you work for yourself, you go up and down all the time. A client comes in and another client leaves you.

You learn to deal with that. You put your faith in yourself and the people you work with, if any, rather than in a big company in which you may have no visibility into the future. You just bob on the water, up and down, and up and down again.

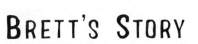

You may have no idea whether your job will persist or not, even if you've worked in the job for years. Is that security?

BRETT'S STORY

Brett is a virtual assistant. He works from home. Brett works for himself. He says, "I wake up unemployed every day! That way I only report to myself."

Brett earned more money at each of his three corporate jobs than he earns now. However, when Brett averages his income over the times that he worked in his three corporate jobs and the time he spent looking for jobs when each of those jobs went away, he sees that he earns more money now, working for himself.

Also, he has tax deductions that only self-employed people get, and he decides how much vacation to take each year rather than following a corporate vacation schedule.

What are your thoughts about Brett's story? How does it apply to your situation? Write about that in your Mojo Journal.

The more you can see yourself as a person who follows your path and the opportunities that present themselves to you at every moment, versus a person who needs job security from an employer (which doesn't exist anyway) and to stay at one job for a long time, the more control of your life you will retain!

What are your thoughts about your need for a full-time, secure job with benefits versus other kinds of jobs (or versus working for yourself)? Write your thoughts in your Mojo Journal.

QUESTIONS AND ANSWERS

My company has a defined career advancement program. I already know which job I'll be eligible for in my company once I learn certain things in my current job. Should I shoot for that promotion, or not?

That's up to you. The question to ask is, "What do I want from my life and career?" Please don't follow any path just because someone sticks the path in front of you and says, "Follow it!" You get to make your own path.

Do I have to start my own business in order to adapt to the changing face of work?

No! You don't have to start your own business. If you work for other people, for large or small organizations, or a combination, you can still adapt to the changing work world. You can still run your career like a business.

When you do, you will grow the same muscles that entrepreneurs grow. You won't fall asleep on your career again, I hope! That's why I wrote this book—to wake you up and keep you from falling asleep again. It's your career to manage! That part isn't going to change. If you don't manage your career, no one will.

Would you lend your car to someone who said, "I'll pay every day to drive your car, but I'm not going to take care of it, put gas in it, or pay attention to where I drive it. I might drive through snow and ice or drive through deep mud or tar. That's okay with you, right?"

You'd say, "No way! I'd charge you a lot more if I thought you were going to abuse my car! You have to take care of it. You have to check the tire pressure and a lot of other things."

We know how to take care of a car, but most of us haven't learned how to maintain, much less drive, our own careers! That's why we let our employers manage our careers, and even let them run our careers into the ground.

We trade our energy for a paycheck every week or every two weeks at work. The paycheck is great because it lets us pay the rent and buy food and other things we need. But who's driving the car?

Your employer is not managing your career or taking steps to make sure that you are learning and growing on the job, most likely. That's your job!

It's your job to keep your car in top running condition so that it can take you where you want to go. It's your job to keep your career in top running condition, too, so that it can take you where you want to go to have the life you want.

When you decide to manage your own career whether you get paid through a payroll department or by invoicing your clients, you're taking a big step. At that moment you pick up the keys to your own career. No one else gets to drive! When you take control of your career, you first decide what you want over the long term, and then you make plans to get what you want.

What are your ideas about your long-term vision for your career? Write them in your Mojo Journal and answer these questions:

What themes or topics are you passionate about that have never made their way into your working life?

What are some career paths you've thought might be fun or interesting to learn more about?

What gifts or talents have other people told you that you should be using in your work (or getting paid for)?

Think about the Business Pain you solve for your employers and/or clients and compose another Pain Letter. Whether you are working right now or not, and whether you are job-hunting or not, this exercise will help you zero in on the Business Pain you solve and how to address it in an overture to a hiring manager. Here is your assignment:

1. Choose a local employer.

2. Research the employer's website and its Company Page on LinkedIn (if there is one).

3. Decide what sort of Business Pain you can solve for your selected employer.

4. Find your hiring manager inside the employer. Use LinkedIn to search for your hiring manager by name (using the Advanced People Search page of LinkedIn) or use the employer's own website to identify the manager who will be your boss if you take a job working for this employer.

5. Compose a Pain Letter to your hiring manager, and send it to him or her via mail (post) together with your Human-Voiced Resume.

6. Celebrate with a nice gelato!

AVOIDING THE BLACK HOLE BY SENDING PAIN LETTERS

In the old working world, we had a clear idea of what the word "job" meant. When you got a job, you could expect to keep the job for a while. You could expect to have regular hours. If you worked hard, you might also expect to be able to move up in the organization.

Then everything changed. Now it's not really clear what the word "job" means.

You can apply for jobs online without having any idea whether the job is a full-time or part-time job, or what it pays. You might not know where the actual job is located. The online job posting might not even tell you whether it's really a job or just a situation where you're supposed to work for commissions only. Sometimes you can get a "job offer" and you're not sure how real the company is, how much you're getting paid, or even what you've been hired to do!

BLACK HOLES

The job-search process in nearly every medium-sized and large employer is an absolute disaster. The process for welcoming job-seekers into the company's recruiting pipeline is terrifying at most organizations.

They botch it completely. They use ancient, creaky ATS (Applicant Tracking System) technology that actually repels people from applying for the organization's open jobs, because the language and the look of the Careers site are so off-putting.

I call these awful recruiting sites Black Holes because resumes and job applications go into them, but almost nothing comes out. Black Hole recruiting is a terrible way to hire people. It's insulting to job-seekers.

I am always happy when a CEO or HR leader gets a personal "Aha!" that jolts them into reality where their broken recruiting process is concerned. We at Human Workplace get to observe a CEO or HR leader experience this frame-shaking "Aha!" about once a week.

When they get the "Aha!" that their broken recruiting process is driving great people away from their organization, they say, "Wait a second! This is not a good recruiting process. I wouldn't fill out that awful application form, with nineteen different screens and obnoxious questions on every page. I wouldn't do it. How can I ask anyone else to do it?"

Smart employers are humanizing their recruiting processes more and more, and there are more and more Human Workplace employers every day, but if you need a job now, you can't wait for an employer to start walking the Human Workplace path. You can't wait for employers to get the memo that their 1990s recruiting process is hurting them—but you also can't get a good job lobbing applications into automated recruiting sites. You can't rest your job-search hopes on the broken recruiting apparatus.

I call automated online application sites Black Holes because just like a real black hole in space, when you drop a job application into an automated recruiting portal, it virtually disappears. Maybe its atoms are shredded and sent to another dimension—who knows? All we know is that you don't usually hear anything back from the employer.

Sometimes you hear something back weeks later. They send you a terse auto-responder email message to tell you that they've hired someone else. Sometimes you hear nothing back at all!

What has your experience with automated Black Hole recruiting systems been like? Write about it in your Mojo Journal.

GETTING AROUND THE BROKEN RECRUITING PROCESS

There are times when you have no choice but to fill out an online job application. Grocery stores and big retail stores are some of the places where there is no other way to apply for a job apart from completing an online job application. In the vast majority of situations, however, you don't have to apply for a job using the online application system, even if the company's HR people tell you that you must!

You can write to your hiring manager—the manager of the department where you'd be most likely to work—directly.

Sometimes job ads will say, "Don't contact the hiring manager." You can ignore that. You are an adult. You can write to anyone you like. Sometimes fearful HR people say, "If you reach out to one of our managers directly, you'll be ineligible to work for our company—for life!"

This is a very weeniefied thing to say. It springs from fear. If your company's recruiting system worked, no one would need to find a back door. Your system is broken.

In the corporate and institutional worlds we say, "Feedback is a gift." Job-seekers all over the world are trying to give the gift of feedback to employers who don't realize that their recruiting processes are badly broken. They are not managing their recruiting practices well. That's a disservice not only to job-seekers, but also to the company's customers and shareholders. It is poor leadership.

If job-seekers are so frustrated with your broken recruiting process that they are writing directly to your hiring managers, that isn't a bad thing. It's a gift to those employers! The job-seekers are telling those employers through their actions that they value the company enough to expend their energy seeking a more effective way to reach its managers than the broken Black Hole system allows.

The right move for an HR person who sees how enterprising job-seekers are working around the company's broken recruiting system is not to crack down on those job-seekers, or to threaten them.

The answer is to fix what's broken in their recruiting process!

ANGIE'S STORY

I'm a Director of HR. I started following Liz Ryan's columns a few years ago. I love what Liz has to say about leadership and Human Resources, but it bothered me that Liz always advised job-seekers to avoid our company's formal recruiting portal and told them to write directly to their department manager instead.

I used to get mad about that. I used to complain to my friends in Human Resources. One of my friends, Victor, said, "You know what, Angie? I used to hate the fact that Liz Ryan tells job-seekers to avoid our formal recruiting systems, too. Then we got a few Pain Letters. One of our department managers said, 'I love these Pain Letters. Within a few seconds I can see whether the person who sent me the Pain Letter understands our business or not. Now I love Pain Letters. I'd rather read Pain Letters than plow through a boring stack of almost identical cover letters and resumes.'"

I listened to Victor and I read more of Liz Ryan's columns. Now I get it. I see that my job is to put a human voice in our company's recruiting process and also to put a human voice in our HR practices.

My job is to make my company the greatest place to work in our area. I'm excited about that goal! It's a lot more fun to make a company a great place to work than to enforce rules and policies.

Now we are talking in our company about changing our recruiting process. We will still post job ads, but we won't ask job applicants to complete long, tedious application forms anymore. Instead, we will ask them to write a short Pain Letter, and our department managers and I will read the Pain Letters together.

This change is going to make our recruiting processes faster and more fun for job-seekers. We want people to be excited about working for us—not bored, exhausted, and insulted by our recruiting message!

What are your thoughts about sending Pain Letters directly to hiring managers instead of filling out online job applications? Write your ideas in your Mojo Journal.

DO NOT YIELD TO FEAR

Some fearful HR people will tell you that if you send a Pain Letter directly to a department manager inside their company, they'll never hire you. Doesn't that sound ridiculous? It sounds medieval. Grown-ups don't threaten other grown-ups: "If you break our rules, you'll be barred for life from working for us!"

That reaction to a shifting frame is sad. It's childish and unprofessional. Would the company's customers and shareholders be happy to hear that a fearful person in the HR department was threatening talented job-seekers who might be able to make huge contributions to the company?

It isn't right to threaten people who are merely doing what anyone would do when a path is blocked—namely, finding an alternate path to their goal when foolish bureaucracy has made the designated path inaccessible.

They're making a detour. That is the smart and logical thing to do.

Would someone who had purchased stock in the company be excited to hear that an HR person stuck in fear was telling talented job-seekers, "If you dare to break my rules, you'll never be able to work here!"?

It's hard to imagine that anyone who values a company's success would think that making up arbitrary medieval rules and threatening job-seekers would be a good use of an HR person's time and energy, or a good way for the company to build its reputation as a place where talented people want to work! If a company would bar you from future employment because you wrote to someone inside the company instead of resting your job-search hopes on the broken Black Hole recruiting apparatus, they are not the best place for you to work anyway!

You are *not* responsible for reading job ads to see what weenie rules are included in them.

You are *not* obligated to lob pointless resumes and application forms into Black Hole recruiting sites and sit and wait for weeks or months for someone to contact you.

You can reach your hiring manager a different way and avoid mojo-sucking Black Hole recruiting sites altogether.

PAIN LETTERS

A Pain Letter goes directly to your hiring manager. You can send your Pain Letter using email, but in our experience the most effective way to send a Pain Letter to a hiring manager is to send it in the mail.

You can send your hiring manager a Pain Letter in the mail, directly to his or her desk, together with your Human-Voiced Resume (more on Human-Voiced Resumes in chapter twenty-one).

Why would you try a very different approach to reach your hiring manager? Here are seven reasons to try it!

1. Your hiring manager is used to seeing boring cover letters. Your Pain Letter will not be boring. If you write it and it's boring to read, it needs more work! Your Pain Letter doesn't drone on and on about you. It talks about your hiring manager, his or her organization, and the organization's most likely Business Pain, instead!

2. Your hiring manager has one or more problems, whether he or she has a posted job opening right now or not. Every manager has problems. Your Pain Letter will touch on one of the problems that your hiring manager is most likely to be experiencing now. You will make a Pain Hypothesis about your hiring manager's most likely type of pain, and you'll address that pain right in your Pain Letter. That will get your hiring manager's attention! All he or she has to do is to read your letter.

3. Not every Pain Letter you write will get read by a human being, but some of them will. Some of them will very likely result in email messages coming back to you, or phone calls from either your hiring manager or the HR person who works with him or her. Your Pain Letter is different from the

standard, boring cover letter clichés. In your Pain Letter and Human-Voiced Resume, you will sound like the fascinating human being you are. Real people like to hear from real people—not battle drones!

4 Your Pain Letter will make it clear to your target hiring manager that not only are you awake and paying attention to the local talent marketplace, but you have also anticipated one of the types of Business Pain that your hiring manager is facing. Not only that, but right in your Pain Letter you have shared a story that illustrates how you solved a similar type of Business Pain at a past job or in a non-work situation. You don't have to brag about yourself in a Pain Letter. Your Dragon-Slaying Story makes it clear how you solve problems!

5 Your Pain Letter and Human-Voiced Resume share some of your personality. They make it easy for a hiring manager in pain to say to himself or herself, "This person wrote an interesting letter, and they pointed out a problem that indeed is costing me time and energy. I'll call this person on the phone and chat with him or her. Why not?"

6 Your Pain Letter and Human-Voiced Resume are branding documents. Some hiring managers won't like them. That's good. You don't have time to waste with people who don't want you to be a human being. If they want to hire a sheep to join their department, you don't have time for them anyway!

7 As you research employers in order to compose thoughtful Pain Letters, your muscles and mojo will grow! You will get a reminder every time you write a new Pain Letter that you have already solved a lot of problems and understand quite a bit about the working world. Pain Letter writing is a mojo-boosting activity!

What are your thoughts about these seven reasons to try the Pain Letter approach in your job search? Write your reactions in your Mojo Journal!

Writing and sending your hiring manager a Pain Letter together with your Human-Voiced Resume instead of a traditional cover letter and a traditional, boring resume will set you apart from other job candidates who might apply for a job opening.

This is especially true when you use your Pain Letter to speak sympathetically and knowledgeably about the Business Pain your hiring manager (aka Possible Next Boss) is likely to be facing on the job. Your Pain Letter may be the most exciting communication your manager receives all day!

It is a great experience to receive a well-written Pain Letter, because nearly every manager struggles with problems at work. Most of us don't get enough acknowledgment. We face problems all day long, and we don't have a lot of people telling us, "You're doing a great job!"

Almost nobody gets enough acknowledgment. Most of us don't have people around us telling us, "You are smart! You are capable!" even when we need that reinforcement the most.

When is the last time someone told you "You're brilliant!" or gave you acknowledgment in another way? Write about that in your Mojo Journal.

Writing the Pain Letter

How will I compose my Pain Letter?

Start by finding your hiring manager's name. Search on the employer's own website, focusing on the About Us or Management Bios page. Use LinkedIn to search for your hiring manager, using his or her most likely job title together with the company name.

Read the employer's website and study its LinkedIn Company Page if they have one. Read the LinkedIn profiles of the managers in the organization. Which one of them is the person most likely to be in need of someone with your Pain-Solving abilities?

Now, compose your Pain Letter.

Pain Letter Components

A Pain Letter has four parts:

1. The Hook

2. The Pain Hypothesis

3. A Dragon-Slaying Story

4. The Closing

The Hook

The Hook is the first sentence or two in your Pain Letter, right after "Dear Joseph" or "Dear Carolyn." If you're writing to a hiring manager in the government, academia, law, health care, or the sciences, you may want to begin your Pain Letter with "Dear Ms. Alexander" or "Dear Dr. Xiao."

You'll begin your Pain Letter with "Dear Susan" or "Dear Ms. Alexander" and then jump into your Hook opening.

You'll grab your reader's—that is, your hiring manager's—attention with your Hook by talking about him or her or the organization you are approaching—not about you.

Your Hook is a simple acknowledgment of something cool or praiseworthy the organization is doing or has recently done. It's an outreach that says, "Good job!" Most of us don't get acknowledgment. Who does? Who wouldn't keep reading a letter that starts out by acknowledging your team for their hard work?

You can find a good Hook on the employer's website, in the Press Releases section, or you can search their name and learn tons about what they are doing in their industry and as members of their community.

Here are three examples of successful Pain Letter Hooks:

- I was happy to see that Angry Chocolates is one of Atlanta's Favorites again this year. That's a tremendous confirmation of your team's commitment!

- Congratulation on your Chairman's wonderful radio interview on the growth of zircon-encrusted tweezer technology in dental-floss farming. What an inspiring leader he is!

- Hats off to your team on the ground-breaking for your new Townsville customer care facility. It's exciting to see a local employer thriving and growing.

The Pain Hypothesis

Leave a paragraph break after your Hook and dive into your Pain Hypothesis. This is a simple suggestion that you wouldn't be shocked to hear your reader (your hiring manager) is dealing with a particular kind of Business Pain that most people in his or her situation get into at some point.

Here are three sample Pain Hypotheses from Pain Letters:

- Given your new distribution deal with Walmart, I wouldn't be surprised to find that your marketing team is taxed to the limit.

- I can only imagine that with two new offices in the past two years, your back-end system may be slowing you down.

- In light of the merger with Acme Explosives, you might be dealing with some turnover and training issues as the two teams merge.

A Pain Hypothesis is simple. If it's much longer than the short Pain Hypothesis examples above, it's too long.

The Dragon-Slaying Story

After your Pain Hypothesis, there's no paragraph break. You'll zoom into your Dragon-Slaying Story—the one you chose for this Pain Letter because it's most relevant to the kind of Business Pain your hiring manager is likely to be facing now.

A Dragon-Slaying Story tells the hiring manager why you needed to act, what you did to make things better, and why you did the right thing when you acted.

Tell us the problem first.

Then, tell us how you solved the problem.

Last, tell us why your solution was brilliant (just as you are!).

That's a Dragon-Slaying Story.

PART THREE

Here's an example of a Dragon-Slaying Story from a Pain Letter. Notice that the Pain Letter writer starts the Dragon-Slaying Story by saying in her own way, "Yes, I know something about that type of Business Pain. I've dealt with that pain myself."

When I was at Underwater Seagrass just before its sale to Nike, we had a similar issue. We had to keep our loyal, local customers happy as our business expanded into fourteen states. I supported our resellers to get our products out to thousands of new customers.

The Closing

Now you've got your Hook, your Pain Hypothesis, and a Dragon-Slaying Story in your Pain Letter. You're almost done. Now you just need to get out!

You'll write, "If [this pain point] is on your radar screen, I'd be happy to talk by phone or start an email conversation. All the best, [you]."

A Pain Letter is short. The first thing you want your hiring manager to think as he or she opens your envelope and looks at your Pain Letter is, "Oh, good. This letter is short." It's a visceral reaction. If you send someone a page of dense text, they're not going to read it.

Everybody is stressed and pressed for time. Your Pain Letter must show up as a welcome message of hope, not another imposition in a busy person's day.

Five Things Pain Letters Do

A Pain Letter tells your hiring manager a lot. Here are five things that your Pain Letter conveys to its recipient (a hiring manager on your list):

- Your Pain Letter tells your hiring manager that you are awake and aware—not a passive, Sheepie Job Seeker who can only fill in an online form and then sit back and wait to hear some word from you.

- Your Pain Letter tells your manager that you are paying attention to the manager's company and, more than that, to his or her business situation specifically. That is a very welcome message for a busy and stressed-out manager to get!

- Your Pain Letter tells your manager that you understand through personal experience what he or she is facing on the job—the Business Pain your manager is struggling with.

- Your Pain Letter tells your hiring manager not just that you've solved a similar problem to his or her Business Pain before, but also how you did it!

- Once your hiring manager begins to get excited about you and your Pain-Spotting and Pain-Solving abilities, your Pain Letter ends—but all your manager has to do is flip over your Pain Letter to see your awesome Human-Voiced Resume just behind it!

What are your thoughts about how your Pain Letter might be a welcome piece of correspondence for your hiring manager to receive in the mail? Write them in your Mojo Journal.

Research employers and write a Pain Letter, and if you're job hunting right now, send it out to a hiring manager on your Target Employer List.

PART THREE

WHEN EVERY JOB IS A TEMP JOB

Every job these days is a temp job, whether it's a full-time job or a job that's been designated "temporary."

If every job you hold throughout your career is actually a temp job—in the sense that you have no idea how long it will last—what's your best strategy on the job? Your best strategy on a temp job (which is to say, any job) is to gather up valuable things while you are there. You must get a paycheck, but that's the least valuable thing you will collect on every job you perform.

Your paycheck only gets you through to the next paycheck—if you're like most people, it is basically already spent by the time you get it.

THE GOOD THINGS THE RIGHT JOB GETS YOU

There are good things (apart from a paycheck) that you collect at every job you have. Even if you only work in the job for a few weeks, you can still get some of these wonderful things:

- Contacts
- Learning

- Exposure to tools and methods

- New ideas

- References

- Ideas for your own path

- Credibility

- New muscles

- Tricks of the trade

- "Aha!"s

What do these terms mean? Let's break them down!

Contacts

Every new job gives you valuable contacts, but only if you seek them out! Part of your job at every salaried or hourly-wage position you hold, as well as every consulting opportunity, contract, or temporary job, is to meet people and strike up conversations with them. That is easier to do at some jobs than others, but nearly every job gives you opportunities to grow your network!

Learning

There are opportunities to learn new things on almost every job, but some jobs give you more learning opportunities than others do.

Exposure to Tools and Methods

The real world outside your office, factory, showroom, warehouse, or institution's walls is always changing. New methods and new approaches are always popping into view. A great job is one that teaches you new ways to solve problems and new tools all the time.

New Ideas

We learn new ideas at work. We hear new perspectives on old information. Our conversations at work get us thinking differently about ourselves, our goals, and the best ways to accomplish things.

References

The people you meet at work are your contacts. If you have been working for some time, you may have dozens or even several hundred professional contacts. There is an important and much smaller group of people you'll want to keep in touch with after you leave each job. These are your

PART THREE

professional references. It is important to collect at least one professional reference from each job if you can. Your reference-givers are people who can speak knowledgeably and from their direct, personal experience about your work.

Ideas for Your Own Path

Your mind is always working, even when you're not aware of it—and even when you're sleeping! We can get new ideas for our lives and careers from almost anywhere. One thing that lots of people get at work is new ideas for their own path.

You might hear someone talking about his or her career path and think, "Wow, that person has an interesting story. Maybe I could try something like that for myself!" You might hear a speech or see a presentation or meet someone at work who inspires you to try something new in your own life or career.

Credibility

Professional credibility can come from many different sources. You build your credibility when you do a great job at work, no matter what kind of job you have. Your credibility grows when you teach other people how to do things you've already learned how to do.

Your credibility also grows when you accomplish something especially challenging at work, or when you speak up and make a suggestion about how to solve a problem. One of the best things about working is that in the right job, your muscles and your credibility keep growing all the time.

New Muscles

When you're in the right job, your muscles grow quickly! You try new things all the time.

Tricks of the Trade

Tricks of the trade are the parts of a job that you have to learn on the job. You can't learn them in a book. They are how-to elements of a job that experienced people know. The people who know the tricks of the trade teach them to people who are newer in the job than they are.

"Aha!"s

"Aha!"s are realizations that hit you all at once or that creep up on you. Sometimes an "Aha!" hits you like a thunderbolt. At other times, you'll suddenly see how the pieces of a confusing puzzle fit together.

Your brain was working in the background and then suddenly, you realize that you've found a solution to your problem or made an important discovery.

In your Mojo Journal, write about each of these good things a job can bring:

1. Contacts—Write about a person you met at work that you kept in contact with after you and he or she no longer worked together. That person is a member of your network and you are a member of his or her network, too!

2. Confidence—Write about accomplishments at work that grew your confidence.

3. Clarity—What are some of the things you've learned about yourself and your path while on the job?

4. Exposure to tools and methods—Write about new methods and tools you've learned to use at a job you've held!

5. New ideas—Write about some new ideas you've come up with at work.

6. A Creative Outlet—Write about how you've used your creative juices at work!

7. Affirmation—Write about feeling reinforced or acknowledged for something you did at work.

8. Feeling of Accomplishment—Write about one of your favorite accomplishments at a past job or your current job.

9. Credibility—Write about how your professional credibility increased because of something you did at work.

10. Stories—Write about one or two of your favorite Dragon-Slaying Stories.

11. Alignment with your mission—Write about an experience you had at work that felt like a step toward your mission!

12. Intellectual stimulation—Write about how you've used your brain at work!

You can see that the right job gives you much more than just a paycheck. In the drawing here you can see some of the important good things the right job gives you, apart from a paycheck.

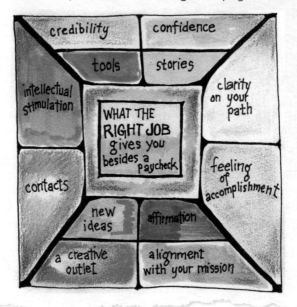

Anything that takes up eight or more hours of your time per day should give you good things in return, shouldn't it? Your paycheck is not enough compensation for the heart cells, brain cells, energy, and mojo you bring to your work. The right job will give you much more than a paycheck.

The right job will give you intellectual stimulation, creative expression, and social affirmation as well. That's why you can't let anyone tell you that it doesn't matter what kind of job you get—that you should be happy to have a job at all.

Which of the elements in the diagram above are most important to you? Which ones have you gotten on the job already and which ones are you still looking to bring into your work?

Anybody who tells you that it's not important or worth your time and energy to look for the right job (as opposed to just any job) doesn't understand the incredible benefits that the right job gives you—or the damage that the wrong job can do to your resume and more importantly, your precious flame.

 Write about your experience in the best job you've had so far in your career. What good things did you get from that job, apart from your paycheck?

It's the new millennium, and we are all turning the crystal together to see our work differently. We can see that our work is a big part of our life—but our work is not our life.

It is a big goal to set—to make the commitment, "I'm going to get the kind of work that celebrates me and grows my flame"—but there is no downside to working toward that goal.

If you keep working at it, listening to your body and learning all the time, you can't fail. There's no way to fail in your career as long as you are always learning from every experience.

MARTHA'S STORY

I worked as a church secretary for 15 years, and it was a fantastic job. The job paid next to nothing, but it was heart work for me, and I loved spending so much time with the people in our congregation.

I got divorced and I couldn't live on my church salary anymore, so I had to leave that job, and it killed me to leave because I was so comfortable there. When I left my job, I was adrift. I took the first job I could get, which was a retail job. My job pays better than most retail jobs, but it's still hard on my feet. I work a lot of hours, and because of my overtime, I earn more now than I did at the church—but I know this job is not my calling or my passion.

I felt very lost because I had thought I would get a "career" job right away when I left the church, and it didn't work out like that. I didn't realize how dramatically the job-search process had changed since the last time I job-hunted.

I'm working at my retail job and applying for every administrative job I see, but I'm getting very few responses. I'm so discouraged!

Now that you've been walking the Reinvention Roadmap path, you can see why Martha's job search is so hard and so frustrating for her. How full or empty do you think Martha's Mojo Tank is? What advice would you give to Martha? Apart from quitting her job and starting a new job that keeps Martha on her feet all day, what else is going on in Martha's life that might increase her stress level and deplete her Mojo Tank even further? Write your thoughts in your Mojo Journal. Here are some more questions to respond to in your Mojo Journal:

· Does Martha know what she wants to do professionally?

· Is Martha's career direction clear and aligned with her passion?

· Since Martha doesn't know what she wants to do next, she has been applying for administrative jobs. However, Martha hasn't heard anything back from the jobs she has applied for so far. What do you suspect is going wrong in Martha's job search?

As she steps into her new life after a huge, disruptive life event (Martha's divorce), Martha is learning at a much faster rate than most of us are. We could judge Martha and say, "Martha, you should have kept that church gig until you found something that pays more and doesn't give you sore legs and feet!" but that horse is out of the barn. Martha has already quit her job. She can't undo that decision now.

Imagine how depleted Martha's mojo level is. Everybody knows the feelings Martha is experiencing now. She feels hopeless. She feels like a failure. She fears that her career may be over and that no one might want to hire her.

When we go through shocks and shakes in life, we get knocked down. We get the wind knocked out of our sails, as they say. It takes time to bounce back. Almost all of us have experienced a Mojo Drop at some point.

In your Mojo Journal, write about a Mojo Drop that you've experienced. Despite her Mojo Drop, Martha is, of course, still smart and funny and vibrant and awesome. She's been an incredible advisor and friend and honorary mom to her church congregation. What other kinds of jobs could Martha do, as she contemplates leaving her retail job and getting back into office administration? Write your ideas in your journal.

Martha is undoubtedly qualified for dozens or hundreds of different job titles—too many job titles to list. Here are just a few of them:

Administrative Assistant	Office Manager	Events Planner or Manager
Guidance Counselor or Coach	Tutor	Department Manager (of any number of possible departments)
Trainer or Instructor	Marketing Person	HR Person
Manager of Administration	Operations Person	Trainer
Admissions Counselor	Victim Advocate	Substance Abuse Counselor
Mediator	Virtual Assistant	Communications Specialist

Martha is amazing, but there are three big obstacles in her way. Keeping Martha from getting a great job—a job that deserves her talents—are the following three roadblocks:

1 A powerless resume

Martha's resume is pale and wan. It lists the jobs she's held so far. It uses awful zombie language like most resumes do. None of Martha's amazing strength and humor and goodwill come shining through. Martha needs new branding materials.

2 A losing job-search strategy

Martha's job-search approach is to lob applications into faceless ATS (Applicant Tracking System) recruiting portals. Martha needs to change up her job-search approach and learn to take charge of her own career by reaching out directly to hiring managers (who might become future bosses or future consulting clients).

3 Depleted Mojo

Martha's last roadblock is emotional and physical. She needs to build up her Mojo Fuel Tank. Naturally it got terribly depleted during her divorce. Now Martha is working a demanding retail job, conducting a part-time job search, and worrying about money. Her mojo is nearly gone and she needs to get it back.

When Martha steps through, over, or across these three obstacles, she will see her own power and be able to get a great job.

Martha is going to take simple steps to change her career and life situation in a big way. First, she's going to dramatically change her branding. Second, she's going to broaden the scope of her job search to focus on more jobs than the ones she's targeting now. Third, Martha is going to put a human voice in her resume, so she won't sound like every other job-seeker anymore. Fourth, she's going to practice writing Pain Letters to reach each of her possible next managers directly, at their desks. She's not going to waste time applying for jobs online anymore, because she's seen how well that method works for her! (It hasn't worked at all.) Lastly, Martha is going to make a serious (but fun) project out of her own Mojo Fuel Tank refilling process.

Martha is not waiting for someone else to give her career back to her. She's taking it back by herself!

She's going to look at all the possible jobs she could perform—and there are dozens of them—and decide on one group of similar jobs to focus on first. That way, she can create one version of her Human-Voiced Resume and only tweak or adjust it slightly each time she sends it to a new hiring manager.

If she isn't happy with the results that come from her focus on her first-choice group of similar jobs, Martha will shift her focus. She is flexible! She is listening to signals from the talent marketplace. She knows that if she's working hard on her job search and her approach isn't working, it would be pointless to keep doing the same things she's already done many times without success. She knows that silence from the talent marketplace is a loud message telling her to change her methodology.

Martha is excited about taking a big step up in her career by taking control of it, but she's a little nervous, too.

Martha says, "I have to break some rules by taking control of my career. I have to take the chance that not everyone will like my approach to my career or my approach to job-hunting."

Martha is right! Not everyone will like the human voice in her resume or the nontraditional way Martha reaches out to hiring managers using Pain Letters.

Not everyone will like the fact that Martha ignores the instructions in some of the job ads she reads—instructions that tell her to apply for the job opportunity by completing an online application at a certain website address. Martha ignores that instruction and sends a Pain Letter directly to her hiring manager working at each possible next employer, instead. She breaks a crusty old rule that says, "Don't you dare contact a hiring manager directly!"

GETTING ONE'S MOJO BACK

Your mojo is your life force. It's forward motion. It's the energy you feel when you know where you're headed and you're ready to roll! When your mojo level is high, you can do anything. When your mojo level is low, you don't feel like you can accomplish a thing.

How do you get your lost mojo back? It's a process. Here are the steps:

- Give yourself a break. That's the first step! Everything you've done up to this point in your life was supposed to happen just the way it did. It's fine, and you are fine. There's nothing wrong with you. People get hit with tough breaks. It doesn't mean you did anything wrong.

- Get a journal. Start to write in it every day or as often as you can. Don't worry about what to write. Write whatever pops into your mind!

- Don't worry about how perfect your handwriting is. You can type into a journal on a device if you can't read your handwriting or don't like to write by hand. Some people prefer to journal longhand (writing on paper with a pen or pencil) because it takes some time to write by hand, and that time gives your brain an opportunity to come up with ideas.

- Your goal as a "journalist"—a person who keeps a journal—is to write enough that you stop thinking as you write. Just write, and don't judge your writing. Your goal is to open a channel so that ideas start flowing down from wherever (the collective intellect, or your higher self, or the spheres, or whatever you like to think about) and down through your arm and out through your fingers and the pen onto the page.

- Write about your life so far. Tell your story on the page. Write everything you can remember and want to write about, including stories from your school days, your most vivid memories as a kid, and what you liked to do when you were little.

- The process of recalling your path so far is called Retracing Your Steps. There is a lot of power in it! You will remember times when you felt strong and powerful, even if you don't feel that way right now.

- Get as much sleep as you can and as much exercise as you can. Triumph in every choice to be healthier (like walking up the stairs instead of riding the escalator). Don't beat up on yourself. You are inviting your mojo back in—you can't command it to return!

- Collect your Dragon-Slaying Stories. Write them down in your journal. Dragon-Slaying Stories are times when you took action and made good things happen, at work or somewhere else. Maybe it was at your child's school or during your own school days. Maybe it was in a volunteer assignment.

- Spend time with people who boost your mojo, and minimize the time you spend with people who bring you down. Remember, your mojo is your fuel source! You can't change your work or life situation with a depleted Mojo Fuel Tank.

 What ideas do you have for growing your mojo? Write them in your Mojo Journal.

If you have depleted mojo, here are some activities that might help you get your mojo back:

Gardening	Dancing with the TV or radio or YouTube	Reading your favorite book
Riding your bike	Visiting the library	Watching a free lecture on YouTube
Cooking a special meal	Inviting people over to visit	Volunteering
Running or walking	Creating art or a craft project	Listening to music you love
Spending time at the park or in nature	Playing music	Teaching a friend or family member how to do something new
Creating a scrapbook	Writing poetry	Writing anything!

EIGHT MOJO BLOCKERS

Here are Eight Mojo Blockers that dam up the good energy—the Team Mojo—in organizations and keep them stuck and unhappy. From the top of the Eight Mojo Blockers diagram, let's review the Eight Mojo Blockers in clockwise order.

1. Role and Cultural Confusion

Look for the man and the woman in very different costumes at the top of the Eight Mojo Blockers diagram. Role confusion is very common and a big Mojo Blocker in large and small organizations. People aren't clear about their roles. They aren't always clear about the expectations the organization has for them, and very often no one talks about expectations, so who could be surprised?

We all come from different backgrounds and bring our perceptions and beliefs with us to work. When we don't talk about the culture at work and pretend that culture is not a factor in our work, the Team Mojo energy is immediately blocked.

2. Disturbance in the Energy Field

Maybe there's big news looming in your workplace but nobody is talking about it. Maybe two people hate each other and everybody is suffering from their hate-vibes flying around the workplace. When there's a disturbance in the energy field, it's foolish to ignore it and pretend it will go away on its own. Disturbances in energy are amazingly effective Mojo Blockers! No one will be able to get anything done at work or plug in to their personal power source when there's a disturbance in the Team Mojo energy that no one addresses.

3. Crossed Wires

Signals can easily get crossed at work. Then people get angry and confused and start pointing fingers. Crossed wires are common Mojo Blockers!

4. Red Tape

Bureaucracy is excess policy and protocol beyond what an organization really needs. Bureaucracy is sometimes called "red tape." When every process is slow and boring and prescribed to the finest detail because somebody decided that employees can't think on their own, then a leader can forget about Team Mojo, because there won't be any. We have to trust the people we hire—which means that we have to trust ourselves to hire brilliant people and then trust them.

5. Approvals for Everything

If six people have to sign off on every decision, no one will care about the mission and the Team Mojo level in a workplace will plummet. Huge decisions with big impact require lots of conversation and careful thought. At the same time it shouldn't require the signatures of the Dalai Lama and God or an archangel to get a new ID badge when you lose your old one. Too many approvals for stupid things kill the Team Mojo at work.

6. Elephant in the Room

The elephant in the room is any important topic that isn't getting airtime, and everyone knows it. The elephant topic expands to nearly suck the air out of a room. Your job is to name every elephant you see in every corner of every room at work. Thoughtfully and with compassion, name the elephant. You can ask, "Should we talk about the new overtime policy, which it seems a lot of folks have questions about?"

7. Fear

Fear is the greatest Mojo Blocker. Managers who use fear to get things done kill the Team Mojo on their teams and get only grudging compliance with their orders, which is the least effective, least exciting, most expensive, and most mojo-crushing form of activity known to humankind.

8. No Vision, No Plan

For you as a working person and for any team you become a member of, everything starts with the vision. If there's no vision, how will team members know which way to travel? You need a vision for yourself, and every team, group, task force, committee, and club you belong to needs a mission, too.

Everybody on the team needs to know what the mission is and how he or she can help the team realize its vision. Without a clear vision and a team to get there, how can Team Mojo grow?

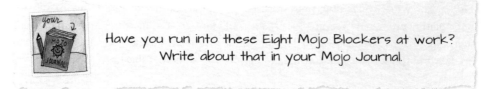

Have you run into these Eight Mojo Blockers at work? Write about that in your Mojo Journal.

THE IMPORTANCE OF BEING HUMAN

We saw earlier how Mojofied Job Seekers can take control of their job searches using Pain Letters and their Human-Voiced Resumes. It's easy to see why a hiring manager would rather see a live human being coming through the page, and receive a letter that talks about him or her (and his or her likely pain points) versus a traditional cover letter that drones on and on about a job-seeker's accomplishments.

Your hiring manager can't possibly care about your accomplishments until you make a connection with him or her, and open an aperture in his or her head.

What can you say in your Pain Letter to open that aperture—to get a hiring manager to care about your message? You can talk about something he or she cares about—namely his or her situation at work.

You can talk about him or her, instead of talking about yourself.

Your hiring manager can begin to care about you only when he or she gets the message, "This person understands what I am going through. Maybe this person can help me!"

Some managers won't contact you when you send them a Pain Letter. That's okay! They are not the right manager for you, at least not at this moment.

Life is long and the world is big. There are plenty of other employers, and there are plenty of other organizations who could engage you to complete a consulting project for them.

You may have your heart set on a particular opportunity or a particular employer, but we don't always know what the universe has in store for us. We don't always know in advance which experiences will be the most flame-growing experiences. Sometimes Mother Nature knows better! As long as it grows your flame and pays you what you're worth, all work is good work!

When you're working in a job that doesn't do any of those things, that's okay too. You know you can't stay in a job that doesn't pay you enough to live on, doesn't teach you anything, and doesn't move your career forward, but for now, even an unexciting job can be a resting place.

You can use your time in the less-than-sensational job to plan your next move! When it comes to managing your career, planning is at least as important as actually "doing."

It is easy to beat up on ourselves and to say, "You should have a better job than this job!" It is easy to criticize ourselves. That's a bad idea. Criticizing yourself only depletes your mojo supply.

If you have an unexciting job right now or at some point in your journey, that's okay. Who's to say the "meh" job isn't going to give you the most amazing learning experience or the best idea you've ever had?

Some people believe that the way to be successful in your career is to keep making more money year after year, and to keep getting promoted to bigger and bigger jobs.

If you know that you're doing the work you were born to do, making more money every year and getting promoted over and over again could be a great thing for you. For many people, though, a successful career has less to do with getting promoted and earning a huge salary than it has to do with bringing yourself to work and performing work that speaks to you.

Write a list of the names of people who boost your mojo. These are people to spend as much time with as you can!

Write a second list. This time, list the names of people who deplete your precious Mojo Fuel Tank. (Make sure your Mojo Journal is in a private place or use code names if you're worried about someone finding your journal and reading it.)

How can you arrange your schedule to spend less time with the people who deplete your mojo and more time with the people who boost your mojo?

STEPPING THROUGH REINVENTION

The grand prize for you or any working person is to line up your career path with your life path so that you are always growing, always learning, and always bringing yourself to work all the way.

Reinvention is a process. It doesn't happen all at once.

Reinvention is not a crossword puzzle or a logic puzzle. It happens at a different level. Your body is involved in your reinvention—not just your mind!

Sometimes we think we can puzzle out anything and solve any problem by using our minds. That isn't always true. Sometimes we have to stop and listen to our bodies!

What would it mean to line up your career with your life path? How could you bring more of yourself into your work and take a step toward the life and career you want? Write your thoughts in your Mojo Journal.

REINVENTION CAN BE EXHAUSTING AND CONFUSING

In the following table are common things people in reinvention say about their in-between state. In your Mojo Journal, write a comment about each statement.

THINGS PEOPLE IN REINVENTION SAY

I just want to be done with this reinvention! I hate being indecisive about my career. I want someone to tap me on the shoulder and say, "Here is your new career path." I hate not knowing what my next step will be!

My feelings go up and down, hot and cold. One day I feel excited and fearless and the next day I want to curl up in bed with the covers pulled over my head. I hate that up-and-down feeling!

I feel like a baby learning to walk again. I'm not going to lie. It's hard! I felt so competent in my old working life and now I feel totally unsure of myself.

One day I think I know for sure what I want to do with my life, and the next day I feel just as certain about a totally different idea. I think my brain is just grasping for certainty. I don't like being in this state and I want it to be over!

I had a dream about being a little kid the other night. I remembered very clearly pushing my baby sister on a swing when those bucket-type swings first came in for babies. I remember my mom saying, "You're so good with little kids." I must have been about four years old. Why did I have that dream?

What are your thoughts about the feelings and reactions to reinvention that our four reinventionists shared in the table? Write them in your Mojo Journal.

The Desert of Reinvention

I call the confusing, rootless phase of reinvention the Desert of Reinvention. That is the part of your reinvention process where you have to wander around for a while before you find your new home. It can be a scary thing to wander in the desert, not knowing what you're supposed to be doing next.

I have been through three big reinvention deserts. The first time I wandered in the desert was just after my former employer, U.S. Robotics, was sold back in 1997. I was out of a job, but much worse than that, my professional identity was gone, too. I hadn't realized how much I'd buried my personality in my job. When I left my job, I realized that I had begun to think (without realizing it) that I WAS my job. When the job went away, I wasn't sure who I was anymore!

I'm an opera singer. In the summer of 1997, I was pregnant and had three little kids at home, so I didn't look for a new job right away. I helped a friend of mine who was starting a new opera company. I started writing columns for the newspaper. I started doing anything I could think of to stay busy. I thought that staying busy was my best course of action. The busier I could keep myself, the less time I would have to worry about the looming question, "What's next?"

When we stay very busy, we keep our thoughts at bay (somewhat!). We keep our fears at bay. We say to the gods, "Look how busy I am! I must get a gold star for effort, right?"

When we stay terribly busy and overbooked, we don't have time to think. We don't have time to look into the abyss and ask the hard questions, like, "What is my life supposed to be about?"

When you were working at your old job or going to school or doing whatever you were doing before your reinvention began, you didn't have time to stop and look over the precipice.

When the train stops suddenly and you are thrust out of the train into a new station, you are shocked into awareness again. You are pushed by the universe to look into the abyss, but most of us don't want to do that. I certainly didn't want to look over the edge!

Most of us don't want to look at the question, "What is my life about?" We'd like to find another safe, cozy burrow (a job that takes care of our financial needs) and make ourselves comfortable in it, but sometimes the universe has other ideas!

There is a reinvention waiting, and it's got our name on it.

Why is it so appealing for people wandering in the Desert of Reinvention to keep busy? Write your thoughts in your Mojo Journal. Have you felt the urge to stay very busy in order to slip through your reinvention without having to stop and look at your path behind you and ahead of you? Write about that in your Mojo Journal.

VIJAY'S STORY

I was in the Desert of Reinvention, and very frustrated. I left my job as a Hardware Engineer because my last six projects were all exactly the same. I was pigeonholed.

I signed up with several contract agencies in hopes of getting contract work, but the market was really dead.

I ended up running out of money, so I got a job fixing hardware bugs for a manufacturing company. I knew that job was a stopgap—a lily pad with a very slim stem. It was a job to keep me afloat while I crawled through the Desert of Reinvention!

I retraced my steps. I wrote about my path in life so far. Once I started writing, I couldn't stop. I wrote seventeen pages! I remembered that before I went to school for engineering, I was very interested in cars. I was crazy for cars, motorcycles, and trucks. I'm a Hardware Engineer, but I don't know anything about product engineering or manufacturing. I don't know much, because I've been designing circuit boards for 20 years.

I started to look for ways to use my mechanical smarts and my curiosity about moving parts in my job—more than I had done before. I found a small device-manufacturing company about 20 miles away from my house and I sent a Pain Letter to the head of

Product Development. I wrote about the pain of getting new products to market. I just got a voicemail message from the VP, AJ. I'm excited to talk to him live!

Vijay found a Place to Put His Canoe in the Water. He is going to focus his initial Pain Letter activity on growing manufacturing firms that might have pain around getting products out the door. Vijay has been a Hardware Engineer for years.

He had never thought of himself or described himself as a product development person, a manufacturing person, or a mechanically inclined person before, but he is doing that now!

 Why hadn't Vijay ever described himself as a product development person, a manufacturing person, or a mechanically inclined person before? Write your ideas in your Mojo Journal.

Phase Transition

We change all the time. All living things change. When water is getting ready to boil in a pan, the water molecules in the pan start moving faster and faster. The movement of the water molecules becomes chaotic and unpredictable. The water begins to boil and the liquid water turns to vapor. The water has stopped being a liquid and has started a new existence as vapor, or steam. Scientists call this transformation from liquid to vapor "phase transition." When water is getting ready to stop being liquid and start being vapor, the movement of the molecules becomes chaotic. The same thing happens to people in reinvention. Our movements can become chaotic and unpredictable, too.

On Monday we think, "I know! I'll go back to school." On Wednesday we think, "I'm going to go back to my old career path." On Friday we think, "I'll start my own business!" We might be jittery and anxious. We can't settle down. Who could blame us? Phase transition isn't easy.

 What feelings or physical reactions has your reinvention created in you so far? Write about that in your Mojo Journal. Answer these questions in your Mojo Journal:

· How did I feel about my reinvention when I first realized that things were changing?

· How have my feelings about my reinvention shifted since then?

- What emotions have I felt during this reinvention? (Fear, confusion, excitement, nervousness, etc.)
- What can I learn about myself by noticing the passing clouds of emotion rather than letting them control me?
- What can I do when strong emotions hit me, to stay calm and feel better?
- How can I manage my time to watch my mojo level and keep my Mojo Tank full?

Other People and Your Reinvention

While we wander around in the Desert of Reinvention, often our family members and close friends get anxious about our state. They want us to settle down and get a job and stop blathering

about our path. They liked us the way we were before. We can be sympathetic to them—they may not have voted for our reinvention any more than we did!

Still, it is important to spend time around people who support you and your reinvention. Sometimes talking about reinvention can qualify as a sticky topic. Some of the people in your life might not want to hear about your reinvention.

It can be hard to say, "I'm looking at my career and life from altitude now. I'm looking at things more broadly than I have for a while. I'm thinking about my path."

Can you enlist people around you to help you in your exploration? They might be interested in the same topics you're investigating in your Reinvention Roadmap process.

Most of us don't spend much time looking back at our path so far, or asking, "What do I want from my time on this planet?" We can walk through reinvention individually, but it's much more fun and affirming when we can talk about what we're experiencing and feeling in reinvention.

Who can you talk about your reinvention with?

Write in your Mojo Journal the names of those you can talk to about reinvention, and answer these questions:

1 How can you arrange your schedule to spend time with people who get you and your reinvention and don't put pressure on you to take the first job you can get?

2 How can you gently set boundaries with well-meaning and loving people who tell you, "You should just go back to your old job!" or "You should go down the street and get a job at the store on the corner—they're hiring!"

PART THREE

NGHIA'S STORY

I quit my job to go to a new job, and then the new company went out of business. I laughed about it because it was too hard to say, "I'm devastated." I loved that new job. I didn't really look before I leapt. I was ready to leave the old job, but I had a feeling that the new job opportunity might be too good to be true, and it was.

I didn't want to be in reinvention. I wanted a new job fast. I didn't want to stop and look at my path, because I knew that if I did that, I'd see that I have no path. I've let other people make a lot of my career decisions for me. I know that, okay? I didn't want to know more about it than that.

I didn't see a way to change that situation, anyway. My dad is a big influence in my life. So is my mom. My wife has certain ideas about what my career path should be, and so do her parents. I have all kinds of people telling me how to manage my career. I didn't know what I wanted for myself, so I took the first job I could get after I got laid off. It was a job in a liquor store.

Amazingly, I learned a lot in that liquor store job—but I didn't earn any money. I talked to the vendors who came in—the wine and spirits salespeople. We hit it off. I asked them how they got their jobs. One of the salespeople said, "You could make a lot of money selling wine and spirits," but I told him I don't know anything about alcoholic beverages. I've never been much of a drinker.

A couple of weeks later the same sales guy, named Eric, told me that his company is looking for an Inventory Supervisor at their distribution center about 20 miles from my house. I got excited and asked him, "Would you mind putting in a good word for me?" I went home feeling pumped up about the possible job opportunity. I told my wife about it. "No way!" she said. "You can't take a job that far away from home, and anyway you don't know anything about that industry!"

I was surprised by her reaction. I realized that people can love you and still not want you to change. I told my wife I would play it out and see what happened. I went to the job interview and it went really well. I came home even more excited. My wife said, "If you want to take the job, do it, but at least look at other possibilities, too."

I wasn't sure I would have time to look at anything else. The warehouse manager was excited to meet me the same way I was excited to meet him. But I got online and started looking at job ads anyway. I saw three or four of them that I figured were worth more investigation. I told my wife, "I want to make big decisions in partnership with you, but I need a job that I will enjoy and thrive in more than I need just another job."

We had a more honest talk about my job search than we've had in a long time. Of course my wife is stressed with me earning half what I was earning before. Of course I'm stressed, too, and neither of us is probably thinking clearly. At least we are communicating. I told my parents that I need to find my next job on my own and that I appreciate their advice but have different needs in my career now than I did before. I need to explore and try new things. My wife's parents continue to offer unsolicited advice, and I smile and ignore it. For me, that's the best approach.

I'm still considering the inventory job, but I'm setting my sights higher. I'm still feeling a little bruised about losing my job so suddenly, but I have accepted the fact that taking the first job I can get is not a great idea, unless it's a survival job like my job in the liquor store. It's a job that I can perform and still keep my "career"-type job search going. I told my boss at the liquor store that I would work for him for a year, even if I get a new job, which of course I hope to do before too long. I can still work at the liquor store on weekends.

I rely on my family members, but so far I've relied on them too much to guide my career. Now I'm taking steps for myself.

What are your reactions to Nghia's story?
Write them in your Mojo Journal.

Exercise: Grow Your Career-Coaching Muscles!

In this Reinvention Roadmap journey you have read many stories like Nghia's. In this exercise, you'll pick two of the stories in this book and write coaching responses to each of the storytellers. You'll write your responses in your Mojo Journal.

In each coaching response, write directly to the storyteller about his or her situation. Here is an outline to guide you as you write:

- First, acknowledge the storyteller for sharing his or her thoughts. Acknowledge his or her feelings.

- Next, lay out the scenario or the problem as you see it.

- Now, share some possible solutions to each storyteller's obstacle. Describe the steps to follow in acting on your coaching advice.

- Finally, give the storyteller (your new coaching client) a mojo boost by reminding him or her that he or she is amazing and talented.

How did you find your virtual coaching experience?
Write about it in your Mojo Journal.

Someone once referred to reinvention as "an unexpected and unwelcome break in your routine." That is a good perspective to keep in mind as you think about your reinvention. Often we think, "I was doing fine until this stupid reinvention thing showed up!" but if we are honest, maybe we weren't doing as well as we thought.

Maybe this shake-up will be good for you. Could that be the case?

Think about these questions and answer them in your Mojo Journal.

- What would you have said was your biggest problem or obstacle before you woke up or were shaken awake regarding your career?

- What is your biggest problem or obstacle now?

- If you lost your job, that may have been a painful experience. You might feel that there couldn't be any positive aspect to that jarring and disruptive event. As you think about it, could there be a positive side to losing your job?

- What possibilities can you imagine for yourself that you weren't thinking about before you got the nudge or the shake that started your reinvention?

- Reinvention is a passage between one chapter in your life and the next one. What gifts could your reinvention give you?

Gifts Your Reinvention Can Give You

Your reinvention can give you . . .

The gift of awareness.

When you fall into a rut, you fall asleep. You buy groceries and pay bills and don't think much about your life. Waking up is a gift!

The gift of possibility.

When your circumstances are fixed, it's easy to stop dreaming about what is possible. When you are shaken awake, you know that you have to create a new reality to live in, so you get permission to dream about a fantastic reality rather than a small, ordinary one. Why not? The gift of infinite possibility is an enormous blessing!

The gift of permission.

When a rug is pulled out from under you, you realize that upsetting things can happen and do happen every day. You realize that nothing is permanent and that the real world is always in flux. You get a reminder that Mother Nature calls the shots, and with that reminder comes an invitation: "Why not design the life you want and step into it? You thought your old life was fixed and unchangeable, and look how it changed! You can make changes that will bring your real life into alignment with your purpose here on earth. That's the message I'm sending you through this reinvention!"

If you cling to the cliffside you know so well and try to keep your old life as intact and unchanging as you can, you will find it harder and harder to stay on the wall. Pieces of rock will start to fall off and hit the canyon floor below.

Eventually you will turn your face away from the forbidding rock wall that used to feel so solid, and you'll look out at the canyon and the valley beyond it and say, "Why am I clinging to this

HOW DO I SURVIVE?

Liz, I'm in a weird place. Half of me wants to listen to your motivational imagery for hours, and the other half is terrified that I'm going to lose my apartment and be destitute. The fear side of me often wins the battle. That's when I pick up the Reinvention Roadmap *book. I can't sleep because I'm worried about money, but I don't want to abandon my career-type job search to get a survival job that wouldn't pay my bills—and that's only if they'd hire me at all. What should I do?*

Here are the three steps we recommend that every job-seeker take to allay his or her fears about money:

1. Get a consulting business card and actively network as a consultant, not a job-seeker. The moral support you'll get consulting will be helpful and you will grow your consulting and conversational muscles, too!

2. Write in your Mojo Journal often. Write every day if you can. Write about your job search, your ideas for your career, your reactions to your reinvention, and anything else you want to write about. Get your thoughts out on paper where you can look at them, versus rattling around in your head where all they can do is distract you and drive you crazy!

3. Take control of the areas of your life that are most easily controllable while you're job-hunting. Clean out your closets and throw away or donate things you don't need anymore. Work in your garden or follow a YouTube exercise guru's program and work out to YouTube videos every day. Tackle a part of your life that doesn't require the patience and steady application of pressure that your job search requires. Invest this time in you and your new chapter!

rock wall, anyway?" Since the rock wall and the valley and the canyon live in your imagination, you can decide how to leave the rock face.

You can parachute, or spread your wings and fly out over the canyon and the valley, or summon a magic carpet to take you wherever you want to go. The rock face felt solid but you are learning that you are more solid than any cliff wall is. You can rely on yourself more than you can rely on any job or employer.

That awareness may be the greatest reinvention gift of all!

YOUR ASSIGNMENT

In your Mojo Journal, write about your feelings. Write about your nervous, excited, happy, or anxious feelings toward your reinvention. Draw, paint, sing, dance, sculpt, bake, or find another creative way to get your feelings out. Your feelings are a big part of your reinvention. Don't ignore them!

CONGRATULATIONS—YOU'RE A CONSULTANT NOW!

In the new-millennium workplace, we are all consultants. If that sounds scary, I understand! For years, people said to me, "You should work for yourself at some point—you have a lot of ideas."

I always said, "No way! I'm not doing that." I was a corporate Sally. I thought working for myself sounded like the scariest thing ever.

It isn't.

Actually, we all work for ourselves. If we get paid a regular paycheck every two weeks or if we get paid by our clients for completing projects, we still work for ourselves. We are all entrepreneurs now!

The muscles that all of us need to survive and thrive in this new workplace are the same muscles entrepreneurs grow. All of the steps you're taking and the energy you're expending will pay off!

CONSIDERING CONSULTING

An easy way to step into entrepreneurism is to start a consulting practice. You can consult part-time or full-time. You can consult alongside a full-time or part-time job.

You can consult while you're job-hunting. Anyone can consult. Nearly everything that you can do in a regular job can also be done for other people as a consultant!

People and organizations have problems. They have pain! You can solve their pain as a consultant. When you do, you'll grow your muscles and find your voice, little by little.

Here's Rita's story about the steps she took to become a part-time consultant.

Rita's Story

I got laid off from my job at the school district's foundation after 20 years. It was a shock to get laid off. The bigger shock was how difficult it was to find a suitable new job.

I didn't feel like I was asking for the moon. I wanted a decent job working with good people, a reasonable salary, and relatively interesting work. I don't think I am especially choosy or hard to please. But every step of my job search felt like a huge pain.

I had to write my resume first, and that was hard. I never wrote my resume before. I filled out a paper application to get my job at the foundation 20 years ago. I worked hard on my resume and I thought it was pretty good. I started applying to jobs online and I heard nothing back. I applied for 20 jobs and I got two very short, terse auto-responder messages back. They said, "If we're interested in interviewing you, we'll contact you."

I networked. I talked to everyone I knew. I went to two networking events in town. I just ran out of steam for my job search and I felt like taking a retail job just to have a job. Not that there's anything wrong with working at a retail job, but I had been managing money and projects, and I have a ton of office experience. I had expected it to be easier to get the attention of employers.

I decided to start a part-time consulting business. If I started consulting even a little I would at least have some income, and I'd learn something new. I got business cards online and I put "Rita Morehouse, Consulting" on them, along with my phone number and email address.

I put my LinkedIn profile URL on the card, too. I started to hand out my business cards.

I told my friends about my new consulting business. One of my friends said, "You're a consultant? Do you know anything about after-school youth ministries?" I had to catch myself before I said "No" automatically. I said, "A little," and my friend Dorothy said, "I want you to meet our pastor."

I met the pastor of Dorothy's church, who needed to organize an after-school youth ministry. I'd been around kids and educational programs for my whole career.

I'd never set up a program before, but it's a project, so I knew I could break it down. I explained to Dorothy's pastor, Richard, how I would manage the youth ministry project if he wanted me to do it.

He said yes. I was amazed! Richard was my first client. I charged him almost nothing for the project because I was happy to have the chance to start consulting. It was great practice for me. We set up a Tuesday- and Thursday-afternoon youth ministry using three classrooms and the gym in our local middle school, which is right across the street from the church building.

We marketed the program to local schools and even got a few corporate sponsors to help us fund it. I gave Richard the biggest hug when the program launched with 76 kids. "You showed up just at the right time to make this happen," he said.

"You showed up for me, too!" I said.

Now I consult and I'm still job-hunting, but a crazy thing has happened. I don't feel like a needy job-seeker saying, "Please hire me!" I know I can make things happen.

I know how to do a lot of things—tangible things that people and organizations need. What I mean is that I feel my value to the people I work with even more now than I did at the foundation. After a while the foundation job just felt like any job. Now I feel like myself.

I'm going to be 57 in a month, and I feel a lot like I did in my twenties. Every day is different. The learning is incredible. I incorporated my consulting business. I did it online for seventy bucks. I had no idea it was so easy.

My friend Blake and I traded services. He's a lawyer and he created my contract for client work. In exchange I created a marketing brochure for Blake's law firm. That was my first marketing brochure. Over the years I had seen and worked with lots of marketing brochures, but I'd never designed one on my own.

You don't know what knowledge you've accumulated that's just hiding up there in your brain waiting to be tapped. You have to tap the keg to know what's in there!

What do you think about Rita's consulting story?
Write your thoughts in your Mojo Journal.

TYPES OF CONSULTING WORK

As a consultant, you could work for organizations (companies, government agencies, and not-for-profit organizations) or for individuals. Everybody has pain! What kind of consulting business could you start, whether it's a full-time or part-time business? For help, consult the table on the next page.

POSSIBLE CONSULTING OPTIONS FOR YOU

Virtual assistant or administrative work	Childcare	Writing or editing	Office or home organizing
Bookkeeping or accounting	Education-related work	IT work or web design	Party or event planning
Social media or marketing	Sports or exercise coaching or training	Graphic design or illustration	Public relations or advertising
Health care or health insurance	Gardening or landscaping	Legal or legal services work	Arts-related work
Counseling or coaching	Moving or hauling work	Financial planning or investment help	Musical instruction or coaching
Home or office maintenance	Database or records management	Customer service or telephone/email/web-based customer support	Fundraising

Could you consult in any of these areas? Write in your Mojo Journal about your consulting ideas.

You don't have to know exactly what kind of consulting you want to do. You can keep your consulting persona very open as you explore the consulting world. Keep in mind that everybody has problems. Everybody needs help with something!

JEREMY'S STORY

I got my degree in music and I worked as a youth music pastor for seven years. I loved that job, but I couldn't pay my bills on the salary. I worked more than full-time, and my wife, who does childcare, earned more than I did. Plus, neither of us had any benefits, and we didn't make enough money to pay for health insurance.

I couldn't think of anything else that I could do to earn money. The only thing I could think of was to work at a retail store, and that would pay even less than my youth music pastor job did. My wife, Andrea, said, "Get a consulting business card," so I did that.

I just put "Consultant" on it. I didn't know what else to put on the card, so I just called myself a consultant and I put my phone number and email address on the card, too.

I started to give out my card. People asked me, "What kind of consulting do you do?" and I said, "Business, youth ministry, and music." I left things kind of open.

My wife's aunt asked me if I would give a quote on a project at her job. She works in a library. I went and talked to my wife's aunt and the Library Director. They wanted someone to organize a series of talks from leaders in the community. I jumped on that. The project paid $1,000, and I have never felt better about money that I earned than I did about that project.

I organized 12 talks by 12 prominent people in our community. I couldn't be there to hear the actual talks because I was working at the church, but I organized everything and did the marketing and publicity, too—promoting the free, public talks all over town.

The turnout from the public was great, and the library asked me to do another project. I also stayed in touch with the 12 local leaders who had presented the talks. I proposed to them that I could create YouTube channels for them to share their ideas with more people. Three of them asked me to do that, and now that is my consulting business! I videotape, edit, and produce YouTube videos for my clients.

I owe everything to my wife's aunt, who got me started in consulting.

 Jeremy can't quit his day job just yet. His goal is to earn $10,000 consulting in the next year. That's a lot! That's eight hundred dollars per month. Jeremy's consulting job could lead to a full-time job or could get big enough that Jeremy can consult full-time. What advice would you give Jeremy on his path? Write your ideas in your Mojo Journal.

BASICS

What Would I Put on My Consulting Business Card?

You could create a consulting business card for just a few dollars at www.vistaprint.com, and have the business cards shipped to your house. Here's a simple model for your consulting business cards:

- Your name

- A simple brand, like "Consultant" or "Business Consulting" or "Home and Office Organizer" or "Freelancer" or anything you like

- Your mobile phone number

- Your location (city and state)

- Your email address

- If you use LinkedIn, you can also include your LinkedIn profile URL, like this: http://www.linkedin.com/in/lizryan

You can include a graphic element on your business cards if you want to, and if there is room on the card. You can change your business cards later if you decide to make changes. You can have new cards printed up at any time. They aren't expensive, so it won't cost you a lot of money if you decide to make changes to your consulting business cards later.

Who will I give my consulting business cards to? Give a card to everyone you come in contact with—your friends, your neighbors, and your relatives.

If you work at a job where you feel comfortable passing out your consulting business cards to your co-workers, do that, but if you aren't sure whether your manager would approve of your after-hours consulting, then don't hand out your business cards at work. You can say, "I started a consulting business, in case you know anyone who might need my help."

If you already know what kind of consulting you want to do, you can mention it. If you don't, then you can leave the topic wide open, the way Jeremy did!

Supposing Someone Calls Me about Consulting, What Do I Do Next?

Let's say that you give out your consulting business cards to two or three dozen people. Somebody might send you an email message and ask you about your consulting business. Here's a sample email correspondence to illustrate how you could respond.

Dear Jeremy,

I hear that you consult with clients for internet projects. I need someone to design a website for me. Can you help me?

> *Thanks,*
> *Alicia*

Dear Alicia,

Thanks for your message! I am not a website designer, but my friend Frank is one, and I can introduce you to him if you are interested in that.

   I work with my clients on their YouTube channels and their social media presence. If you are looking to expand your presence on social media (Facebook, Twitter, Instagram, and LinkedIn, for instance), I can help you with that.

> Thanks,
> Jeremy

Dear Jeremy,

Thanks for your message! Honestly, I don't know what I need. I don't know anything about the internet. I'm a poet. I only know that I need to get the word out there about my poetry. I just had my first "professional" poetry reading after two of my poems were published in a poetry journal. Do I need a website? I'm not sure.

> *Thanks,*
> *Alicia*

Dear Alicia,

I understand what you're saying. Social media and an online presence are new topics to a lot of people. Let's have coffee together and talk about what you need. There's no charge for the coffee meeting.

I can help you figure out what you need to do to let more people know about your poetry.

Congratulations on having those two poems published in the poetry journal, and on your poetry reading! Those are huge accomplishments. Looking forward to meeting you.

> Thanks,
> Jeremy

Dear Jeremy,

You are so kind! I'd love to have coffee. Since I wrote to you, I've had one more poem accepted by a different poetry journal and I'm very excited! How about coffee at Café Zip next Tuesday morning at 10 A.M.?

> *Thanks,*
> *Alicia*

Dear Alicia,

I'll be at my day job on Tuesday morning but how about Tuesday late afternoon, around 5:30 P.M. at Café Zip? Thanks!

> Jeremy

Dear Jeremy,

That sounds great! See you then!

> *All the best,*
> *Alicia*

PART THREE

A very long-standing rule of thumb in the consulting world is this:

Whatever the clients say their problem is, that isn't what their problem really is.

This rule doesn't mean that clients are lying to you or trying to be evasive. They just don't know! Alicia is a perfect example.

ALICIA'S STORY

Alicia thought she was looking for a website designer. Why would Alicia need a website? She thought that she needed a website now that her poetry career is taking off.

Most people will not go looking for Alicia's poetry website, and it will cost her time and money to create and maintain that website, although her poetry so far is not earning her much money.

When Alicia and Jeremy met for coffee, they decided together that Alicia doesn't really need a website. She can use a Facebook page to let people gather and talk about her poetry and to promote her poetry readings and the journals that publish her poems.

Alicia paid Jeremy a small amount to create her Facebook page for her, and now she is reading poetry on her own YouTube channel, as well!

 How does Alicia's experience relate to your situation?

How Should I Set My Consulting Rate?

An easy rule of thumb for establishing your consulting rate is to take your target annual salary and divide it by 2,000. We use the number 2,000 because most full-time employees work about 2,080 hours per year.

Jeremy earns $36,000 per year at his church job, which is not a lot of money for a person with a degree and seven years of tremendous experience working with kids. However, a lot of churches don't have much money, and Jeremy's church is one of those.

Here's the math that Jeremy used to establish his hourly consulting rate:

Annual salary: $36,000
Divided by 2,000: $18/hour

Jeremy earns about $18/hour at his church job.

Because he won't be billing anywhere near 40 hours per week as a consultant for some time (and because $18/hour is a very, very low rate for any sort of consulting in the US), Jeremy bumped his hourly rate from $18 to $30/hour for his consulting clients.

Most consultants add a 30 percent to 50 percent "cushion" to the hourly consulting rate that they get by dividing their annual salary by 2,000 hours. Other consultants add a one hundred percent "cushion" to cover their business expenses.

Thirty dollars an hour is still a very reasonable consulting rate, and Jeremy's clients are happy to pay him that amount. After all, Jeremy's social media help and YouTube videos are doing great things for his clients! What kind of hourly consulting rate could you establish for your services?

Let's build your consulting persona right now! Write in your Mojo Journal your answers to the following:

- What is the name of your consulting business?
- What kind(s) of Business Pain will you relieve for your clients?
- What will you charge your clients for your services?

Write about your consulting business in your Mojo Journal and share your ideas with a friend.

Your assignment is to get a consulting business card and start giving it out to people you know. You can buy your consulting business card online at www.vistaprint.com and have the cards shipped to your house.

Congratulations! You're a consultant now (although you've been a consultant for a long time—it's just that you're giving yourself permission to call yourself a consultant now, at last)!

PART **THREE**

CHECKING IN: TAKING STEPS

You have completed Part Three of your Reinvention Roadmap journey, Taking Steps. Write in your Mojo Journal about the steps you're taking to move into your next career and life chapter!

Fantastic job completing Part Three and three-quarters of your Reinvention Roadmap experience—you are mighty! How will you celebrate your accomplishment?

You're three-quarters of the way through!

PART 4

GROWING MUSCLES and MOJO

Part Four of the Reinvention Roadmap is called Growing Muscles and Mojo. Part Four is the final section of the Reinvention Roadmap. In Part Four we'll talk about keeping your reinvention muscles and mojo growing throughout your career and your life.

Your career is not an equation. It is a not a break/fix scenario, or an event. It is a process. When you stay open to the learning that the world has for you, you will never stop growing!

Let's dive into Part Four!

STEPPING OUT

We've noted many times along this journey that the old working world is dead, and job security is something you carry about with you now. You build up your own job security.

Your job security is in your reputation, your ability to spot an organization's Business Pain and articulate it, your ability to get work as a consultant and/or as an employee, and your ability to keep learning and growing all the time.

Wow! These are different activities than the activities that led to career success in the old working world. Those activities were very different:

- Following instructions

- Completing procedures precisely and repetitively, and fast

- Being "self-motivated" (i.e., making as little fuss and asking as little of a manager as possible)

- Working well with other people

- Accumulating training hours and certifications

- Getting a positive performance review

We still need to be able to work well with other people. That hasn't changed, but the rest of our Old-Working-World Success Factors list has changed dramatically.

Getting a gold star from your manager at your performance review doesn't turn out to mean beans when the whole company could be gone tomorrow.

When you focus all or most of your energy on pleasing other people, including your own manager, you weaken your muscles. Your brain changes and you can easily become very fearful. You can lie in bed at night thinking, "I hope my manager is happy with the report I gave him."

That is not a good state. It's not healthy. When your principal concern is, "What does another, particular adult—my boss, that is—think about me?" you are not in your power.

It's cute when a kid hopes the teacher likes his or her project, especially if the kid has a great teacher who gets excited about the kids' hard work. It is one thing to work hard to impress a teacher when we're 10 years old, but another thing completely to work to impress a boss when we are 25 or 55 or 68 years old.

It's not appropriate or healthy for adults to lie in bed and worry about what another human being thinks of them. We think it's normal because we all grew up with the same ideas about the working world.

We grew up with this idea, especially: "Your boss is in charge, and his or her opinion of you matters more than anything." We grew up believing that we have to please the boss.

The Old Working World Success Factors come from an earlier time. Those days are gone! If you can't buy job security, how do you build job security in yourself? It is a muscle-building exercise.

You have to look at some important topics you might not have dwelt on in the past. Then you have to take steps. You can do it. You are an athlete!

Here are the steps to take to build your own job security into yourself.

BUILD YOUR OWN JOB SECURITY, STEP BY STEP

The kind of job security you want is that you can get work when you need it—and not just any kind of work, but good work that inspires you and that pays you what your talents are worth. Self-contained, self-powered job security is the only real job security there is.

Here are the steps to building your own self-contained, self-powered job security by becoming a champion Pain-Spotter and Pain-Solver!

Answer the Question, "What Business Pain Do I Solve?"

You have to know what kind of Business Pain you solve. Maybe you solve the Business Pain called, "Our company has no IT Security Plan and we are vulnerable."

Or maybe you solve the Business Pain called, "We know how to build great products here, but not how to sell our products effectively."

Become an Expert on "Your" Flavor of Business Pain

You have to know a lot about that type (or those types) of Business Pain. You have to know what it looks like when it shows up. Maybe it looks like inside salespeople so overwhelmed that they can't return phone calls from prospective buyers.

You have to understand "your" type of Business Pain so that you can spot it in your environment. You can learn about your Business Pain specialty online or by asking people you know, or by reading books or the newspaper.

It's worth noting that we don't tell farmers, "Learn about the sun and the rain—they're important to running your farm." If we told a farmer to pay attention to the sun and the rain, the farmer would be insulted. He or she would think we were crazy. Of course farmers know about sun and rain!

Why don't all of us know how the business world works and how people and organizations make money and lose money, develop products and sell them, and invest their money?

These topics affect us all, so why are they so poorly understood by so many people? We think we don't need to know about business, but that's like thinking that we don't need to worry about the weather.

We have to know about everything that affects our lives and our health, and of course the business world and the mechanics of it are critical topics to each of us individually as well as to our families and communities.

Study Your Talent Marketplace

As you work to build your new-millennium career muscles and portable job security, you have to look at the local talent marketplace to see where your Business Pain is most likely to exist. Is your particular kind of Business Pain found in small, large, or medium-sized organizations?

Does it show up when a business is growing, or shrinking, or it is something that afflicts every organization? Once you have an idea where "your" type of Business Pain shows up, you'll create a Target Employer List to focus your job-search efforts.

Brand Yourself for the Jobs You Want

You have to develop your brand. That includes creating your Human-Voiced Resume, your LinkedIn Profile, your consulting business card, and a list of ready Dragon-Slaying Stories for your first Pain Letters.

Zero In on Target Employers and/or Clients

You'll begin to explore and research each of your Target Employers. You'll focus on their current business situation, the trends and news swirling around them, and everything else you can learn about their leadership, their goals, and their challenges.

You'll research your Target Employers online and ask everyone you know what *they* know about each organization on your list.

Find Your Hiring Manager in Each Organization

You will locate your most likely hiring manager in each organization. If you are going after Purchasing Agent jobs, your hiring manager will be the Purchasing Manager. Or instead he or she might be called Materials Manager, Procurement Manager, or Director of Operations. You can use LinkedIn to conduct searches on the Advanced People Search page to find the LinkedIn profile of the person you'll work for in your new job, if this is the right place for you.

If you can't find your exact hiring manager (the person who will be your boss or your client if you go to work for the organization), don't panic. Just go "up" the organization chart and approach your boss's boss, instead. In the case of our Purchasing Manager, that next-higher-level boss might be the Director or VP of Operations, or a Director or VP of Procurement, Materials, or Supply Chain.

Scout around and see who's called what at the organizations on your Target Employer List! You are learning how organizations are structured and what their managers are called.

Customize Your Human-Voiced Resume for the Specific Hiring Manager You're Writing To

There is more than one side to you, and your fantastic experience can't be captured in a one- or two-page resume, even your powerful Human-Voiced Resume.

Every time you send out your Human-Voiced Resume or give it to someone, you'll customize it slightly for the opportunity you're pursuing. You might adjust the Summary at the top of your Human-Voiced Resume for a particular opportunity, or switch Dragon-Slaying Stories in or out of your resume to make it as relevant to your hiring manager's Business Pain as it can be.

Send Your Pain Packet in the Mail

You'll enclose your Human-Voiced Resume and your Pain Letter together in one envelope and send them through the mail to your specific hiring manager working at a particular organization. You'll follow the same process whether you're looking for a job or a consulting assignment.

Track Your Progress and Pat Yourself on the Back

You'll track your outgoing Pain Packets on the same spreadsheet that lists your Target Employers, and then you'll celebrate!

I recommend a nice gelato.

PUTTING THE PIECES TOGETHER

Now you'll think about what you learned as you composed your Pain Letter. Another piece of the big puzzle called "How does this whole Pain-Spotting and Pain-Solving thing work?" has been filled in. Managers will read your letter or they won't; either way is okay, because the right opportunity will find you!

PART FOUR

ARIANA'S STORY

Ariana is a new-millennium working person. She is constantly on the hunt for pain she can solve in her local talent ecosystem.

Ariana worked as a marketing person for a wireless device manufacturer for several years, and when she lost that job she became a marketing person for her local community college.

Now Ariana is job-hunting again. She wants a job that's more interesting and pays more than her community college job did. She would be fine taking a consulting project instead of a job, because she can charge more as a consultant than she'll be likely to earn in a full-time job.

Ariana is learning the fine art of Pain-Spotting. She knows from her two long-term marketing jobs that a lot of organizations have trouble getting people interested in their products and services. She saw the direct correlation between her marketing activities and the customer inquiries and sales that resulted from them.

Ariana doesn't know the statistics that relate marketing expenditures to new sales and she doesn't care about those statistics anyway, because she can only say with certainty that in her two marketing roles, her employers generated a lot more money in new-customer sales after Ariana worked her marketing magic than they paid Ariana. That's okay with her! Ariana wants her employers and clients to prosper.

Now Ariana is looking for marketing pain in her talent ecosystem. She's looking for companies that may not be getting the word out about their products and services as effectively as they might be doing.

Ariana reads the business section of her local paper. She's interested in learning about new businesses. One day she spotted an article about a company that had hired 15 new

team members. *Is all that hiring to keep up with demand for their products, or to spur the demand so that more people buy the products?* she wondered. Ariana figured she'd research the company, called Angry Chocolates, to see what she could learn about them.

She found that Angry Chocolates had won some awards at a national chocolate and candy trade show. It had gotten a lot of new orders in the door from supermarkets and candy shops across the country.

Ariana wrote a Pain Letter to the VP of Marketing at Angry Chocolates, Nelson Jones. Here's the Pain Letter Ariana sent to Nelson:

Dear Nelson,

Congratulations on the Best New Taste award you and the Angry team brought home from Chocoholic Expo 2016! That's a huge feather in your cap.

I can just imagine that with new orders coming in from all over the country and the planet, your talented Marketing team must be taxed to the limit. When I was at Wiggly Devices just before their acquisition by Microsoft, we had a similar problem.

We had to meet demand from resellers around the globe while keeping our loyal domestic customers happy. We created a two-pronged strategy that grew sales 40 percent in one year, to $15M.

If you've got a moment to talk about your plans for Angry's growth, I'd love to hear more.

All the best,
Ariana Vasquez

How did Ariana find Nelson's name and job title? It was easy. Ariana just looked at the Angry Chocolates website, where the names of their managers were listed. She could also have found Nelson's name by searching on LinkedIn. Ariana knew about the Best New Taste award by reading the press releases on the Angry Chocolates website and by Google searching the company name.

Ariana came up with her Pain Hypothesis—the idea that Angry might be stretched having to service new customers they acquired at the Chocoholic Expo while still taking care of their old customers—by thinking about her days at Wiggly Devices. Even

if Ariana hadn't worked at Wiggly when she did, it stands to reason that any company would be stressed by coming home from a trade show with a lot of new customers to service. That's only logical!

Ariana did not have a high-level position at Wiggly Devices. She never said she did! Her title there was Marketing Coordinator. So what? Ariana was part of the marketing team that helped Wiggly Devices grow its sales to $15 million per year. Ariana was part of the team that came up with a two-pronged strategy to take care of their new customers and their old customers at the same time.

How does Ariana's story relate to your story? Write about that in your Mojo Journal.

Ariana's story about her success at Wiggly Devices is an example of a Dragon-Slaying Story. We looked in Part Three at how a Dragon-Slaying Story is a story about a time when you solved a problem at work and came out on top! We all have Dragon-Slaying Stories, but often we don't know we have them. We don't think about them, because we were just doing our job while we were accumulating our Dragon-Slaying Stories.

Long before Ariana wrote her Pain Letter to Nelson, she had made a list of Dragon-Slaying Stories from her career.

You can make a list of your own Dragon-Slaying Stories. You can use your Dragon-Slaying Stories in your LinkedIn profile and in your Human-Voiced Resume.

You can use them in your Pain Letters, the way Ariana did, and use them in job interviews.

ARIANA'S STORY CONTINUED

Ariana composed her Pain Letter, got a white 8.5 × 11-inch envelope, stapled her Pain Letter to the front of her two-page Human-Voiced Resume, and slipped the three pages of information for Nelson into her envelope. Then she got a black Sharpie and printed Nelson's name, job title, company name, and street address on the front of the envelope, right in the center. She printed her own name and address at the upper left of the envelope, took it to the post office, and had the post office clerk weigh and stamp the envelope for her. The clerk took Ariana's envelope, and Ariana went to get a nice gelato. She had sent her first Pain Letter!

Nelson took a week to get back to Ariana. She had started to get nervous during that week. Before Nelson replied to Ariana, her first reaction was, *I won't ever do that again. I won't sit and wait for someone to respond to my Pain Letter. I'll research and send out three or four more Pain Letters, instead of waiting around!*

When Nelson sent Ariana an email message, he said, "Great letter, Ariana. I can tell you're enthusiastic. I don't have any openings right now, but if you want to talk by phone next week, I can make time for that."

Ariana jumped on Nelson's offer of a phone call. A keyhole is a keyhole, after all! Maybe on the phone, Ariana could get Nelson talking about his pain.

She wrote right back to Nelson: "Next week sounds great for a phone call. How is Thursday afternoon?"

Ariana wasn't working, so she could have talked to Nelson at any time, but she wasn't about to say, "I can talk to you at any time!" Ariana already saw herself as a consultant—not as a desperate, needy job-seeker.

Nelson wrote back to say, "Let's do Thursday at 2 P.M."

On their phone call, Nelson told Ariana that he didn't have any openings in Marketing but that he could use some consulting help. "Could you help us out part-time until we figure out whether we'll be able to hire someone new?" he asked.

Ariana thought about that. She didn't want to stop her job search or her consulting outreach for a part-time job, but then again, a keyhole is a keyhole!

"Sure, I can do that," said Ariana. "If you are okay with my consulting rate of thirty-five dollars an hour, I can help you part-time, although my availability does vary somewhat from week to week."

"That's fine," said Nelson. "Come in and meet the team next week!"

Ariana wasn't disappointed that Nelson didn't have a full-time job opening for her. She knew that she got something very valuable when she first got Nelson on the phone and then got a part-time consulting engagement in one of her target firms, Angry Chocolates.

Ariana told her boyfriend, Evan, "Nobody else interviewed for the consulting job I got. It was just me. Isn't that great?"

What are your thoughts about Ariana's Pain Letter and her call with Nelson? Write them in your Mojo Journal.

Here is Ariana's Human-Voiced Resume. Do you see how it sounds like Ariana is a real person, rather than a cardboard cutout or a robot?

Ariana Vasquez

Fayetteville, Arkansas
ariana.catherine.vasquez@gmail.com
303-555-0100
http://www.linkedin.com/in/arianacvasquez

Marketing Specialist

I'm a Product Marketer whose mission is to make tremendous, emerging brands bigger by building excitement through traditional marketing, social media, and hands-on customer events.

At Wiggly Devices, I helped grow the company from $2M to $15M in annual sales. At Northern Community College, I launched marketing programs that vaulted our certification programs from zero sales to $400K in two years.

Northern Community College, Fayetteville, Arkansas
Certificate Programs Marketing Coordinator
2011–2015

I was recruited to Northern Community College to build enrollment in our certificate programs. We worked hard to get our top three certificate programs to peak enrollment—the maximum number of students our facility could support.

We did that within two years and got huge acclaim from students, graduates, and employers for the high quality of our programs and their value. We reached prospective students online, at live events, through email and via social media, and we created a huge buzz around our programs.

Wiggly Devices, Fayetteville, Arkansas
Marketing Analyst
2005–2011

I joined Wiggly when it was growing out of its first office/manufacturing space and selling $2M in devices per year. I helped Wiggly grow to $15M/year in sales by building training tools for the sales force, creating sharp marketing materials, and listening to our customers and salespeople.

Education

Townsville State College, Rogers, Arkansas
B.A. Marketing, 2005

Interests

Volunteer, Habitat for Humanity since 2010
American Marketing Association member
La Leche League Education Committee chair, 2012–2013

Begin writing about yourself. You can write in your Mojo Journal or work on your LinkedIn profile. Write about yourself the way Ariana described herself in her Human-Voiced Resume—that is, with a human voice instead of standard corporate or institutional zombie language.

CHAPTER

TWENTY-ONE

WRITING YOUR HUMAN-VOICED RESUME

What makes a resume a Human-Voiced Resume?

A Human-Voiced Resume sounds like a living person is talking, rather than a machine. Most of us have been taught to write as though we're machines, instead of people. That's not good for us, or for the poor people who have to read our resumes! You aren't writing a resume for a machine—an automated applicant tracking system. You're writing for a human reader (your hiring manager).

Humans like to read interesting things, and who can blame them? Your Human-Voiced Resume will be a lot more fun to read than an awful, zombietastic traditional resume!

HOW TO PUT A HUMAN VOICE IN YOUR RESUME

To begin writing your Human-Voiced Resume, think about the Business Pain you solve. Think about "your" flavor of Business Pain the way the person who's experiencing the pain (your hiring manager) thinks about it.

How does "your" flavor of Business Pain show up? How does a manager become aware that he or she is suffering from the kind of Business Pain you solve?

DID YOU BRING THE PAIN RELIEVER?

- Does it show up in the form of unhappy customers, or falling sales?

- Does it show up in the form of frustrated employees and staff turnover?

- Does it manifest itself as increased expenses?

Ariana began her Human-Voiced Resume by explaining that she's a marketing person who is very interested in increasing sales. Although every Marketing department in the world was launched to increase sales, very few Marketing people brand themselves as people who understand that sales are important and that increased sales are a very good thing. Instead, most Marketing people use their resume to tell you what you already know—that they create marketing programs! They tell you that they know how to create marketing brochures, write press releases, and organize events.

Sadly, nearly every Marketing person brands himself or herself the same way, so that in the end they all sound alike. It's not just Marketing people who brand themselves in the most fall-asleepy way they can. Nearly everyone does it!

Why do you think most people write about themselves in the same boring way? Answer that question in your Mojo Journal!

Most of us have been taught to write about ourselves as though we were just bundles of skills and credentials. We are not! We have powerful stories to tell. Each of us is completely different from everyone else. Ariana told her story in her Human-Voiced Resume. You can do the same thing!

Once you are clear on the kind of Business Pain you solve, you can begin writing your Human-Voiced Resume Summary. In the first sentence, tell us what function you perform and how you view your function.

Ariana used the first sentence of her Human-Voiced Resume Summary to tell us that she markets products for small brands that want to get bigger.

Ariana took a chance. She didn't say, "I want to do Marketing for some company—any company!" She focused her sights on small companies like Angry Chocolates. That's the kind of Marketing that interests Ariana the most. She uses the word "exciting" in her Human-Voiced Resume Summary. She is a human being and she has emotions, and she brings her emotions to work with her. She wants people to get excited about the products she markets, but first she has to get excited about them!

Once Ariana communicated her function (marketing) in her Summary and told us how she views her marketing mission, Ariana told a short Dragon-Slaying Story—right in her Human-Voiced Resume Summary!

She knows that hiring managers like Nelson are busy. Their attention spans are short. She jumped right into a story—but why? Ariana wants Nelson and every hiring manager she approaches in her job search to know that she sees how the dots are connected in the organizations she works for.

She doesn't just understand marketing—she also knows why her marketing projects are important to her employer, and in particular to her manager. That's the person who must know the value of Ariana's work—not to the world in general, but to himself!

Once her Summary was completed and Ariana was happy with it, she set to work writing short descriptions of the two marketing jobs she's held so far. Ariana told the story of each job.

She told us what she came to accomplish at each organization and how she fulfilled that mission.

Notice that Ariana doesn't brag or praise herself in her Human-Voiced Resume! Here are three more things she doesn't do in her Human-Voiced Resume:

1 Ariana doesn't use zombie words or phrases like "Results-oriented professional," "Motivated self-starter with a bottom-line orientation," or "Meets or exceeds target requirements."

2 Ariana doesn't tell us about her daily or weekly tasks and to-do items on two jobs she's held so far. She knows that we are smart enough to figure out what a Marketing person does without her help.

3 Ariana doesn't tell us about her trophies. She doesn't mention that she got an excellent performance review or that she was voted Employee of the Month one time at the community college. There is nothing wrong with acknowledgment from other people, but Ariana is not content to brand herself by saying, "Look how well other people like me!"

Ariana wants her story, her voice, and her personality to take the reader (Nelson, in this case) to a different place—seeing in her resume a possible answer to a problem that's bothering him.

Ariana doesn't want Nelson to be focused on her as he reads her Human-Voiced Resume, but rather on himself—and the pain that Ariana could solve for him!

WRITING YOUR HUMAN-VOICED RESUME, STEP BY STEP

To write your Human-Voiced Resume, you'll need to know a few things.

Determine Your Brand

You'll need to know what sort of work you want to focus on as you brand yourself in this edition of your Human-Voiced Resume. You aren't stuck with just one brand. You can write as many versions of your Human-Voiced Resume as you want, but keep in mind that you can only have one LinkedIn profile at a time. Hiring managers who receive your Human-Voiced Resume and who are interested in learning more about you are going to jump to your LinkedIn profile right away, so your LinkedIn profile has to bear some resemblance to every version of your Human-Voiced Resume.

In order to begin writing your Human-Voiced Resume, you need to know which area of career focus this version of your Human-Voiced Resume will emphasize. For our example, let's pretend that your name is Alex and that you're writing your Human-Voiced Resume with not-for-profit fundraising jobs in mind.

You've done some not-for-profit fundraising before and you've also worked in a few corporate Marketing jobs. You're going to use both of these experiences to make the case in your Human-Voiced Resume that you can raise money for the not-for-profit you intend to work for next.

Have Your List of Jobs Handy

You need a list of the jobs you've already held and the approximate starting and ending dates for each job. You don't have to include every job you've ever held in your Human-Voiced Resume. You don't have to go back to the beginning of time. It's up to you how far to go back in your career history as you compose your Human-Voiced Resume. Keep in mind that your Human-Voiced Resume can be one or two pages long and no longer.

Your Human-Voiced Resume's job is to get you a job interview—not to share every detail of your life so far.

Write Your Contact Information

Once you've got an idea how you want to brand yourself in your Human-Voiced Resume (in Alex's case, that brand will be "not-for-profit fund-raiser"), and once you've got the details about your past jobs handy, you're ready to start writing!

You'll begin your Human-Voiced Resume by writing your name and contact information at the top. You don't need to include your street address, like "123 Park Avenue." You can skip that information and simply include your city and state. Few if any employers are going to send you snail mail at home. You'll include your name and your telephone number, email address, and LinkedIn profile URL. Be sure to customize your LinkedIn profile URL so that it shows your name, like this: http://www.linkedin.com/in/lizryan (see box at the top of the next page for instructions). You are rocking and rolling now!

Here is the Contact section at the top of Alex's Human-Voiced Resume.

Alex Vega
Montclair, New Jersey
alexconradvega@gmail.com
Alex's phone number
http://www.linkedin.com/alexconradvega

CUSTOMIZING YOUR LINKEDIN PROFILE

You can customize your LinkedIn profile URL by clicking on the Edit Profile page and then clicking on the little gear-shaped icon below your profile photo. That will take you to a page where you can customize your public LinkedIn profile, and on that page you can create your customized LinkedIn profile URL, the one with your name in it. You can use that customized LinkedIn profile URL on your Human-Voiced Resume, your consulting business cards, and your email signature.

Compose Your Human-Voiced Resume Summary

The next part of your Human-Voiced Resume that you'll compose is the Summary at the top. To compose your Human-Voiced Resume Summary, begin with a sentence (not a zombietastic sentence fragment!) that tells the reader what you do professionally and either why or how. Here is the first sentence of Alex's Human-Voiced Resume Summary:

> I'm a not-for-profit fundraiser whose mission is to help donors make a tangible difference by supporting causes that speak to them.

Alex tells us he's a not-for-profit fundraiser right away. That's vitally important. Maybe in another version of his Human-Voiced Resume, Alex will emphasize his Marketing background and his views on Marketing, but today Alex is in his not-for-profit fundraising persona. Alex can do more than one thing well—the same way you can!

Alex has told us in his first sentence that he's a not-for-profit fundraiser, but a lot of people do the same kind of fundraising work that Alex does. Alex tells us a little more. He tells us why he does what he does. He's passionate about giving a voice to the people who donate to his organization's work. Everybody wants to have influence on this world we live in, and why shouldn't they? People get to choose how to spend their money. A lot of people choose to contribute to worthy causes, and Alex views his fundraising work as an almost sacred responsibility to connect the donors who want to help with the good work his not-for-profit agency employer is doing.

Not every single not-for-profit Executive Director will like Alex's approach to telling his story. That's fine! Alex doesn't need every Executive Director to appreciate his brand of jazz. His Human-Voiced Resume is a branding document. Its purpose, like every branding message, is to attract the right people and repel the wrong ones. Alex doesn't have time to waste talking with people who aren't likely to resonate at his frequency and vice versa.

Alex's Human-Voiced Resume Summary is three sentences long. It packs a lot of power into three sentences. Here is Alex's full Human-Voiced Resume Summary:

PART **FOUR**

Not-for-Profit Fundraiser

I'm a not-for-profit fundraiser whose mission is to help donors make a tangible difference by supporting causes that speak to them. I began fundraising for my university alumni association as an undergrad and have raised over $4M in donations from corporations, foundations, and individuals. At the Frog and Toad Society, my fundraising events and social media campaigns generated $1.2M in donations in one year, doubling the organization's operating budget.

Any Executive Director reading Alex's Human-Voiced Resume will see that Alex has a knack for fundraising, and also that Alex works on the modest end of the fundraising spectrum, dollars-and-cents-wise. Four million dollars is a lot of money to you and me, but many large not-for-profit organizations raise many times more money than that. That's okay!

Alex is not trying to compete with multi-skillion-dollar fundraisers for his next job. He is looking for a smaller agency where an extra $1.2 million coming in the door would cause everyone to bust into an impromptu dance party. Alex doesn't need to make excuses or apologize for his background or his accomplishments, and neither do you.

Most people undervalue themselves. You have done amazing things in your life so far. I hope you are writing about them in your Mojo Journal to remind yourself of some of the incredible things you've done.

Add Your Career History

After the Summary, Alex is going to move on to his career history. Alex will list his past jobs in reverse chronological order. He'll start with his most recent job. That job wasn't a not-for-profit fundraising job, but Alex is not deterred. His last job was a corporate Marketing job. Alex is going to talk about how he got his tight-fisted bosses to part with $30,000 to fund Alex's ambitious community-involvement program. That program was a big success, so naturally Alex wants to tell the story!

Angry Chocolates, Fayetteville, Arkansas
Marketing Director
2009–2014

I was brought on board at Angry Chocolates, a $10M specialty chocolate maker, to bring the company to national prominence. We had just begun selling our chocolates at Whole Foods across the U.S. and had a much bigger market to support.

First, Alex tells us his mission. He tells us why he was asked to join Angry Chocolates. He sets the stage for the reader, who may never have heard of Angry Chocolates. Now, Alex lists his three favorite Dragon-Slaying Stories from his Angry Chocolate days.

- I conceived a community involvement program to introduce Angry Chocolates to our consumer fans, sold the program to our CEO, and secured $30,000 in funding for the launch. The Angry Facebook fan page is now responsible for 40 percent of the company's direct-to-consumer online sales.

- To support the national Whole Foods launch, my team and I built an interactive "How can chocolates be angry?" page with video featuring our team members and a tie-in to in-store promotions at over 250 Whole Foods stores. In one weekend we generated one million page views and our highest two-day revenue number ever (over $500K).

- I left Angry Chocolates when I moved to New Jersey, where my partner lives.

Why did Alex talk about moving to New Jersey in his third bullet point? Alex wants to answer the question nearly every hiring manager will have: "Why do you live in New Jersey now, if you had a job in Arkansas last year? What happened in your life, that got you to New Jersey?"

Alex didn't have to share his personal information, but he wanted to. He thought that it would be silly to leave the question, "Did this guy get kicked out of the state of Arkansas, or what?" hanging in the air while a hiring manager read through his Human-Voiced Resume.

Alex is a marketer. He knows that one of the principal functions of communication is to reduce uncertainty. Alex wants to reduce any uncertainty that a reader of his Human-Voiced Resume might feel when they see that he worked in Arkansas but now he's living in New Jersey. If Alex had wanted to, he could have explained his cross-country move in his Summary instead of in the final bullet under Angry Chocolates.

In that case, here's how Alex's Human-Voiced Resume Summary would have read:

Not-for-Profit Fundraiser

I'm a not-for-profit fundraiser whose mission is to help donors make a tangible difference by supporting causes that speak to them. I began fundraising for my university alumni association as an undergrad and have raised over $4M in donations from corporations, foundations, and individuals. At the Frog and Toad Society, my fundraising events and social media campaigns generated $1.2M in donations in one year, doubling the organization's operating budget. I've recently returned to New Jersey, where I grew up, and am looking for my next adventure.

Alex will continue describing his past jobs as he writes the remainder of his Human-Voiced Resume. For each job, he'll list the employer name and location, his job title, and the dates he held each job. Alex will only list the years he spent at each job—not the months. He'll use the location where he worked, not the company headquarters, which may be located somewhere completely different.

Alex will add page numbers to his Human-Voiced Resume. He's learning to brand himself in a human way!

Alex's most recent job was his job at Angry Chocolates. That was a corporate Marketing job. Yet Alex is branding himself a not-for-profit fundraiser. That's fine—because Alex is a not-for-profit fundraiser, and a really good one! Many executive directors who head up cash-starved not-for-profit agencies would kill to meet a sharp corporate Marketing person who can translate what they know about corporate Marketing to the not-for-profit world.

Undoubtedly there are some not-for-profit executive directors who will turn up their noses at Alex's non-cookie-cutter fundraising background. Alex isn't worried about that.

Alex has been around the block a few times, as the saying goes. He has worked with many different people.

He doesn't have the emotional energy to waste on trying to be someone he's not in order to please people who wouldn't find the "real Alex" acceptable. Alex says, "God bless those people, but I don't want to work with them. I have to bring myself to work, or I don't want the job."

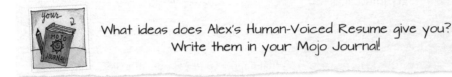

What ideas does Alex's Human-Voiced Resume give you?
Write them in your Mojo Journal!

I invented Human-Voiced Resumes, Pain Letters, and the rest of the Whole Person Job Search approach you are learning because I saw that the traditional job-search approach was broken beyond repair. Our species has been evolving since we showed up and we're not through evolving yet—thank goodness! We are evolving away from zombietastic resumes and talent-repelling online application systems. We are waking up to remember that only human beings powered by mojo fuel our organizations' forward motion.

Don't panic if your first attempt at writing your Human-Voiced Resume doesn't thrill you. Writing takes time. You can work on your Human-Voiced Resume for a few minutes at a time, whenever you have a little time to spare. You can get your friends' help on your Human-Voiced Resume, too, but don't let them talk you into reverting back to zombie-speak language!

AVOID ZOMBIETASTIC RESUME PHRASES

Make sure that the traditional zombietastic resume phrases listed below (and their fifty gazillion cousins and offspring) don't creep back into your Human-Voiced Resume!

- Results-oriented Professional with a bottom-line orientation
- Motivated self-starter
- Superior communication skills
- Savvy/seasoned/strategic Business Professional
- Meets or exceeds expectations
- Skilled at leading cross-functional/high-performing teams
- Proven track record of success
- Progressively more responsible positions
- Strategic visionary
- Dynamic Industry Leader

You can give permission to step out of the traditional how-to-write-a-resume box and sound like yourself in your Human-Voiced Resume. When you do, you'll feel stronger and more powerful. You'll feel more confident as you remember that only the people who get you, deserve you—so why write zombie-speak language in an effort to try and please or impress people who don't deserve your talents in the first place?

Begin composing or continue working on your Human-Voiced Resume.

Take your time. You can work on your Human-Voiced Resume for a few minutes every day, or all in one sitting. You'll never be "done" with your Human-Voiced Resume, because you can change it, reframe it, or rework it at any time. So, enjoy the journey!

CHAPTER
TWENTY-TWO

A PLACE TO PUT
YOUR CANOE IN THE WATER

If reinvention were out of our hands, we wouldn't have to look in the mirror or retrace our steps. We can imagine an alternate universe where somebody else—a top-secret branch of the government, let's say—managed our careers and told us which jobs to do.

In that alternate universe, you might file a Form R (for Reinvention) on a government website and then wait six to eight weeks to get a letter in the mail telling you what your new job and your new career path would be. You wouldn't have any choice in your career path in that alternate universe, but at least you wouldn't have to do any work to decide on your new career! Somebody else would make your career decisions for you.

Here in our universe things don't work that way. There is no government agency that tells people what sort of work to do. If you wait for the government to put you into a job, you will wait a very long time!

You have to find work—and the right work, not just any random job—on your own.

You don't have to know your dream career path in order to start your talent-market exploration. You can choose a place to start your career research. We call this spot A Place to Put Your Canoe in the Water.

The real world changes all the time. You can think about your path so far and think about what's important to you, then use that self-reflection to narrow your new career direction from "I just want a job—any job!" to a smaller patch of ground.

You might not know exactly which jobs to focus your job-search efforts on. That's okay! You can begin your job search as soon as you have an idea of at least one type of job that you would enjoy, that can pay you enough to live on and that would make great use of your talents.

 Can you think about and list job titles that meet these three requirements? Write your ideas about possible job titles in your Mojo Journal.

HOW MUCH WILL I GET PAID?

Before you can begin a job search, you have to know what your talents are worth. You will benefit by conducting enough salary research to understand what your background and talents will be worth to employers in the jobs you're most interested in!

A great way to begin the salary-research process is by searching familiar job titles on salary-research sites. Salary.com, Payscale.com, and Glassdoor.com. Salary.com and Payscale.com are sites that share salary information on lots of different job titles. Glassdoor.com is a site where current and past employees rate their employers, but lots of people leave comments on Glassdoor that include salary information, too. Think of job titles you've held already and other job titles that you are interested in learning more about. There's almost never a salary range in the job ad, but researching these sites will allow you to know what a given job should pay.

Take a break from your Reinvention Roadmap and go conduct online salary research now.

 Which job titles did you search for on Salary.com, Payscale.com, and/or Glassdoor.com? Write about them in your Mojo Journal, and answer these questions:

What did you learn about your talent-market salary range through your online research?

What impact on your job search or your career path will your new salary information have?

Did your salary research project shift your thinking about your career path?

Researching job titles to learn what other employees get paid is a basic form of research that every job-seeker should perform. It's important to know what people get paid in the job titles you are most interested in or most likely to pursue in your job search.

There are other ways to research your market compensation value, too!

COST OF BUSINESS PAIN EXERCISE

One important exercise for you to conduct is called the Cost of Business Pain exercise. This is an exercise that involves a series of questions about the value you create for employers and/or clients when you solve their problems. Write your answers to the Cost of Business Pain questions below in your Mojo Journal.

You can make reasonable assumptions about the cost of the big problem—the Business Pain—that you will relieve for your next employer, and use those assumptions to estimate the cost of the Business Pain you will solve for your employers and/or clients. To complete the Cost of Business Pain exercise, choose a hiring manager on your Target Employer List, and answer these questions about him or her:

1 What is the Business Pain you intend to relieve for this hiring manager?

2 Why is this type of Business Pain a big enough problem for the manager that he or she would consider paying you to relieve it?

3 How does this type of Business Pain cost your target hiring manager's company money?

4 How much money is your hiring manager's company wasting as the Business Pain goes unresolved?

BASIA'S STORY

I work as a National Accounts Supervisor for a computer supplies distribution company. I spend most of my day on the telephone and using email to track down orders for my clients. I like my job, but I'm pretty sure I could earn more money doing something else. I'm not in a rush to get a new job, but I'm bored, and when I think about spending another year or two on this job, the thought is very depressing.

There is nothing creative in my job, and when I try to stretch my job description to do something more interesting, my manager tells me to "stick to my knitting." That's her way of saying, "Don't do anything that isn't specifically required by your job description!"

I want to start a job search. I'm interested in three different career areas so far. One of them is marketing communications. I know that I could be successful writing marketing copy, creating marketing plans, and working with website designers and developers. I haven't done that kind of work before, but I would like to explore it.

The second area I'm interested in is education. I do a lot of coaching and training in my job, on the phone and using email. I coach and teach my customers and the account reps in my department. Lastly, I'm interested in leadership.

I'm called a National Accounts Supervisor, but as I mentioned earlier, my boss is a very commanding and controlling person. There's no room for me to do more than check in on the account reps in our department and make sure they have what they need to hit their numbers every week.

Basia completes the Path Exercise and gets several powerful "Aha!"s from that experience. Here's how she describes her "Aha!"s after completing the Path Exercise:

I realized as I wrote about and thought about my path in life that I am a natural teacher. When I was a little girl I wanted to be a teacher, but that wasn't possible because when I moved to the country where I live now, I didn't speak the language. I couldn't be a teacher without being fluent. Now I am fluent, but I don't think I want to teach in a classroom.

I can teach people in many different settings. I know that I want to do some kind of teaching or training in my next job. I also realized while working on the Path Exercise that I like to work in a group. I don't like solitary work. I realized that not everyone can easily teach other people something they've learned. Thinking about my path made me a little less interested in marketing and more interested in coaching, training, and leadership.

There's nothing wrong with marketing and I'd still like to learn more about it. If I can get a leadership job with some coaching or training in it, I wouldn't need for my job to involve marketing.

I do like communicating in writing and I think that's one reason I talked about wanting to get into marketing before I completed the Path Exercise. Now I realize that I'll be communicating ideas in writing in almost any job.

Basia decided that she wanted to focus on leadership jobs that involved coaching and/or training. She wrote this LinkedIn Summary for her LinkedIn Profile:

> I'm a coach and trainer to my teammates, who are account reps for Excellent Computer Products. My colleagues and I take care of our company's national accounts by expediting their orders, keeping them up to date on new products and making it easy for them to work with us.

Basia isn't going to mention in her LinkedIn profile that she's job-hunting, because her boss or anyone at Excellent Computer Products might see her LinkedIn profile. She doesn't want anyone to know that she's job-hunting until she accepts a job offer and gives notice to her boss.

Still, Basia knows that hiring managers who receive her Pain Letters and Human-Voiced Resumes will jump straight to her LinkedIn profile and read her Summary. She will make it easy for them to do that by including the URL (website address) to her LinkedIn profile in her Human-Voiced Resume.

Basia decides to begin her job search with just one prong, or career direction. She writes her Human-Voiced Resume Summary this way:

Supervisor/Team Leader and Coach

I'm a Supervisor who's passionate about training and coaching my teammates so they excel at their jobs and feel good about their work. I've been managing the National Account Management team at Excellent Computer Products, a $100M computer supplies distributor with clients all over the world.

I hired, coached, and trained my 14 teammates to beat their sales targets for the last nine out of 13 months. I'm ready for a new challenge and excited to help build a team or take it to the next level.

Basia isn't sure what kinds of supervisory jobs she'll apply for. That's okay! She will read job ads and respond to some of those she finds. She'll also research employers that don't have job ads posted—employers that she's interested in learning more about or possibly working for.

How will Basia find those employers?

Basia creates a Target Employer List for her job search. She uses a spreadsheet program for her Target Employer List, but she could have created her list on paper, too.

She begins her Target Employer List by reading her local newspaper's list of fastest-growing companies. She's interested in working in a fast-growth company, since she hasn't done that before. Excellent Computer Products has been about the same size (in annual sales) since Basia started working there five years before. Basia starts her Target Employer List with six of the 50 fastest-growing companies in her town from the newspaper list.

Basia chooses her first six Target Employers from the 50 organizations on the newspaper's list by reading about each fast-growing company in the newspaper's story and then visiting the websites of the companies she's curious about.

Basia is happy to have the first 10 employers listed on her Target Employer List. She wants to build her Target Employer List to 50 organizations before she starts her job search. Her plan is to work at her current job during the day and to job-hunt at night and on the weekends.

Her job search will be a stealth job search. She won't tell anyone except her closest friends and family members that she's job-hunting until she gets her new job. Basia isn't about to invest the time and energy her stealth job search will require just to get a change of scenery! She has five items on her New Job Wish List:

- I have to work in a more open, human environment. I need to get out of Excellent Computer Products and into a Human Workplace! I'll be able to tell through the interview process whether or not each company I meet with is a Human Workplace.

- I need to be in a real supervisory position, where I can work closely with my teammates and build the sense of community that my current team lacks.

- I need to earn at least $10,000 per year more than I'm earning now.

- I need to work around people who are excited about a mission—something I don't get to do now.
- Lastly, I need a new job where I can continue to learn and grow.

Basia knows that not all of the 10 companies she has just added to her Target Employer List will have published job openings for Supervisors (or for anyone, for that matter). She doesn't care about that.

She's not worried about whether any of the organizations that end up on her Target Employer List have posted job openings or not.

Basia is going to reach out to a hiring manager or decision-maker in each company on her list whether they have a posted job opening (or more than one) or not.

If the organization is very small, Basia will write directly to the CEO or President of the company. She will send each CEO or President a Pain Letter composed just for him or her.

If the organization appears from its website to be bigger than 100 employees, Basia will look for a hiring manager inside the organization who leads a large enough team that he or she might have supervisors or team leaders to help him or her out.

Why doesn't Basia write to the HR Manager at each of her Target Employers? Basia might write to a few HR Managers. She wouldn't mind working in HR, a department that often has needs for people to train and coach employees. When Basia is researching each employer on her Target Employer List, she'll look to see whether the organization has an HR Manager or not. Still, unless Basia is pursuing an HR job, she won't focus her job-search efforts on any organization's HR Manager. She knows that sadly, many HR people would only take her Pain Letter and put it into a pile and send her a "no thanks" message back—if she got any reply at all. Basia knows that the recruiting process in many or most organizations is broken. She isn't relying on HR people in her Target Employers to find a manager who could use Basia's talents. She is looking for those managers on her own!

What are some job titles or career paths Basia could investigate in order to get more involved in marketing, leadership, and coaching or training? Write your ideas in your Mojo Journal. What items are on your New Job Wish List? Write them in your Mojo Journal.

How will you find your new career direction? You'll look at what you do well, what you love to do, and what employers or clients will pay you to do. You'll look for the point where your passions (the things you care about), your talents (things you do especially well), and the Business Pain you solve all come together.

In your Mojo Journal, make a list of things you love to do. Include things you love to do at home and things you love to do at work! Now, make a list of things you're good at—at work and at home.

DON'T GET DISCOURAGED READING JOB ADS!

As you browse published job ads, don't get discouraged by job ads that ask for long lists of qualifications and certifications. No one has all those qualifications and if they did, they probably wouldn't take the job anyway! You can apply for any job for which you possess 40 percent of the listed qualifications. Don't be afraid to apply for a job just because you don't have every requirement listed in the job ad. Go ahead and send a Pain Letter anyway—it can't hurt you!

HOW DO I FIND MY PLACE TO PUT A CANOE IN THE WATER?

To figure out which of the things you love to do and the things you're good at that will also solve Business Pain for employers, we need a research tool. Luckily, we've got one! Go to Indeed.com and search the available positions in your area (or any region where you might be interested in living and working). Use terms from the lists of Things I Love to Do and Things I'm Good At that you wrote earlier for your search on Indeed.com.

HEATHER'S "AHA!" STORY

I love to do conflict resolution, but I'm an IT person. I didn't expect to see "conflict resolution" in many IT job ads, but I was surprised! I found three IT job ads that all included the phrase "conflict resolution." It hit me that if three different IT hiring managers used the phrase "conflict resolution" in their IT job ads, I should mention my experience with and interest in conflict resolution in every one of my Pain Letters. Surely every IT Director or CIO must have the same issues to face. Maybe I can use my conflict resolution experience in my IT career after all!

What are your thoughts about Heather's conflict-resolution "Aha!"? Write them in your Mojo Journal.

EZRA, TIERNEY, AND DIETER PUT CANOES IN THE WATER

EZRA'S STORY

I got way too analytical when it came to choosing my new career direction during reinvention. My old career direction was gone. My field went away—there aren't any jobs, so I knew I had to choose a new career path. I'm 45, so I have a lot of years to go before retirement, if I ever retire.

I was too analytical at first, but then I thought, "I just need to get this job search started!" I rebranded myself as a Project Manager, because that's what I love to do. I'm writing my Human-Voiced Resume to emphasize my project management experience.

I don't know if I'll end up doing a Project Management job or something else. I'm just exploring. It's fun to write Pain Letters and send them out. Every time I write a new Pain Letter, I feel more competent and more confident. I'm stepping into my consulting persona by writing Pain Letters!

What are your thoughts about Ezra's story? Write them in your Mojo Journal.

TIERNEY'S STORY

I was a college athlete. After college I was a ski instructor, a swim coach, and a nanny. I did that for 10 years, hoping that one of my three career paths would take off.

That didn't happen. I guess I didn't go about my career the right way, but I learned a lot.

When it finally hit me that my career was going nowhere, I decided to step back and look at my options. I know that sports and athletics are my first love, career-wise.

I looked into a Fitness Management certificate at college but I talked to several Athletic Directors who told me that they wouldn't hire someone with a certificate unless they also had a lot of athletics leadership experience.

I decided to focus on getting the experience and think about a certificate later if I still needed one. I took a part-time job managing the swim instructors at a health club near my house. The job was a lot like my other part-time jobs, except it was a leadership job instead of hands-on coaching with young swimmers.

I made that half-time job the focus of my path. I took my leadership role very seriously, so seriously that my boss Rachel said, "I appreciate your professionalism, Tierney."

After four months I got a three-quarter-time job running the aquatics program at a private school. Now I had two swimming-related jobs and I stopped being a nanny and a ski instructor.

I told both my bosses about my desire to work full-time in aquatics management. I told them that I very much appreciated both of my part-time jobs (which added up to more hours than one full-time job) but that I needed to pursue a full-time job in aquatics leadership. Both my bosses took my request seriously. Rachel at the health club said, "I could make you the full-time Aquatics Team Leader if you would also teach the moms-and-tots swim class for me. That way I could justify your full-time salary."

So, that's what I did. I took the Aquatics Team Leader job and quit my job at the private school. Now I'm in the field of athletics leadership, 10 years after college, but that's okay!

I Put My Canoe in the Water in the actual water, and now my goal is to learn all I can here and then run an aquatics program overall for a community center, parks department, or fitness club.

I love my new job and I especially love the fact that I have a goal for my career now. I'm driving my career from now on!

 What are your thoughts about Tierney's Canoe in the Water story? Write them in your Mojo Journal.

DIETER'S STORY

I had no idea where to begin my job search. I know what I love to do and what I'm good at, but I wasn't sure how to wrap those things into my job search.

I'm good at organizing complicated systems and taking massive amounts of information and analyzing them to help people make better decisions.

I knew I had to zero in on a specific career direction for my job search, or else I wouldn't be able to brand myself for specific jobs I might be interested in.

I found a job opening that I thought would be interesting for me and that would really use my abilities. It's a Senior Data Analyst job. Spotting that Senior Data Analyst job ad helped me figure out where to Put My Canoe in the Water, because it was the exact kind of job I know I could do well and not everybody can.

I sent a Pain Letter to the hiring manager for that job. I couldn't find the exact hiring manager because the company is fairly large, so I sent my Pain Letter to the Chief Technical Officer and it worked.

I got a call back about an interview with the actual hiring manager for my target job. His name is Harold, and I'm meeting him next week.

 What are your thoughts about Dieter's story? Write them in your Mojo Journal.

 Where will you Put Your Canoe in the Water for your reinvention job search? Write your thoughts in your Mojo Journal!

QUESTIONS AND ANSWERS ABOUT PUTTING YOUR CANOE IN THE WATER

What if I have absolutely no idea how to zero in on the kinds of jobs that would be a good fit for me? I know more about what I don't want to do in my career than what I do want to do.

That's okay! You can read job ads until you find one or more that look interesting or make you think, "I could do that job!"

Write a Pain Letter and send it to your hiring manager. Most of the learning in your job search will come through trying new things. Try applying for a job that's different than the jobs you've held so far. Your clarity around your new career path will come in time as you step into new territory and learn more and more about it—and about yourself!

I keep changing my mind about my new career direction. Sometimes I think I want to go one way, and then the next day I have a different idea. What should I do?

You can have as many career directions as you want to! We call these career sub-direction Prongs. You can have three, four, or five prongs in your job search, but you have to manage each prong separately. (We'll look at prongs more in the next chapter!) You'll need a separate version of your Human-Voiced Resume for each prong you are pursuing in your job search.

Think carefully before you decide to create several different prongs for your job search, though, because the more clearly you can brand yourself for the specific jobs you want, the more successful your job search will be!

Where will you Put Your Canoe in the Water for your reinvention job search? Write your thoughts in your Mojo Journal.

You are getting really good at understanding Business Pain and your own place in the economic ecosystem around you. Now it's time to start taking bigger steps! Can you take one of these steps now?

- Take on a consulting project for a friend or family member and use it to launch your consulting business.

- Reach out to a local businessperson with whom you don't share any mutual friends or acquaintances. Ask him or her to have coffee with you.

- Send out a Pain Packet!

USING PRONGS IN YOUR JOB SEARCH

Greta is using three prongs in her job search. Greta considers herself a marketing person, but she could easily perform a full-time Public Relations job and she's also done some not-for-profit fundraising.

Greta loves marketing, PR, and fundraising. All three of her prongs can take her into jobs she would love and be good at. Greta realizes that she's going to need three versions of her Human-Voiced Resume for her job search.

One version of her Human-Voiced Resume will focus on marketing jobs that might include public relations, but won't be limited to PR projects.

A second version of her Human-Voiced Resume will focus on public relations work.

The third version of Greta's Human-Voiced Resume will emphasize her fundraising experience.

Greta is happy about her three prongs but she also knows that she has to wrap her three prongs together into one LinkedIn profile.

 What are your thoughts about using sub-brands or prongs in your job search? Write your thoughts in your Mojo Journal.

Emily, Joaquin, and Marcel Talk about Business Pain

Emily's Story

I've been an office person since I graduated high school, and now I'm a part-time community college student, too. I never thought about what kind of Business Pain I solve, but now I think about it all the time! I keep a busy office organized. That's a big problem for a lot of companies. They have procedures, but people don't know them.

When your office is disorganized, you can't run your business well. It's expensive for you and awful for your customers!

My consulting clients are small businesses. They hear about me from my other clients. Maybe they never took the time to write procedures—then I'll do it for them! Their staff members don't know how their office works. They don't even necessarily know how the business functions! That's another common problem.

I work full-time, but I also have a part-time consulting business. My business is called The Streamlined Office. I took a photo of a flowing stream on my phone and I scanned it onto my business card. The cards look great! I charge my consulting clients thirty dollars an hour. I write procedures for them, teach their staff members how to take care of things they aren't familiar with, and help them make their offices more efficient. I consult at night and on the weekends, and my clients love it.

I made $6,000 consulting last year, on top of my full-time salary!

 What can you take away from Emily's story and apply to your own situation?

Joaquin's Story

I'm an IT person, and it isn't that hard to find a job, once you have a network. I've been working in IT for five years. The big new thing in IT is information security. Everybody is worried about getting hacked. That's one of the worst things that can happen to a company, large or small. I took two online courses in IT security and I read a lot on my own.

The last time I looked for a new job, it took me four months, and that's a really long time to be without an income. I should have been eligible for unemployment compensation because my last company laid me off, but I wasn't eligible.

I had been working through an agency, instead of directly for my employer, and since I was a contractor, I couldn't collect unemployment compensation. So, I had no money coming in at all for four months. I said, "Never again!"

I went to an IT-focused employment agency and when I filled out the application forms, I emphasized my IT security background. I called myself an IT Security Specialist on the application form. Why not? I realized that I've worked with dozens or even maybe a hundred other IT people, and I can only think of two or three who know as much as I do about IT security.

Here's what happened. A lady from the IT employment agency called me back right away and said, "We don't get a lot of calls for IT security jobs, but when we do, the jobs pay really well."

I said, "I also know other IT topics, of course—networking, hardware, software, and supporting users." She said, "Well, I have an assignment that pays twenty dollars an hour."

My heart was in my throat because I was broke. I needed money bad. I said, "That won't work for me, of course, but I'm sure you have lots of people in your database who can do those jobs." My heart was racing.

"Not really," she said. "Not with your experience. What rate do you need?"

I said, "Forty an hour." I figured the worst she could do was say, "How about thirty an hour?" She said, "Let me call you back."

Two hours later, she called me back and told me about an IT assignment that had nothing to do with IT security—it was a regular PC-network tech assignment. I took the assignment at $30 an hour, and I told her, "I have to let you know that if I get an IT security job, I'm going to take it."

I started the assignment the following Monday. Everyone I met at the client company said, "You're the IT security guy, right?" My brand preceded me! It's all because I chose to brand myself for the job I wanted rather than the jobs I'd already had.

A month later, the client made me an offer to come on board full-time as an IT Security Specialist at $40 an hour. Believe it or not, I turned them down. I figured they'd hire me full-time and keep me for a few months to get their IT Security in order, then lay me off. I said, "Hire me as a consultant to set up your IT Security program," and they did.

What a life lesson! You have to decide for yourself what your talents are worth. No one else is going to pay you what you deserve unless you insist on it and are ready to walk away.

 What would you have done in Joaquin's situation?

Marcel's Story

I am a social worker. It's a government job. It's easy to get burned out. The work is very hard. There are too many clients to take care of. Everyone knows that being a social worker is hard, but it's still difficult to get a good job, because there are a lot of social workers around.

I wanted to stay in the human services field but get out of government social work. It is too draining. I couldn't support my clients the way I wanted to because I was drowning in paperwork.

I hope I live long enough to see the social work system reinvented. I sincerely want to see that, because a lot of people need help and the way we do social work right now is not effective.

But in the meantime, I had to make a change. I had to change jobs, because I was burnt out and hurting my health, and like I said, I wasn't supporting our clients the way I wanted to.

I looked at a lot of job ads and all I got from that was discouraged. Everybody seemed to want a lot of qualifications that I don't have, even though I care a lot about my work and I've been doing it for years.

I decided to get a job completely outside of social work and human services and see whether I could solve some pain in another area. I looked at jobs in the arts and not-for-profit jobs. I saw an interesting job opening for a head of talent development at an international aid foundation. Talent development is kind of like training, I guess. I had no experience whatsoever in that area, but at the same time I felt qualified to do the job. This organization sends young people around the world to do development work.

I could train them for those assignments. I applied for the job using a Pain Letter. I knew the organization had pain or else they wouldn't be advertising a job for someone to train the young people before they start their assignments.

In my Pain Letter, I talked about how sending young people from the developed world out to foreign countries to dive into development work is a lot like going into the housing projects I visited for years as a social worker.

I was amazed that I got an interview. I felt as though my passion for the job and the mission got me the interview, because I had no experience in international aid or not-for-profit work.

I got the job! The Executive Director said, "I've met a lot of talented applicants for this role, but you are the only person who talked about the discomfort and the culture shock our young trainees experience. I feel as though you actually understand what they are going through."

I understood the Executive Director's pain and the pain of the young people who are leaving their home countries to help people around the world. I am so excited.

I'm so glad I stopped worrying about my qualifications on paper and brought my job search down to a human level—or should I say *up* to a human level!?

How did Marcel use his understanding of Business Pain to move his job search forward?

Write your thoughts about Emily's, Joaquin's, and Marcel's stories in your Mojo Journal. Also jot down ideas on how you could use Business Pain in your own reinvention and job search.

Teach one of the Reinvention Roadmap concepts you have learned to another person. Choose a person who wants to learn! Walk that person through one of the ideas in this program and have them write to you to tell you what they learned.

Hurrah for you! Your muscles are growing!

STAYING ON YOUR PATH

Organizations have pain. Individuals have pain, too! They have problems. Most of us have at least one big problem that we'd pay good money to get rid of. Spotting pain in our environment and coming up with a way to solve the pain and get paid for it is not a bad thing. It's a good thing. It's what people have always done! It is not evil to start a business. It's awesome and muscle-building.

Even if you don't start your own business, you will become a business owner. You're a business owner now, because your business is your career. You can run your career like a business, and also you must. The new-millennium workplace requires it, because old-fashioned, sit-at-your-desk-and-do-what-they-tell-you-to employment is going away.

STAYING AWAKE AND AWARE

In order to spot pain in the ecosystem around you, you have to have an awareness of the kind of Business Pain you solve.

Armed with that awareness and your wonderful five (or six) senses, you will talk with people and read the newspapers (online or in print) and pay attention to the world around you in a way you may not have done. The business section of the newspaper or of a website is usually the section that puts normal people to sleep unless they consider themselves businesspeople. A lot of people go to work in the business world every day but they don't follow business news, mainly because it's boring to read.

What do you think? Do you think business news is boring? Write about that in your Mojo Journal.

Most people you talk to don't know a lot about how the business world operates, and part of that is because we've made the topic "How does business work?" as tedious and awful as we possibly could. A lot of high schools offer a few business classes, but they all steep a kid in Language Arts, Math, Science, and Social Studies!

We are teaching out of a very, very old playbook. The world has moved on, but schools have not. That's okay! Business is not complicated. If you get a job in the business world, you will see that there is nothing very complicated about business.

Beware of Weenies

Weenies try to make business sound complicated, but it's not.

What are weenies? They are hot dogs, frankfurters, coneys, or Chicago dogs or any other kind of frank in one sense, but for our purposes a weenie is someone who has found a comfort zone in the rules and structures of the business world or the institutional world. A weenie is someone who has stepped completely out of his or her human form just because he or she is at work. There are a lot of folks like that around, because the business and professional worlds themselves reinforce weenie-type behavior in many ways.

Weenies are people who love rules and policies. They love structure. It makes them feel all cozy. They love to tell other people what to do. They don't like ambiguity. They don't like it when people around them get creative or have fun.

All of us have spent time with weenies! There are a lot of weeniefied people working in corporations, start-up companies, not-for-profit organizations, government jobs, in academia, and almost everywhere. Weenies squash creativity. They don't like people who think outside of boxes.

We all have weenie tendencies. The more fearful we become, the more our weenie tendencies come out. They show themselves when we become overly attuned to rules, schedules, policies, numbers, and algorithms and forget to be human at work.

We forget how to laugh and be ourselves. We forget how to be vulnerable and say things like, "You saved me in that meeting just now!" or "I'm not sure what to do next."

When we become fearful, we devolve out of our human forms and become weenies. I draw weenies to remind you that there is more than one way to be at work.

Bring Yourself to Work

You can bring yourself to work all the way—your ideas, your heart, your passions, your quirks, and your sense of humor. Why not? Your employer or your client is paying for you to come to work—not a clone of you who looks like you but doesn't say the things you say.

We have to be professional at work, of course. We can bring ourselves to work, but work is a human place and that means we operate in a community at work. We can't curse and rail about things that bother us or yell at people or any of that.

We have to be open and friendly, because that's what good community members do for one another, and we'll all be happier when we can work together comfortably without tension.

In the same way entrepreneurs have an advantage over full-time salaried employees because they have to make constant adjustments to keep pace with changes around them, people who practice bringing themselves to work all the way have a huge advantage over people who let their suits or their job titles do their jobs for them.

People who go "under cover" at work show up and do what they're told, but their minds and hearts are far away or crusted over by layers of frustration and apathy. We can sympathize with anyone in that state!

It's hard to be a grown-up. It's not that easy. When we go to work we usually talk about the schedule and the plan and the deadlines and the targets to hit. We seldom talk about how hard it really is to make it, just to keep a roof over our heads and pay the bills, much less to have a good life and take care of the people who are important to us.

It's hard. Being a grown-up is simply hard and we don't talk about it. We don't have support groups for people who feel that it's hard to put all the pieces together, which means everyone.

We do a pretty good job, all in all, of keeping the pieces together. It's praiseworthy. We can make our burden, the regular burden of being an adult and figuring everything out and keeping gas in the car and keeping the lights turned on, easier. We can ease up on ourselves and focus on moving toward the life we want, rather than following old rules and listening to people who may not have our best interests at heart. We can stop worrying about what other people think about us. Only the people who get you, deserve you, after all!

That is a great way to begin taking control of your life and your career.

Do you sometimes worry about what other people think about you? Write your thoughts in your Mojo Journal. Have you started on a big goal only to be sidetracked with another life issue that showed up? Write about that.

GETTING ALTITUDE ON YOUR LIFE

It's simply not that easy to manage everything we have to manage in life, and part of our stress comes from the fact that much of the time, we operate at a pretty low altitude. We have so many demands and issues right in our faces that it's hard to make time to think longer-term or to envision the life we want. We don't dare to ask ourselves the question, "What could my life be like if I changed everything I need to change? What could my career be like if I weren't afraid to shoot for the moon?"

What keeps you from getting altitude on your life and career? Is it embarrassment, or exhaustion, or the fear that you might fail if you set too high a goal? Write your thoughts!

We spend most of our energy and time on the ground. We think, "I have to fill out that field trip permission slip, and I have to get the invitations out for Bob's birthday party, and get my car stereo fixed." We worry a lot about our ground-level issues. We don't spend much time asking bigger questions like, "Where would I live and what kind of life would I have, if I dared to go for my dreams?"

Let's practice high-altitude thinking!

In your Mojo Journal, describe the life you'd have if you could snap your fingers and do whatever you wanted to do. Don't worry about the practical aspects of your high-altitude thinking just yet. Just let yourself dream! Answer these Cloud-level questions about your life and career. Have your views changed during your Reinvention Roadmap journey?

1. What sort of work would you do if you could do any kind of work you wanted to?

2. Where would you live if you could choose exactly the spot you wanted to live in?

3. What would your living situation be like? Describe your dream home.

4. Who would live with you, in your high-altitude plan?

5. How would you fulfill your life's mission, in your dream scenario?

6. How would you like to be remembered, after you're gone?

7. What desire or passion that has been burning in your heart for a long time would come out and be realized in the dream life you're envisioning?

PART **FOUR**

We spend most of our energy and time on the ground—but it is this high-altitude exploration that pays off the most!

When we let our minds feel free to envision what we really, really want and are willing to focus on and step toward, incredible things happen. Obstacles get smaller. Did we make it happen through our strong, positive intention? You got me. I don't know. I've only seen this happen hundreds or thousands of times, so I believe in it.

Your commitment to your path will change your path, simply stated. When you walk out into unknown territory, you grow muscles fast. The only way to grow muscles for this new-millennium workplace is to step out and try something a little scary.

You did it when you were eight years old! You were super tough then. As we grow up, we forget how to take risks. We forget how to stretch ourselves. You can teach yourself again!

 **BABY STEPS**

Here are five Baby Steps you can try to challenge yourself to think about things, and do and say things that at first feel a little scary.

1. Go to a networking event and when someone asks you, "What do you do?" answer, "I'm a consultant. What about you?"

2. Design your ideal job or consulting project. Write about the Business Pain you will solve for your employer or client and how getting past that pain will help their business.

3. Volunteer to speak at a job-seekers' networking group. Share your experiences with them!

4. Write a blog post and publish it on LinkedIn.

5. Write a one-page biography that describes you in your ideal working situation. Write about yourself as though you already have the career you want. Make it real in your mind, first, and then in reality!

Once you get in the groove of running your career the way a CEO runs a business, you'll see opportunities to relieve pain everywhere you look. Some of them will be consulting opportunities. Some will be full-time or part-time jobs. You'll become a champion Pain-Spotter over time!

When you are working, one-half of your brain and heart will be devoted to your job. That is plenty of your brainpower and heartpower to do your job extremely well! The other half of your brain- and heartpower will go to managing your career.

Even if you are passionate about the work you are doing, if you work for someone else you need to reserve some time and mental energy for managing your career, because whenever you are employed, things can change in an instant.

If you start your own business, then your task of dividing your time and energy between your current job and your long-term path becomes easier. Your path and your job are the same or closely intertwined when you work for yourself.

If your business begins to falter or you find that it isn't as fun or as rewarding or financially viable as you thought your business was going to be, you'll be able to spot the signs quickly and make changes. You will never stop managing your career!

As a business owner, whether you work for someone else or work for yourself, you will have your antennae up.

You will be on the alert, looking for Business Pain in your environment and keeping in mind the question, "Where could I plug in to make a contribution, relieve someone's pain, and do what I do best?"

KEYHOLE CONVERSATIONS

One way you'll meet people, grow your Pain-Spotting muscles, grow your network, and become more comfortable talking to people is through keyhole conversations. We call them keyhole conversations because they are entry points. We don't know where these conversations will lead.

In the book *Alice in Wonderland*, Alice goes down a rabbit hole and then drinks a potion that makes her small enough to slip through the keyhole in a locked door. You'll do the same thing, without having to drink a magic potion (although I hope a little of our magic potion slips down your throat while you are following this program!).

You can start conversations wherever you go. You can meet new people almost anywhere without much trouble. You only have to turn your focus away from your phone and your problems, get outside your head, and start a conversation with a person sitting or standing next to you.

You can start conversations with people about Business Pain and solutions very easily.

You can ask them questions about their life at work and what they're dealing with. The first time you start a conversation with a person you don't know, it might be a little scary. It will get easier and easier every time you do it!

When you start a conversation with a person about their work, and about Business Pain and solutions, not knowing at the start of it where the conversation will lead, we call it Slipping through a Keyhole!

You can slip through keyholes all the time. You can start conversations with everyone you know and everyone you meet for the first time—conversations about problems at work and possible solutions to those problems. You can learn a lot about people by asking them about their work.

Your aim in starting keyhole conversations is not just to generate consulting work or to find a new job, although those are wonderful goals! Your aim is broader than that. You are looking to learn more about the business world and your community by inquiring about business situations.

Consultants start keyhole conversations naturally nearly everywhere they go. You are a consultant now!

PART FOUR

Here are some places you can start keyhole conversations:

At your gym	At your kids' school	At the grocery store
In your neighborhood	At the day care center	At your place of worship
At the dog park	At the coffee shop	At your book club
At your child's recital	Standing in a checkout line	At your salon
Waiting for the movie to start	At the library	At the juice bar

 Where else could you start a keyhole conversation? Write your ideas in your Mojo Journal.

Keyhole Conversation Script

What will you say when you begin a keyhole conversation?

Here's a script to give you ideas. In this sample, you're watching your son's seventh-grade basketball game alongside a seventh-grader's mom.

YOU: Go Cougars! Wow, that was a great pass.

MOM: They are really on fire.

YOU: Which Cougar is your child?

MOM: Number Eleven, over there—his name is Corey.

YOU: Does Corey love basketball?

MOM: He does, but he's overbooked, honestly. He loves all sports.

YOU: How fun!

MOM: Yes, but kind of expensive and nerve-racking, too. The little guy has already broken a couple of bones and spent more than his share of time in the emergency room!

YOU: That's hard on you!

MOM: Yes, and I work, too.

YOU: What sort of work do you do?

MOM: I'm the Office Manager for a medical practice downtown. I run the office, and it's hectic!

YOU: That sounds like a cool job! How did you get involved in that?

MOM: I didn't have a health care background, but I ran the back office for an insurance company and when they closed, I applied for this job and got it. I really like it.

YOU: It must be fun!

MOM: It is, but of course there are always issues.

YOU: What kinds of issues do you run into?

MOM: Right now, we're dealing with all the new regulations and requirements for keeping electronic health records confidential. We're upgrading all our computer systems and I'm losing some sleep over it!

YOU: How stressful for you! Who is helping you with that?

MOM: Oh, we have an IT guy, Gary, and he's a sweetheart, but he's learning about software upgrades as much as we are. Why, do you know anything about this kind of thing?

YOU: I'm a software consultant. I've helped a lot of companies step through software upgrades.

MOM: Really? I don't suppose you would have time for a cup of coffee one day?

YOU: If we look at our schedules I'm sure we can come up with a good time to meet.

Does this conversation sound scary? Write your thoughts in your Mojo Journal.

Many people you talk with in a keyhole conversation will not be experiencing the same type of Business Pain you relieve best, at least not at the exact point in time when you chat with them. That's okay! You are networking, and networking is a long-term process, not a quick fix. The more keyhole conversations you have, the more comfortable you will become asking people about their work and about issues they're facing.

You can start your keyhole conversation exploration by sitting down for one-on-one meetings with people you already know. You can grow your Pain-Spotting and keyhole conversation muscles that way!

What if you have a great conversation with someone, like the seventh-grader's mom at the basketball game, but there is no instant, obvious intersection between his or her needs or work situation and your Pain-Solving abilities? What do you do then?

That's no problem! You can ask your new acquaintance if they happen to have a business card handy. Sometimes they will, and sometimes they won't.

A parent at a middle-school basketball game might just as easily have business cards on their person as not. It doesn't matter. If someone doesn't have their business cards handy when you meet them, you can ask them for their name and email address.

PART FOUR

You can also ask them whether they'd be comfortable with you sending them a LinkedIn invitation. If you and they become connected on LinkedIn, you can easily stay in touch.

Some people don't use LinkedIn. That's all right. You can keep their email address and send them a quick note in a couple of days to mention that you were pleased to meet them. If you want to, you can invite them for coffee.

You can sit down with them at a coffee shop and learn about their life, and tell them about yours.

That's networking!

Networking for People Who Don't Want to Network

Networking is not hard. It's very simple, but to get the most out of networking you have to keep these two things in mind:

- Networking is a long-term activity, like tending a garden. You can't expect to walk into a networking coffee meeting and walk out with a new client or a new job lead. You have to be willing to invest the time and energy into networking whether it leads to an immediate benefit for you, or not.

- The point of networking is not to tell your new acquaintance enough about you so that you get them to hire you for consulting or recommend you for a job at their place of employment. The point of networking is to build a stronger relationship, what we call "glue" at Human Workplace, with another person. Focus on them—not on you! Your muscles will grow whether you get advice from your new networking contact or give them advice, or both. Networking is about people, not about transactions.

If you're new to networking, a great way to begin more active networking is to touch base with people you already know.

 In your Mojo Journal, write the names of 10 people you haven't seen or haven't spoken to in a while—people you can touch base with now over coffee, lunch, breakfast, or another kind of get-together, like a walk in the park.

Start Meeting with People

Would it help you grow your networking muscles as well as your mojo to get together with some of the folks you've just listed, over the next few weeks? You can write to them by email, text them, or call them on the phone and invite each of them to meet you for coffee or another kind of meeting.

You can pick a coffee shop that is near each of their houses or workplaces. After all, you're the person reaching out, so you want to be as accommodating as possible! Ask them whether they've got time to meet with you. Here's a sample networking coffee invitation:

Dear Amy,

I saw your LinkedIn profile the other day and thought it's been way too long since we've seen each other. If you have time to meet this month or next month it would be great to get together. What about lunch or coffee? I can't wait to hear what's new with you!

Thanks,
Lisa

When you make a lunch or coffee invitation or any kind of networking invitation, put your networking friend's needs and schedule above your own. It is impolite to write to to someone you haven't seen in a while and say, "I'd love to see you. Let's get together on the fifteenth, at Pete's Bakery." That kind of invitation sounds like you've got everything planned out and you expect your networking partner to fit into your plan. It's more polite to leave the date and place of your meeting (and even the type of meeting) open until you hear from your friend.

After all, your first question is, "Do you have time to meet?" Some people, even if they like you a lot, won't have time to meet you. They may write back to you and say, "Let's get together after the new year. I have my mom staying with us right now and I don't have a spare minute. Thanks for understanding!"

 In your Mojo Journal, write about your experiences with networking coffee meetings, lunch meetings, and other kinds of one-on-one networking get-togethers.

In the diagram below you'll see a star surrounded by 15 planets. You are the star. You sit in the middle of your own solar system! Each of us is the sun in our own universe.

Draw a similar diagram in your Mojo Journal, and in the planets surrounding the star in the diagram, write in the names of 15 of your friends, neighbors, colleagues or ex-colleagues, and other people you could sit down with over a cup of coffee and have a keyhole conversation with very soon.

Was it simple or challenging to think of 15 people to include in your keyhole solar system? Write your ideas in your Mojo Journal.

Can you write to each of these 15 people via email, text them, call them, or see them in person and suggest that you and they get together for a cup of coffee?

Your network is a huge part of your Reinvention Roadmap journey. The people you know are not only fantastic conduits and connectors to consulting work and full-time and part-time job opportunities. They are also critical mojo-builders for you. We feel better about ourselves when we help other people with issues they are dealing with.

You can do that over coffee and give a friend or neighbor fantastic advice that will help them solve one of their biggest problems!

Do you think of networking—that is, meeting with and talking with people about your life and your work, or just catching up with them—as something fun and easy, or something hard and unpleasant—or somewhere in between? Write your thoughts about networking in your Mojo Journal.

CHAPTER TWENTY-FIVE

YOUR REINVENTION, YOUR PATH, YOUR LIFE

You've made it to the last chapter of the book! Good job! Let's review what we've learned thus far.

LONG-TERM EMPLOYMENT IS NOT THE GOAL ANYMORE

Years ago many people got one job and stuck with it and retired from the same job they'd had for years. That was the common career journey when I was a kid and for years after that.

My dad took a job right out of college and kept working for the same company for 35 years. He did the corporate ladder thing. He worked hard and made a big contribution to the company, so he got promoted every few years. My dad retired from that company. Who has a career story like that today? Almost no one!

When is the last time you were invited to a retirement party for a person who didn't work for the government? Government jobs still take a lot of people from the beginning of their careers to the end of them, but fewer and fewer private employers can say the same thing. There is another problem, too. The more likely a particular job is to keep you employed for years on end, the less likely that job is to help you grow your muscles. That's bad!

Full-time employment is going away. Not only are there fewer jobs that a person can walk into at a young age and stay in for years, but the average tenure (the length of time you spend in a job) of a working person in a particular job is getting shorter, too. We can see that the ability to get a job—or to get paying work, such as a consulting gig—is even more important than your ability to do the job once you've got it.

We can say that that's an awful realization, or annoying or unfair or scandalous, but it's true.

It won't do you any good to be an expert in your field if you don't have any way to get a new job when your old job goes away.

You have to know how to perform your work, of course, in whatever career path you choose to follow. However, it's just as important to know how to get a job—or to get work, whether it's a job or a consulting engagement—as it is to know how to perform the job once you get it!

 How do you feel about your ability to perform your work and your ability to get hired into your desired position? Write about those two aspects of your career in your Mojo Journal. I've provided an example to get you started.

MY ABILITY TO DO MY JOB	MY ABILITY TO GET WORK WHEN I NEED IT
I'm confident about some things, like preparing reports, but not so much about other things, like talking on the phone.	I can usually get a job when I need one, but this job search is the worst one I can remember in terms of taking forever.

If it were very easy to get a new job when you need one, or if it were easy to get new consulting engagements when you need some work, we wouldn't need to learn the techniques you're learning in this Reinvention Roadmap program. You wouldn't need to read this book, and I wouldn't have needed to write it and draw the pictures in it.

We wouldn't have to learn how to brand ourselves, how to value our talents, and how to negotiate job offers and consulting deals. All of that stuff would be easy. It would be second nature to us.

Maybe in an alternate universe, little kids are learning these topics starting from the age of five. In that alternate universe, every little kid knows how to spot and solve Business Pain and how to follow his or her own path.

Here in our universe, most of us are exploring these topics for the first time. We didn't learn about following our path or growing our flame or knowing our value to employers and clients when we were kids. Now we are learning how to set a career direction, how to brand ourselves for the jobs we want, and how to grow other essential New-Millennium Career Muscles.

That's what you have been doing in this Reinvention Roadmap program. In this book you have been learning new approaches to running your job search and your career, but the intention of this book and the Reinvention Roadmap program is to give you something more valuable than "how-to" advice.

My mission in this book has been to shift the way you look at yourself, and to remind you of the power that you have to run your own life and career. You are much smarter and more capable, creative, and powerful than you think. You can accomplish the ambitious goals you will set for yourself the minute you give yourself permission to set your sights on the life you really want.

In fact, setting big goals and committing to pursue them no matter what anyone else thinks is the single best way to reach your goals!

You're going to have to work hard to get to the life and career you want, but that's okay—your work to get there is exactly the cost of the vision for your life that you are creating.

Why work that hard for a slight improvement in some minor area or aspect of your life? Why not give yourself permission to dream really big?

Many of us hesitate to set ambitious goals because we fear that the people closest to us will say, "Who do you think you are to set such lofty goals?"

You don't have to tell anyone that you're thinking about making big changes in your life. You don't have to set yourself up to have the people around you poke fun at you for daring to envision a different life than the one you have now. You don't need that pressure.

You can keep your dreams to yourself for now. The key is to envision them, and then to commit to them!

When you start a new job or start a new business, is your reinvention over? No way! Reinventon is forever. It's constant. You started reinventing the moment you were born. You won't stop! Even if you were asleep before, you're awake now and you're tuned in to your own priorities.

You get to decide where to take your career and what sort of life you want to live. Nobody will make those decisions for you, unless you fall asleep again and let your employer decide what kind of career you will have!

 What are your thoughts about these questions? To stay awake and keep focusing on your needs and your goals, ask these questions every month or even more often and write your thoughts in your Mojo Journal:

- Am I happy at my work? Am I doing work that grows my flame?
- Am I learning something new every day, week, or month at work? Am I growing new muscles?
- Am I being paid what my research and my experience tell me my talents are worth?
- Can I see the path ahead at my current job or in my current working situation?
- Can I see more learning experiences ahead at my current job, or have I reached a point where the learning will slow down or stop entirely?
- Do I work among people who "get" me and therefore deserve me?
- Do I get to use my talents on my job, or not?

YOUR WORK IS YOUR ART

Years ago, career paths were well-defined. That isn't true anymore. Work is splintering. Industries are splitting up and merging and morphing in fascinating ways.

Many traditional career paths don't exist anymore. New career paths are not straight, logical, linear paths but hops from one lily pad to another.

It's not just the working world that is losing its traditional boundaries and categories. There were well-established genres and sub-categories for art, music, film, and literature for many years, but these categories are splintering and blending into one another now.

Genres are not distinct. They overlap and merge to create new combinations, new art forms, and new businesses, trends, and social movements all the time.

Your career is a piece of art. It's your creative expression, after all! You don't have to put your career into a preset category. You can bend and stretch your career in whatever direction you like.

You are not "an accountant" or "a software engineer." Whatever kind of art you make, it's yours alone. You have your own distinct point of view, and you are very unlike any other accountant or any other software engineer. Your personality, your beliefs, your worldview, and your creative style all influence your work to a huge degree—as they should!

How does your personality show up in your work?
Write about that in your Mojo Journal.

WE ARE WAKING UP

Now that the traditional corporate ladder is gone and traditional job security is gone, we are waking up. We are realizing that if we're going to have to manage our own careers anyway, we may as well manage our careers so our work suits our life, and not the other way around!

Your work is important, but not as important as your personal life. Your health and your loved ones are your highest priorities. Your work will inspire you and get the time and energy investment it needs to blossom if your work is aligned with your mission.

That's why I wrote this book—to remind you that you can drive your career in any direction you like, and that it isn't presumptuous of you to expect and to work toward a career that supports who you are beyond your resume.

PART FOUR

Your resume is just a tiny sliver of you. A couple of pages of typed information could never convey your spark, your brilliance, or your sense of humor.

That's okay! You are much more than your resume.

 In your Mojo Journal, write about some of your favorite characteristics or traits that don't show up on your resume.

HUMANS GO TO WORK

People are starting to wake up to the idea that since human beings populate every workplace on earth, work can and should be a lot more human than it often is.

We are remembering that when work is fun and stimulating, people get more excited about it and the work is easier and more successful.

You cannot keep Mother Nature out of any system, no matter how gray and steely and boxy that system might be. You can't keep the human characteristics of working people out of the workplace, no matter how hard you try. The wonderful and inspiring human traits of working people assert themselves wherever people gather!

That's a good thing.

Work is a human place, and people are reasserting themselves at work simply by coming to work as themselves, rather than disguised as cardboard cutouts of themselves. That's good for them, their customers, their employers, and their shareholders. It's good for all of us!

They aren't willing to water down their personalities just for a paycheck—and can we blame them for that?

More and more everyday working people are rejecting the tired old frame, "You get paid to work, so it's not supposed to be fun." They're asking the sensible question, "Wouldn't the work be more effective, more productive, and more energizing for everybody if it were more fun and more human?"

People are getting tired of playing a fake character at work. They believe that their hard work is enough to earn them a paycheck. They don't believe they should work hard every day and also play a fake version of themselves when they come to work. That's asking too much of them!

Little by little the human side of work is coming to the forefront. It has been pushed aside and shoved into the background for a very long time.

We have grown up with the idea that work is fake and mechanical and formal, but that is a very old and dusty idea.

It isn't based on anything except the fact that people have been repeating the same old dusty idea for over a hundred years.

There is nothing about work that requires it to be stiff, formal, harsh, rule-bound, or hierarchical. There is nothing inherent in work that makes the work better or more effective when it is routine and boring. Work is better when it is more human.

When work is human, it becomes real to the people performing the work. They can care about the work when they can put their own stamp on it. They care about their work when it's their work rather than just a task that someone assigned to them, and when a win on the job is their own win. Everybody knows that about people!

At work, we often pretend that people are like machines. We put them on fixed schedules and give them fixed procedures to follow. This is a sure-fire recipe to get people to give only the minimum amount of effort at work.

Why should anyone care about work that they've been told to perform exactly the same way a machine would perform it?

Why would anyone care about doing a great job when the definition of a "great job" is to do the job the way any other person would do it? We can be very stupid about leading people at work sometimes!

What are your ideas about how human or how mechanical work should be? Do you feel that you can bring the real you to work, to your business, or to your job search? Write your thoughts in your Mojo Journal.

WHAT YOUR JOB GIVES YOU BESIDES A PAYCHECK

People get excited about work that stimulates their heart and brain. That's why it's important to try to get a job that means more to you than just a paycheck!

Your flame won't grow in a job that allows almost none of your spark and brilliance to show through. Don't you deserve a job that gives you more than a paycheck, after all?

This diagram from earlier in the book shows some of the things the right job will give you.

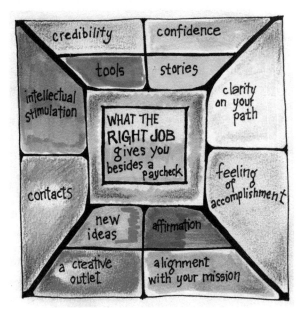

PART FOUR

Which of the elements in the diagram are important to you? Which have you already experienced on the job and which are you looking forward to experiencing? What do you feel you deserve in a job, apart from a paycheck? Write your thoughts in your Mojo Journal.

If you don't feel that you can bring yourself to work all the way right now, that's okay. Almost everyone has felt that way at times. You can take baby steps toward bringing yourself to work all the way. You can give yourself time. You are growing new muscles, and that doesn't happen overnight.

LISTEN TO YOUR BODY

If you want to practice bringing more of yourself to your job, your business, or your job search, you can start by paying attention to your body.

Notice how you feel at work. Notice which activities suck away your mojo and which activities build your mojo supply. Notice which people drain your energy and which people give you extra energy.

Now, pick up your Mojo Journal and answer these two questions:

1 If you're not working now, think back to the jobs you've held before. Which activities at work made you feel the most like you?

2 Which activities at work sucked away your mojo and made you sad, tired, or bored?

We tend to ignore our bodies when we're at work or when we're job-hunting. That's a big mistake! Our bodies are trying to send us signals all the time. If we can't sleep, that's a signal.

If you wake up in the morning with your jaw aching from grinding your teeth all night, that's a big signal from your body to your busy brain.

If you take a painkiller and forget about your aching jaw, you won't see the real issue and you won't deal with it.

That happened to me. First my jaw ached and then my back went out and I had to go on a stretcher in an ambulance to the emergency room. That is the most undignified way I can think of to go anywhere. I was embarrassed and in horrible pain at the same time.

I got the signal, and I made some big changes in my life and career over the next few months. Now I don't have back problems—knock on wood. My back was screaming at me, "You are not on your path!"

Have you ever gotten a signal from your body that told you to slow down and look more closely at your life? Write about it in your Mojo Journal.

FIND YOUR VOICE AND SPEAK YOUR TRUTH

As you grow your truth-telling muscles, you will feel more and more comfortable sharing what you actually think and feel rather than reading from the standard script at work or on your job search.

You'll bring yourself to work, not a cardboard cutout who looks like you but says things the real you would never say.

You'll keep in mind that you have to say "No!" to the wrong things in order to bring the right things in. You'll remember that not everyone deserves your talent. If they don't get you, they don't deserve you!

You are taking steps and growing your muscles. We are all growing muscles together!

What will you do with your new muscles and mojo? Write your ideas in your Mojo Journal!

YOUR ASSIGNMENT

You have come quite a distance in your Reinvention Roadmap journey. Let's look ahead at your path:

· What are your career and life goals for the next 12 months?

· What is the next step you will take on your path?

· How will you celebrate your Reinvention Roadmap experience by sharing what you've learned with someone else?

PART FOUR

- What do you know about yourself now that you didn't know when you began this Reinvention Roadmap program?
- Who's running your career?
- What does it mean to run your career?

Write your answers to the above questions and also your thoughts about each of these Reinvention Roadmap journey topics in your Mojo Journal:

REINVENTION ROADMAP TOPIC
My career direction
My brand
My job-search "prongs"
My market value/target pay level
My Target Employer List
My target job titles
My target hiring manager (by job title)
The Business Pain I solve in my work
My network
How I will keep my mojo level high

CHECKING IN: GROWING MUSCLES AND MOJO

Great job walking the Reinvention Roadmap path! You have completed all four parts of your Reinvention Roadmap journey magnificently! You are incredible. You won't go to sleep on your career again. You're driving now—and there are so many wonderful places to go!

You deserve something special to celebrate taking control of your career and your life. How about celebrating your Reinvention Roadmap journey with a nice gelato? Bring a friend with you and boost his or her mojo, and your own!

A Place to Put Your Canoe in the Water *(page 210)*

The process of finding your perfect path involves trying things out by trial and error, and thus you must start somewhere—but not anywhere. Put Your Canoe in the Water—begin your job search—at a place where you know you can use your brain and your talents, get paid appropriately for your contribution, and have fun. Then stay open to learning and the real world will teach you what you need to learn.

"Aha!" *(page 160)*

An "Aha!" is a realization that stops you in your tracks for an instant or hits you like a thunderbolt. An "Aha!" can be small or great, but it always shifts your thinking in some way. "Aha!"s can be powerful. They can change your life dramatically if you tune in and pay attention to them.

Altitude *(pages xv–xvi, Part One)*

Altitude is your distance from the ground. When you climb out of the weeds of your day-to-day life to look at your life and career from the aerial perspective, you can see where you've been (going all the way back to your childhood) and choose where you want to go next (going all the way forward to as far ahead in your life as you like). As you gain altitude, you get powerful learning about your past choices and great ideas about how to move forward toward your vision for yourself.

Black Hole *(page 148)*

A Black Hole is an automated recruiting system where job-seekers are instructed to fill out an online application form. I don't want you to waste time filling out online application forms. As an HR advisor I hate them and think they've set back the recruiting profession at least 30 years.

Blossom *(pages 241–242)*

You won't blossom if you're stuck in a small box. But in the right situation, you will blossom. Your task is to find that situation by reflecting on your path, getting altitude on your life and career, taking steps, and learning from every new experience. We all need room to grow, sunlight to warm and inspire us, and fresh air in order to blossom!

Brand Yourself *(page xvii)*

We all know that products have brands. People have brands, too! What is your brand? Your brand is the way you describe yourself to people. As a job-seeker, working person, or consultant (or all three), you get to choose your brand. You're going to brand yourself as the vibrant, amazing person you are! Three ways you'll brand yourself professionally are through your Human-Voiced Resume, Pain Letters, and LinkedIn profile. Your brand includes all the signals that people get about you before they know you and as they meet you or encounter you for the first time. The way you dress, talk, laugh, solve problems, and perceive the world are all parts of your brand. Your reputation is part of your brand. Your tattoos and piercings are part of your brand. When your brand represents the real you and not a cardboard cutout version of you, your brand is aligned with the person you are. That's the ideal state!

Business Owner (Hint: You Are One!) *(pages xvii–xviii, 72–74)*

Even if you work for a company, you are a business owner. Your business is your career. You could name your business "Jason's Professional Adventures" or "Abigail's Career in Banking." You will run your career like a business by understanding what kinds of Business Pain you solve for the people who hire you, what that Business Pain costs them, and more.

Business Pain *(pages xvii, 135)*

Business Pain is any problem or obstacle that slows a business down. For example, when customers are unhappy, that's a form of Business Pain. When new products are slow to reach the market, that's another form of Business Pain. When IT systems don't work well, those logjams create more Business Pain. Every organization has Business Pain at every moment. Business Pain is a critical concept for every mojofied consultant, employee, and job-seeker to understand. Most young people know how to solve common types of Business Pain, and your power in the talent equation is your ability to spot and solve Business Pain for employers and clients in your talent marketplace. You gain power when you can solve more and more expensive and hard-to-resolve kinds of Business Pain.

Career Path *(page 24)*

Your career path is your choice and no one else's. If one career path turns out not to excite you anymore or the career path disappears, that's okay; you get to choose a new one! You can change careers at any point. Your parents may have set you on the road to your career path so far, but now it's your decision which way to continue. No test can tell you which career path to follow; however, your own trusty heart and brain can tell you, if you listen.

CEO of Your Career (Hint: That's You!) *(page 98)*

A CEO is a Chief Executive Officer or the top dog of an organization. When it comes to your career, *you* are the CEO. Nobody gets to tell you how to run your career. You are in charge! If other people have been making career decisions for you, be it your parents or your boss, that's going to change. You're going to be making the decisions going forward.

Closing *(page 156)*

The Closing is the last element in your Pain Letter. It tells your hiring manager, "If the issues I've raised are relevant, let's talk."

Come to Work as Yourself *(page 228)*

It is easy to believe that because a job requires a certain costume (business attire, for instance) and comes with a script (the standard conversations a person in your job would typically engage in) that the job itself is like a part in a play or a movie. That's why thousands of working people have told me over the years, "I like my job, but I can't be myself there. I have to play a part." When you come to work as yourself rather than in character—playing the part that you believe your manager or your colleagues expect you to play— you bring the real you, not a fake cardboard cutout version of you, and you begin to grow muscles. You don't censor yourself before you speak. You share your emotions as well as your rational thoughts. You deserve to bring your authentic self to work rather than keeping your personality, your sense of humor, or other facets of yourself hidden from view. Our companies would be more effective and we would all be happier if we came to work as ourselves.

Consultant (Hint: You Are One!) *(page 181)*

These days, we are all entrepreneurs. We may not be running a business employed by others, but we are all running our own careers. We also are all consultants now. When you provide services to other people (either individuals or people who work for businesses, or work for themselves) you are a consultant. A consultant is anybody who can solve problems for other people, and that includes you! You can get a consulting business card and start describing yourself as a consultant right now.

Contingency, Contract, or Temporary Work *(pages 68–70)*

Many of us grew up thinking that there is only one legitimate or "respectable" kind of work: namely, full-time, salaried employment. We were taught in many ways that the best kind of job you can get (and keep forever!) is a full-time salaried position with a big, stable company. This vision for the ideal kind of work is fading fast. Big companies are no more stable than small ones and quite often, less so. Your own knowledge of your value to employers and clients provides a lot more stability than any other kind of employment. In fact, in many ways, long-term, full-time employment can hurt you. It can weaken your muscles. Nowadays many people are working for themselves through contract or contingent employment, meaning that they are not on a company's payroll, but working through a contract or temporary agency, or working for themselves as independent consultants.

Cost of Business Pain *(page 212)*

We all need to know what kinds of Business Pain we solve for our employers and clients. We need to know how that pain typically shows up and what it costs an employer or client until it gets resolved. Business Pain always has a cost. Sometimes it's a "hard" cost; for example, the Business Pain may keep an organization from generating revenue or it may cost the organization money. Some kinds of Business Pain incur a "soft" cost, such as the hidden cost of having unhappy employees. As you learn more about your own Pain-Solving abilities you will zero in on the cost of the Business Pain you solve. That number or formula is a big part of your value to employers and clients.

Culture *(pages 13, 66, 168)*

Every organization has a culture. Every organization's culture is slightly different from every other one, but all cultures fall somewhere on the Reaction-o-meter dial. Some cultures celebrate community and group "wins" and others don't. Healthy cultures are based on trust. Unhealthy cultures are based on fear. You will be able to read the culture of any organization you interview with by noticing how people communicate with one another and with you as a job-seeker or prospective consultant to the organization. Listen to their words and watch their body language. Pay attention to the feeling in the air inside the organization. You will get very good at evaluating culture from outside the organization.

Dead-End Job *(pages 74–75)*

A dead-end job is any job that obviously has no future. Maybe it's a lousy job that pays nothing and one where they tell you, "I doubt you'll last here for more than a year." But now that you are following your own path rather than waiting for an employer to manage your career, a dead-end job could be a great experience for you. So the job has no career path—so what? You don't need your job to offer you a career path. You have your own career path to follow! Every step on your path has something valuable to offer you.

Dragon-Slaying Story *(page 123)*

A Dragon-Slaying Story is a story about a time when you came, saw, and conquered, either at work or somewhere else. You'll use your Dragon-Slaying Stories in several ways in your job search.

Driving Your Career *(page 96)*

You are driving your career now; your employer isn't driving it for you! You are in charge and behind the wheel. Driving your career means deciding where you want to go and pointing your vehicle in that direction. It means deciding every day whether your current job or work situation is still the best one for you. It means investing your time and energy to collect experiences and Dragon-Slaying Stories that will help you move along your path. When you drive your own career, you stay awake and alert, the way any driver must.

Elephant in the Room *(page 168)*

An elephant in the room is a topic that desperately needs to be discussed but isn't. No one wants to talk about it. The topic sits in the room and everyone is aware of it, like an elephant in the corner of the room. Everyone pretends to ignore it. An elephant in the room is an energetic disturbance. It's a logjam. How can people get anything important done together if they pretend not to notice a huge, critical issue? It's there, but they won't talk about it. People don't talk about the elephant in the room because they are afraid to. We all experience fear at work, but we are not talking about it and instead pretend it doesn't exist.

Energy *(page 75)*

Every human being sends off waves of heat as well as emotion and other signals. You give off one kind of signal when your Mojo Tank is full and a different signal when your Mojo Tank is nearly empty. Company culture is a manifestation of the energy field created by the interactions of the people who work in the company. When your body signals to you that you need to pay attention to something amiss in the energy field around you, pay attention!

Energy Disturbance *(page 168)*

A disturbance in the energy field is a problem in any workplace. Energy disturbances don't solve themselves, because there is pent-up energy behind the obstacle, sometimes called an energetic logjam. When people don't talk about topics that need airtime, the team's forward energy is impeded. It's important to clear away energy disturbances before they overwhelm Team Mojo. To clear away the obstacle, you need to talk about it.

Falling Asleep on Your Career *(pages 5–6)*

When you fall asleep on your career, you merely do your job. You forget that you have a career to manage and that you are the CEO of your life and career. You don't think about your career. You stop planning for your future and staying tuned in to the external market for your talents—the people who could hire you apart from whichever company you work for now. You stop thinking about whether and how much you're learning at work, and about collecting powerful Dragon-Slaying Stories.

Fear *(pages 75, 79–80, 169)*

Fear is the most significant topic in the workplace that no one talks about. We all feel fear at work. People at work are afraid of making a mistake, afraid of looking bad, afraid of getting in trouble, and afraid of getting fired. Everyone is afraid, from the loading dock to the CEO's office, but no one talks about those fearful feelings. When I was an HR VP, I regularly had adrenaline shooting through my veins, and I always wondered, "Am I the only person who feels this way?" It is time for us to talk about fear at work and about replacing fear with trust. It is time for us to talk about leading through trust rather than fear, and about talking frankly about fear and trust in the workplace and their effects on Team Mojo, customer service, productivity, profitability, and the communities in which organizations operate.

Five Stages of Career Change *(page 49)*

Career change is not a one-step process. You have to decide what you want to do next in your career before you can begin taking steps to start working in your new career path. Enjoy the stages you will work through—all the learning you'll need to do brilliantly in your new career is in the five stages you will experience getting from Point A (your old career) to Point B (your new one). Following the steps ensures that when you've settled on your new career path and you begin stepping into it, your brain, body, heart, and soul—all of you—will be unified and aligned behind your new path. Give the process time! It isn't an equation to solve. This is your life we're talking about. Enjoy the stages in your career change. The journey is the point, not the destination!

Flame *(pages 91–92)*

Your flame is your personal power. When your flame is high, you are feeling great about yourself and feeling confident. When your flame is low, you might feel uncertain or discouraged. Whether you work for yourself or work for someone else, your job must grow your flame! You deserve more from your work than just a paycheck.

Frames and Frame-Shifting *(pages 77, 123)*

A frame is a mental model that we construct to make sense of the world. We all learn frames as we are growing up. By the time we are adults, we have assembled lots of frames in our minds. We know a lot about how the world works, or how we think it works. A big part of your Reinvention Journey is the process of stepping out of frames that were set in our minds. For instance, we might have believed for years that the world worked a certain way. Then one day we had an experience that shook our frame—an experience that showed us a new way to look at something we thought we already understood completely. Frame-shifting is a critical step in moving to a higher altitude in your life and career.

Hiring Manager *(pages 115–120)*

Your hiring manager is the specific person in an organization who can hire you to help him or her solve some kind of Business Pain. You can find the name of your hiring manager by using an employer's website, LinkedIn, and/or Google.

Hook *(page 154)*

The Hook is the first part of your Pain Letter. It is the Hook's job to grab your reader's attention so that he or she will read the rest of your Pain Letter and flip over the page to read your Human-Voiced Resume.

Human Voice *(pages 12, 111, 201)*

Your power will come across most strongly through any medium when you speak your own words rather than reading from a script. So your Reinvention Roadmap project and your job search will have a human voice—*your* human voice, to be exact. You'll drop the formal, stuffy, robotic "business language" and speak to prospective employers and clients in a human, conversational tone. Your Human-Voiced Resume, your LinkedIn profile, your Pain Letters, your correspondence, and your conversations will also use the same human voice.

Human-Voiced Resume *(page 111)*

Your Human-Voiced Resume is a resume that has a human voice in it, the same way you do when you speak. It's written on one or two pages like a traditional resume, but it tells your story rather than listing your skills and credentials. It doesn't use any weenie jargon like "motivated self-starter" or "experienced business professional." Instead, your Human-Voiced Resume uses a conversational tone and Dragon-Slaying Stories to get your personality and your power across on the page.

Human Workplace Employees *(page 149)*

Human Workplace employees are working people who are walking the Human Workplace path. They know why they have their jobs and where they're headed. They know how to pay attention to their feelings and the energetic signals that hit them all day long. They know how to talk about fear, trust, conflict, and other "sticky topics" at work. Most of all, they know how to maintain their mojo supply and bring themselves to work.

Human Workplace Employers *(page 149)*

Human Workplace employers don't force job-seekers to fill out pages of soul-crushing online forms. They don't treat prospective customers badly, and they don't treat prospective employees badly either.

If They Don't Get You, They Don't Deserve You *(pages viii, xviii, 228)*

If you meet people who don't resonate at your frequency, don't see your background and your worldview as valuable, don't like you, or send off vibes that you are unwelcome in their midst, you know one thing for sure: those people don't get you. And only the people who get you, deserve you. You are a brilliant and talented person. You deserve to work with and among people who see the incredible gifts you bring. Anybody who doesn't see your talents, treats you badly during your job search (or in a consulting-related business development process), or disses and dismisses you is not someone you have time for.

The world is big. You don't need everyone to resonate at your frequency—only a small number of them. Go and find them! Leave the people who don't get you in your rearview mirror.

Job Security *(page 35)*

Job security is gone, but you don't need job security anyway. You need something different; you need *income security*. You need to know that you will be able to work. You'll gain the knowledge and security you need by walking the Reinvention Roadmap path.

Keyholes and Keyhole Conversations *(pages 231–233)*

A keyhole is an opening for a conversation. Keyholes are important for anyone who is taking control of his or her own career (like you!). You slip through a keyhole when you start a conversation with someone who might be able to help you, or who you might be able to help. You might have a keyhole conversation at your child's baseball game, at the gym, at your place of worship, or at a block party. Nearly everybody likes to talk about himself or herself. When you start a keyhole conversation you'll ask another person about his or her work and life. Any keyhole conversation is a way to build relationship "glue" between you and another person, and a way for you to learn about other people and their lives, including the kind of work they do. It's also a way to learn about the Business Pain that people and organizations face. So in these conversations, be on the lookout for Business Pain. And know that whether or not you spot or hear about Business Pain, it's very mojo-boosting to have conversations with new people!

Leading with a Human Voice *(pages 201–209)*

We are all leaders, whether or not our jobs require us to manage other people. We are all leading our own lives and managing our own careers. We are all developing new leadership muscles as we go through life. And we are always learning. When we speak to people, when we work with other people, when we teach our children, and when we interact with people around us, we always have the choice to lead in a human way or to lead in a way that is mechanical and inhuman. We always have the choice to remember that likely everyone is overworked, confused, and unsure of themselves, the same way we are. We always can choose trust over fear and lead with a human voice. We can lead in a human way at home, at work, and everywhere we go.

Levels of Altitude *(pages 40–41)*

There are three levels of altitude for you to focus on as you think about your path and your next steps: the Cloud level, the Hilltop level, and the Ground level. The Cloud level is the highest level of altitude. From the Cloud level, you can look down at your path and see where you've come from and where you're going. A step down in altitude from the Cloud level is the Hilltop level. From the top of a hill you can look down at your path and make decisions about which way to go forward. The lowest level of altitude is the Ground level. That's where we take steps by putting one foot in front of the other. Many of us spend almost all our time down at the Ground level, focused on our to-do lists and overwhelmed by obstacles in front of us. When we get altitude, we can see where we're trying to go and find alternate routes to get there. High-altitude thinking is getting above your day-to-day "to-do" list to think about your life and career from a higher level. You'll think about your life goals and the kind of life you want to live. You'll ask yourself questions like, "Am I moving forward on my path, or stuck in place?" If you are stuck, you'll think about how to get over, under, or around the obstacle in your way. We all have to deal with day-to-day issues, but it's important to take the time to think about your life from a higher altitude, too.

Lily Pad *(page 69)*

Frogs sit on lily pads in ponds, and brilliant people like you sit on lily pads in the talent marketplace. A job, a temp assignment, and a consulting engagement are lily pads. We don't expect a lily pad to support us forever, but it's a place to rest and check out the landscape around us. We always have our eye on the other lily pads arrayed around us in the water. We sense the moment when it's time to jump to a new lily pad. That's how we keep moving and stay above water in the new-millennium workplace.

LinkedIn *(pages 116–117)*

LinkedIn is a business-focused networking site. LinkedIn has hundreds of millions of users. LinkedIn membership is free. LinkedIn is a tremendous tool for working people and job-seekers in their networking, branding, business development, and learning. I encourage everyone over age 16 to create a LinkedIn profile and start exploring LinkedIn's many features!

Mojo *(page xiv)*

Your mojo is your life force. It's your sense of self and your forward momentum. Your mojo is your fuel source for everything you want to accomplish in your life. When you're tired and overworked, your Mojo Tank can empty quickly.

Mojo Drop *(page 163)*

Most of us have experienced at least one Mojo Drop. A Mojo Drop is the terrifying event that sucks your mojo away completely and leaves you feeling hopeless, useless, and worst of all, worthless. Your mojo will come back—give it time, and don't put pressure on yourself!

Mojo Journal *(page xi)*

Your Mojo Journal is any notebook that you like and can write in. Writing in your Mojo Journal will help you work out obstacles and issues, show you how far you're traveling, and remind you that you solve big problems every day. Your Mojo Journal is an important part of your Reinvention Roadmap journey.

Mojofied *(pages xiv, 169)*

When you are mojofied, it means that your Mojo Tank is full. You feel energized and ready to take on the world.

Mojofied Job Seeker *(page 169)*

A Mojofied Job Seeker is a job-seeker who understands his or her value in the hiring equation. Mojofied Job Seekers know they don't have to beg for jobs, because if the talents and gifts they bring aren't valuable to those employers, then there's nothing to talk about. A Mojofied Job Seeker understands the saying, "Only the people who get you, deserve you!"

Mojo Tank *(pages xiv, 76, 79, 86)*

Your Mojo Tank is your personal reserve of mojo. One of your jobs as CEO of your life and career is to manage your activities in a way that keeps your Mojo Tank full. Sometimes you'll experience a Mojo Drop, but remember: You are more than worthy, more than capable, and perfectly equipped to carry out your mission. Your mojo will return.

Muscles and Mojo *(page 191)*

As you follow your Reinvention Roadmap journey, you are growing new muscles and building up your mojo supply. Your growing muscles and mojo reinforce one another. Every time you step out of your comfort zone and try something new, you'll feel a little stronger—that's how your muscles grow. You also will feel more confident—that's your mojo growing.

Networking *(page 234)*

Sometimes networking can seem like a scary thing. But all it means is connecting to people you already know and new people you're meeting for the first time. One way to think about networking is "organized friendship." Your network is important for moral support, new ideas, and guidance on your path. And you provide the same kinds of support to the members of your network. If you are new to networking, you can take baby steps. Get together with people you already know well and talk with them about their path, and tell them about your path, too. Like the rest of your new-millennium workplace muscles, your networking muscles will get stronger with use.

New Deal vs. Old Deal *(page 107)*

The "old deal" for working people was that you got a job, kept the job as long as you could, and, for the most part, didn't think about your career. The "new deal" for working people is that we are all CEOs of our own careers.

New-Millennium Workplace vs. Old-Millennium Workplace *(pages 10–13, 24, 73–75, 99)*

The old-millennium workplace (what work was like in the 1900s) was very different from the new-millennium workplace. Now, jobs look very much like consulting engagements and job security is a thing of the past. We now build our own security in ourselves and carry it around with us.

Pain Hypothesis *(pages 129, 155)*

Your Pain Hypothesis is the second section of a Pain Letter, after the Hook. Your Pain Hypothesis lets the hiring manager know that you have some understanding of what he or she is living through.

Pain Letter *(pages 119, 152–157)*

A Pain Letter is a letter that you send to a specific hiring manager along with your Human-Voiced Resume. You'll write each Pain Letter specifically for one hiring manager you've identified—a real person, not a recruiting machine. A Pain Letter talks about the Business Pain your hiring manager is most likely to be facing. There are four parts of a Pain Letter: the Hook, the Pain Hypothesis, your Dragon-Slaying Story, and the Closing.

Pain Packet *(page 256)*

Your Pain Packet is the set of documents you will create and slip into an envelope to send directly to your hiring manager. It includes your Pain Letter and your Human-Voiced Resume.

Pain-Spotting *(pages 136–139)*

Pain-Spotting is the activity of noticing the world around you and paying special attention to the problems and obstacles that people and organizations face.

Path

Your path is the road you travel in your life and career. When you are on your path, you're doing what you feel you were born to do. You're plugged in to your personal power source and learning something new every day.

Path Exercise *(pages 38–39)*

Your path is your story since you were born. The Path Exercise is an exercise that asks you to look back at your life story and remember as much as you can about it. When you think about your path so far in life, you'll remember events, people, feelings, and ideas that influenced you over the years. These exercises form a powerful learning experience.

Permission *(pages xvi, 178)*

In order to walk the Reinvention Roadmap path, you will need permission to think about and do things differently than you may have thought about them and done them in the past. You'll need permission to step out of one conception of your life and career and to create a new vision for yourself. Who will give you that permission? You will give it to yourself. You'll give yourself permission to dream as expansively as you want about your life. You'll give yourself permission to take steps that might make you feel a little foolish or afraid. You'll give yourself permission to decide what you want from your life and then to go get it.

Personal Growth *(page xix)*

Personal growth is the process of learning about yourself and your place in the world—your relationships with other people, your path, and your mission. Personal growth involves self-reflection. It's different from other kinds of learning, like learning to use a new piece of technology. All learning is great, but learning to use a new phone or device doesn't require you to stop what you're doing and look inward, whereas personal growth usually does.

Phase Transition and Reinvention *(page 174)*

Phase transition is the physical process that takes place when a substance changes from one form to another. When ice melts, that's a phase transition. When water boils, that's a phase transition. When substances are getting close to phase transition, their molecules begin to move in chaotic and unpredictable ways. You are in reinvention, and so you may experience the effects of phase transition, too. You may feel confident at times, panicky at other times, and shaky in between. Let your body experience all the feelings that phase transition brings. There's nothing wrong with you; you're simply stepping out of one skin and into a new one.

Plug In

When you plug in, you feel like yourself and you take an active role in your job search and your career. You won't stand by as events unfold. You'll actively direct events and take steps as often as you need to in order to keep moving down your path. You are not waiting for anybody to solve your problems; you are solving your own problems.

Prong *(pages 219, 221)*

A prong is a sub-direction in your career path. Maybe you love the field of marketing and see yourself as a marketing person, but you are interested in several different types of marketing jobs. You might choose three prongs for your job search: an all-purpose marketing prong, a public relations prong, and a fundraising prong (for not-for-profit organizations specifically). You'll create a separate Human-Voiced Resume for each of your three prongs, and you'll combine elements from each prong into your LinkedIn profile (since you can only have one of those at a time).

Reaction-o-meter *(pages 78–80)*

The Reaction-o-meter illustrates the most common reactions people will have when you shake up their traditional thinking—when you rattle their mental model or frame. The Reaction-o-meter is a critical Human Workplace tool to study as you work your Reinvention Roadmap path. You, too, will have reactions to new ideas. Pay close attention to your reactions and write about them in your Mojo Journal. Your reactions will likely change over time as you become more comfortable with the practice of stepping out of old frames.

Reclaim Your Path *(page 31)*

When you reclaim your path, you look back and get the powerful learning that your path has to give you. You start by thinking about your life, going all the way back to your childhood and asking yourself, "What was important to me when I was little, and as I got older? What did I know about myself back then, and what has changed in the meantime?"

You look back and think about every step you've taken in your life, and especially when you choose it—when you say, "Whatever has happened, happened for a reason." You are not a victim of circumstance, although we all sometimes feel that we are victims. We all sometimes feel that things have happened to us randomly and we have no control—but we do have control! We exercise our control by choosing how to react to the crazy things that just happened to us, and we get to choose to follow the path that works best for us. That's reclaiming our path.

Reclaim Your Power

You reclaim your power when you understand, not just in your mind but also in your body, that you are a unique, talented, and incredible person with a story that no one apart from you can tell. You reclaim your power when you realize that no matter what has happened to you, what negative or limiting messages you have heard, or what doubts you may have felt, you are fine and whole. You are perfect right now, and only the people who get you, deserve you.

Red Tape *(page 168)*

Red tape is excess process; that is, procedures and policies that don't move an organization forward but hold it back instead. A company policy that says you have to get a manager's approval to get a new pen when your old pen runs out is an example of red tape. Human Workplaces work hard to keep the red tape to a minimum. Red tape is strongly associated with fear in an organizational culture. The more red tape you see in a company, the more fearful its culture is.

Reinvention *(page vii)*

Reinvention is change. When we reinvent, either by choice or not, we step into a new persona or identity. When you are in reinvention, one chapter of your life is ending and a new one is beginning. Reinvention can be a scary and uncomfortable place to be. This book will help!

Reinvention Roadmap *(page viii)*

Reinvention Roadmap is a path. You'll start at the beginning and move through your own Reinvention Roadmap to the new place where Mother Nature wants you to be. Don't try to rush through your Reinvention Roadmap process; you'll have a better experience when you take your time.

Roadblock *(pages 43, 164)*

A roadblock is any impediment in your way. We all run into roadblocks all the time. Often our first reaction to a new roadblock in our path is an "Oh, dang!" reaction. We think the last thing we need is a new roadblock to surmount. But the funny thing about roadblocks is that they help us. They teach us. How would we get stronger and grow our muscles without new challenges to take on? You can think of roadblocks as pieces of exercise equipment at the gym. You'll have higher and higher walls to climb on your way, but as you continue climbing, you're building muscles, so you'll have an easier and easier time climbing the walls, perhaps even rocketing or sailing over them. Some you'll tunnel under, and some you'll break down. You're clever and resourceful, so you'll have victory around every roadblock you run into!

Safe Jobs *(page 11)*

We often think we need a "safe job," meaning one that is secure. But nowadays, there are no safe jobs and no safe career path. Nature changes constantly. Our task is to learn to deal with changes rather than to avoid them. Instead of looking for a safe job, we can grow muscles and step into new situations with confidence. We can seek out change rather than shying away from it.

Setting Boundaries *(pages 87, 175)*

We are growing new muscles for the new-millennium workplace. One of the muscles we are growing is our Setting-Boundaries muscle. We are learning to set boundaries with people at work and at home. You can't please everyone, and you will exhaust yourself trying to do it. It is not your mission to make everyone around you happy while ignoring your own needs. You can set boundaries with your manager at work, with your family and friends, and with people you interact with on your job search or in your consulting business. Setting boundaries is a critical life skill! No one will value you more than you value yourself.

Sheepie Job Seeker *(page 156)*

The traditional job-search approach still taught in many schools, workforce development centers, and career services centers teaches a job-seeker to beg to get a job. The emphasis in the traditional approach is on pleasing the employer, rather than looking for an intersection of interests between the job-seeker and the employer. The assumption behind the traditional job-search mindset is that every employer is flooded with qualified applicants and has the luxury of picking and choosing among them, but that's not true. A person who has drunk enough of the toxic lemonade that teaches us "You are nothing as a job-seeker, and every employer is mighty" can easily become a Sheepie Job Seeker and forget his or her own value.

Step *(pages 42, 58, Part Three)*

Everything you're learning in your Reinvention Roadmap journey equips you to choose your own path and then to follow it. The key to your success on the Reinvention Roadmap and in your life and career generally is your willingness to take steps. You have to try new things, to be willing to fall on your face and make mistakes, and to keep learning in order to grow. That's what this book is all about!

Takeaway

A takeaway is an idea or a feeling that you gain from an experience. It's something that remains with you after the experience, whether the experience is a conversation, a sunset, a job interview, or a walk around the lake. Sometimes takeaways hit us right away and sometimes they don't hit us for weeks or months— or even years!—after the experience. Pay attention to the signals you're receiving, no matter where they come from. A random sign that you spot on a wall as you drive to the grocery store may have significance for you. Every signal can be a takeaway.

Talent Marketplace *(pages 7–9)*

The talent marketplace is any place (virtual or physical) where people arrange to perform services for other people or for organizations.

Target Employer List *(page 260)*

Your Target Employer List is a list of the employers you might reach out to. You'll use your Target Employer List as a way to start your job search.

Team Mojo *(page 13)*

Team Mojo is the collective energy on a team of people; for instance, the people who work together in the same company. The Team Mojo level in an organization is the most important indicator of how well the organization is performing or is likely to perform in the future. Team Mojo increases when the trust level in an organization is high and decreases when trust disappears and is replaced by fear.

Tricks of the Trade *(page 160)*

Every profession and career path has methods and tools associated with it. Now you are learning new tricks of the trade, with the trade not being your profession per se but "living the life I choose and having a career that supports my life."

Two-Lane Highway

A two-lane highway is a particular career strategy. It's the career strategy that you employ when you work at one job while planning your next career move as a side project. When you work at a full-time job while planning the launch of your consulting business, you've got a two-lane highway going. When you are consulting on your own full-time and planning the launch of a start-up business, you're driving on your two-lane highway. Any combination of a current gig or work situation and the construction of the next work situation is a two-lane highway. As you walk the Reinvention Roadmap path, you'll see many opportunities to use a two-lane highway strategy in your own career.

Undercover at Work *(page 83)*

As you walk the Reinvention Roadmap path, you'll ask yourself, "What kind of work and what kind of working environment will support me best?" You'll grow muscles and set boundaries so that you don't end up in a bad working situation—the kind of situation where you have to pretend to be somebody you're not in order to perform the job. When you can't bring yourself to work and speak with your own voice, you are in an undercover situation. Sometimes that can be manageable and even fun for short periods, but over time you need and deserve a workplace where your flame can burn brightly.

Weenie *(page 227)*

A weenie is a person in fear who believes that by sticking to the rules, making tiny distinctions between things, telling other people how to act, and generally controlling his or her environment to an extreme degree, he or she won't feel so fearful. We all fall into a weenie state at times, because we all get fearful. When we hear ourselves bossing other people around, we know we're feeling fear. We can take a deep breath, trust in ourselves and the people around us, and ask, "How can I learn something new in this experience, instead of being bossy and stubborn?"

Weeniefied *(pages 150, 227)*

Weeniefied people are people who have forgotten that they are still human, even when they're at work. All of us can fall victim to our weenie tendencies at times. When we fall into a weeniefied state, we can become very concerned with rules and policies and use whatever power or authority our job title gives us to put other people down. The higher your mojo level remains, the less likely you will be to devolve into a weeniefied state.

Whole Person Job Search *(page xviii)*

The Whole Person Job Search is the job-search approach you are learning in *Reinvention Roadmap*. It is a job-search worldview that focuses on your individual personality, goals, voice, and talents. In your Whole Person Job Search, you don't approach employers with the message, "Please find me worthy." You approach them a different way, with the message, "Let's get your biggest problems moved out of the way and let's both of us grow our flames in the process!"

You Are a Whole Person

Don't let anybody talk you into the lie that only your years of experience matter. Don't let anyone get you thinking that only having the "right" kind of background makes you significant and worthy. Don't let anyone confuse you and give you the idea that they are mightier than you or that a corporation or institution has the right to dim your flame, because none of those things are true. You are *not* a bundle of skills, credentials, and qualifications. You are a whole, amazing, brilliant human being unlike anyone else—a person the likes of which the world has never seen! You have incredible talents, some of which you have already tapped and explored, and others you're waiting to try.

You Are Not Your Job

Your job doesn't define you. Your business card and your job title don't define you. You are much more than your job! You are a complex and amazing person, and your job is part of you. Whatever job you do, it has to fit into your life. Your job may be close to your passion or some distance away from your passion; that's okay. As long as you are on your path and moving toward the vision of your life you've designed, you're in great shape.

You Get to Choose

All the important choices in your life are yours to make. Your employer doesn't dictate your career. Your family members don't, either. You do. All that decision-making power can feel scary. Often we get comfortable with our own constraints. We like to be able to say, "Well, that's not my decision." But what would happen if every major decision about your life and career was your decision to make? That is a good question to ponder, because in reality every big decision *is* yours to make!

Your Body and Your Life *(pages 244–245)*

Your body is your best friend, but most of us treat our bodies pretty badly. We wear our bodies down and yell at our bodies. We say, "Body, go to the gym!" and "Body, stay up and pay these bills!" When it says back, "I'm tired," we ignore it. We treat our bodies like beasts of burden. But our bodies are very wise. In fact, our bodies may have more wisdom than our brains do. Learn to relax and listen to your body and receive the messages it is sending you. Your body is your partner in your mission.

Your Consulting Business Card *(pages 185–186)*

You are stepping into your consulting persona, and you need a consulting business card. Your consulting business card will present you to the world as a consultant rather than a job-seeker. You can make your consulting business card an expression of your style. Have fun choosing just the right words and design for your consulting business card!

Your Credibility *(pages 124–125)*

Your credibility is not something that anyone can confer on you. Your credibility is something you build in yourself and carry around with you. Perhaps you were promoted at work and became a manager. That's a great triumph for you if you take the new learning that your new position will provide you. If you seek external validation like promotions, titles, degrees, and accolades in order to feel more credible, then true credibility will elude you. Instead of speaking with your own voice, you'll fall into line with whatever you feel your job title and your business card require you to say. That's not credibility; that's fear in action. Real credibility comes from speaking your truth and living your life according to your values, whether other people approve of your choices or not.

Your "Flavor" of Business Pain *(pages 193–194)*

No one can solve every kind of Business Pain. Most of us can solve one or several kinds of Business Pain, once we reflect on our experiences and the Business Pain we've already solved in our careers and other areas of our lives. You need to know which kind(s) of Business Pain you solve—that's your "flavor'" of Business Pain!

Your Mission *(pages 41–48)*

You are here on planet earth for a reason! You have a mission. What is that mission? That's a great question to ponder. When you know what you came to this planet to do, to bring about, and to contribute, your path becomes much clearer. Understanding your mission can make everything you do easier, because you'll know what's important to you and what isn't. As we grow up, we don't get a brochure or a letter that tells us what our mission is, but the exercises and stories in this book can help you figure out your mission.

Your Network—Beyond Your Work People *(pages 118, 159, 234)*

Your network is made up of the people you know, and with luck you'll be meeting new people all the time. They are part of your support system, and you are part of their support systems, too.

Your personal friends and family members are part of your network, and so are your neighbors, your kids' friends' parents, your parents' friends, and everyone else you know. Your network is much bigger than just the people you know from your professional life.

Your Power *(pages 124–125)*

You have enormous power. Most people are afraid of their power and/or afraid of the way other people will react if they start to use their power. But as you exercise your power, your muscles will grow. Your power grows when you begin to use it. For instance, when you speak with your own voice and say something that feels a little scary to say, your power muscles grow the minute you speak up. When you make a hard decision, you use (and grow) your power again. When you take an unpopular view or speak up as the lone voice in the room, you use your power. The more you use your power, the easier it will be to use and grow your power the next time.

Your Story Is Your Brand *(pages 125–126)*

Your story is the most important part of your brand. Your story is the most powerful thing you can tell someone about yourself on paper, on a computer screen, or when you're talking by phone or face-to-face.

Your Sweet Spot *(page 55)*

Your career sweet spot is the point where your passion, your talents, and the real world intersect. Your sweet spot is the place where you can perform work you'll be good at and enjoy, and where that work will also solve someone else's Business Pain. That part is important, because you have to solve someone's Business Pain in order to get paid what you're worth. Understanding what type of Business Pain you solve for employers and/or clients is one-third of the sweet spot puzzle. The other two-thirds are finding work that aligns with your passion and finding work that you'll be good at (or perhaps are already good at). The place where those three elements intersect is your sweet spot. It's a great place to be!

Your Work Is Your Art *(page 241)*

Your work is more than a way to make money. It's your art. It's your contribution to the community of people who hold up our global society together. Everybody has a part in that effort. Your work is your creative expression. You deserve to perform work that speaks to you and that exalts your talents.

You're the Star of Your Movie *(pages 36, 55)*

Many or most of us grew up with the message, "You're okay, but don't start thinking you're anything special." We can keep our flame very dim because we fear that other people won't like it if we start to have a high opinion of ourselves. But you are the star of your movie; no one else is! Your life is up to you. Your career is under your control. So don't be afraid or embarrassed to think or to say, "This is what I want. I know what's best for me."

Zombietastic Resume *(pages 201–209)*

A zombietastic resume is a traditional, boring resume that sounds like it came out of an automated resume-writing machine. A zombietastic resume sounds like it describes a zombie or a robot, not you! You need a human voice in your resume to bring your power and personality across on the page.

ACKNOWLEDGMENTS

I am enormously grateful to Glenn Yeffeth and the team at BenBella Books for their tremendous work on *Reinvention Roadmap*; and to our literary agent, Peter Miller, CEO of Global Lion Management, who has been a champion for this book and the Human Workplace mission.

Reinvention Roadmap would not exist without the advocacy and support of Jon Zakin, who has been my mentor and friend for over 20 years. I am grateful to Sir Ken Robinson for his Foreword, for his leadership in shifting frames around the world, and for recognizing the Human Workplace mission as congruent with his. I would like to acknowledge my business and life mentors, Ray McAlpin, Dr. Dave Thompson, Michael Seedman, John McCartney, Jon Zakin, and Casey Cowell; and my guides, Francis X. Gregory, Eileen Krause, Susan O'Dell, Winifred Faix Brown, Walter Blazer, and Agnes and Marie Ryan. I am grateful for the incredible support of our dear friends Ania and Jacek Rzadkowski, the Adventure Barbies, and our lifelong friends Alice and Patrick Forsyth. I would like to thank my parents, siblings, brothers- and sisters-in-law, and nieces and nephews for the love and good energy they've given me. Finally, this book would not be possible without the wisdom and friendship, insight and inspiration, of Molly Campbell and Dr. Jim Campbell; my husband, Michael Wilcox; and our children, Caty, Cormac, Eamonn, Declan, and Darrien Wilcox.

ABOUT THE AUTHOR

Liz Ryan is the CEO and Founder of Human Workplace, a publishing, coaching, and consulting firm, and the world's most widely read career advisor. Liz ran Human Resources for Recycled Paper Greetings as the company grew from $2M to $180M in annual sales, and then led the HR function at U.S. Robotics as it grew from $15M to $3B in sales. She co-founded the VC-backed technology startup Ucentric Systems, which is now a unit of Motorola, and founded WorldWIT, the world's largest online community for women in business and technology.

Liz's nontraditional and very human take on leadership, job search, career management, and Human Resources has made her a beloved advisor to millions of readers and listeners around the world. They follow Liz's columns on Forbes.com, LinkedIn, and many other publications, listen to her sparky and mojo-boosting podcasts, and watch her videos. Liz teaches job-seekers to find their voices and take control of their careers with the reminder, "Only the people who get you, deserve you!"

Liz Ryan is an operatic soprano who studied at the Manhattan School of Music and has sung professionally throughout the United States. Liz brings her theatrical flair to her live appearances around the world. Liz is a graduate of Loyola University of Chicago and Northwestern University. She lives with her husband and their five children in Boulder, Colorado. Liz draws the illustrations for her stories and Human Workplace instructional materials, including the illustrations for *Reinvention Roadmap*.

Follow Liz Ryan and Human Workplace on Twitter: @humanworkplace

To access more exercises, please visit www.humanworkplace.com/growyourflame. To download the exercises, you will need to provide your email address and this code: MOJO.

Liz Ryan's
MOJO JOURNAL

I have everything
I need to have the
life and career I
want. Not everyone
will like my brand of
jazz and that's fine. Only
the people who get me
deserve me!